Achieving TABE® Success in Language

in Language

Level A

Mc Graw Hill **Wright Group**

Executive Editor: Linda Kwil
Marketing Manager: Sean Klunder
Production Manager: Genevieve Kelley
Cover Designer: Vickie Tripp

 **Wright Group**

ISBN: 0-07-704458-4

Send all inquiries to:
Wright Group/McGraw-Hill
One Prudential Plaza
130 East Randolph Street, Suite 400
Chicago, IL 60601

Printed in the United States of America.

10 11 12 MAL 15 14 13

The **McGraw·Hill** Companies

Table of Contents

Table of Contents continued

To the Learner

If you have had problems expressing your ideas, particularly in writing, Contemporary's *Achieving TABE Success in Language* will help. The workbook will explain basic grammar and composition skills and let you practice those skills in focused exercises. *Achieving TABE Success in Language* will build your confidence in your ability to communicate, both orally and in writing.

How does using Contemporary's *Achieving TABE Success in Language* improve your language skills, particularly your writing skills? The workbook covers the following areas:

- grammar and usage
- sentence formation
- paragraph development
- capitalization
- punctuation
- writing conventions for special forms, such as letters and quotations

Included in the workbook are a Pretest and a Posttest. The Pretest will help you find your language strengths and weaknesses. Then you can use the workbook lessons to improve your skills. When you have finished the lessons and exercises, the Posttest will help you see if you have mastered those skills. Usually mastery means completing 80 percent of the questions correctly.

Achieving TABE Success in Language will help you develop specific language skills, especially writing skills. The workbook is self-contained with the Answer Key at the back of the book. Clear directions will guide you through the lessons and exercises.

Each lesson in the workbook is divided into four parts:

- **The first page** clearly defines, explains, and illustrates the skill. The examples prepare you for the work in the following exercises.

- **Practice** lets you work on the skill just introduced. If a skill requires additional explanation, this page may add to the information.

- **Apply** gives you a different way to practice the skill.

- **Check Up** provides a quick test on the skill covered in the lesson.

How to Use This Workbook

1. Take the Pretest on pages 7–14. Check your answers using the Answer Key on page 15. Refer to the Evaluation Chart to find the skills on which you need to work.

2. Take each four-page lesson one at a time. Ask your teacher for help with any problems you may have.

3. Use the Answer Key, which begins on page 212, to correct your answers after each exercise.

4. At the end of each unit, read the Unit Review and complete the Unit Assessment. These pages provide an opportunity to combine all the individual skills you have worked on and to check your progress on them. After you finish the Unit Assessment, your teacher may want to discuss your answers with you.

5. After you have finished all six units, take the Posttest on pages 203–210. Check your answers using the Answer Key on page 211. Then discuss your progress with your teacher.

Pretest

Decide which punctuation mark, if any, is needed in each sentence.

1. Isaac pedaled energetically nevertheless, he could not overtake the leader in the race.

   A : **B** , **C** ; **D** None

2. Have you ever watched the community access channel

   F , **G** ? **H** . **J** None

3. Would you bring me the needle-nose pliers?" Ramsey asked.

   A ' **B** " **C** , **D** None

4. I checked out books, magazines and videos from the library.

   F , **G** . **H** ? **J** None

5. The contracts of three of the players run out this year.

   A ' **B** ? **C** " **D** None

6. Because much of Montana was once underwater the land shows ancient shorelines.

   F ; **G** ' **H** , **J** None

7. The Renaissance, which was a turning point in history began in the fourteenth century.

   A , **B** ; **C** : **D** None

Choose the word or phrase that best completes each sentence.

8. Diana couldn't find _____ dog anywhere, so she reported it missing.

   F it

   G his

   H her

   J hers

9. This record from the 1940s is the _____ one in my collection.

   A old

   B older

   C oldest

   D most oldest

10. Nobody in my family _____ amusement park rides that turn riders upside down.

    F has never enjoyed

    G hardly enjoys

    H has ever enjoyed

    J won't enjoy

11. Rhonda's uncle _____ her how to play guitar.

    A learned

    B was learned

    C taught

    D was taught

Choose the sentence in each set that is written correctly and shows the correct capitalization and punctuation. Be sure the sentence you choose is complete.

12. F Last weekend we are taking a walk next to the old canal.

    G Long ago, merchants have brought goods by canal boat.

    H Parts of the canal are still here.

    J Before the walk ended, I will be learning about the canal.

13. A Where did uncle Joe move?

    B His new One-floor Condo is near route 49 and Baxter road.

    C He sold his handsome but bulky victorian furniture to my Cousin.

    D Let's visit him early in June.

14. F "How does the furnace look?" Teresa asked the repairman.

    G "In here, the repairman pointed, "dirt is interfering with ignition."

    H He went on, "That explains why the furnace wasn't working.

    J He also said that "the furnace needs an annual checkup."

15. A Andrew plans to start his own business this year.

    B One of his problems is health insurance for hisself.

    C Nobody he knows has their own business, so they can't help him.

    D Them problems with insurance and taxes might stop his plans.

16. F Some days you feel as if you should have stayed in bed.

    G One stormy day, Bea stepped off the bus into a wet puddle of water.

    H Being blown across the street, Elise watched her umbrella.

    J Later she moaned about losing an umbrella and to be drenched.

17. A Most fast food places sell burgers, pizza or hot, dogs.

    B Many people want healthier foods, and they look for salads.

    C Even so not everything on a salad is healthy.

    D As you might expect dressings add calories and cholesterol.

18. F When you peel the potatoes.

    G We're having leftovers, do you mind?

    H For dessert, that pie that we started on Saturday.

    J Actually, I prefer cake.

19. A Two children, on a nice day, is looking at the shapes of clouds.

    B One boy says the clouds above his house looks like a duck.

    C Then a flock of geese flies past.

    D What does the clouds look like to you?

Pretest continued

Read each set of underlined sentences. Then choose the sentence that best combines those sentences into one.

20. Mr. Adler cut down some overgrown forsythias in front of his house.

    He planted two azaleas in front of his house.

    F   Mr. Adler cut down some overgrown forsythias in front of his house and planted two azaleas in front of his house.

    G   Mr. Adler cut down some overgrown forsythias in front of his house and planted two azaleas there.

    H   Although Mr. Adler cut down some overgrown forsythias in front of his house, he planted two azaleas there.

    J   Mr. Adler cut down some overgrown forsythias in front of his house, although he planted two azaleas there.

21. The weather was stormy.
    Marty drove out of state anyway.
    She drove to visit relatives.

    A   The weather was stormy, and Marty drove out of state, and she visited relatives.

    B   The weather was stormy, although Marty drove out of state and visited relatives.

    C   Although the weather was stormy, Marty drove out of state, and she visited relatives.

    D   Although the weather was stormy, Marty drove out of state to visit relatives.

22. Marc watched his kitten.
    The kitten was three weeks old.
    It was playing with some string.

    F   Marc watched his three-week-old kitten, and it was playing with some string.

    G   While Marc watched his kitten, it was three weeks old and playing with some string.

    H   Marc watched his three-week-old kitten playing with some string.

    J   Marc watched his kitten when it was three weeks old and playing with some string.

23. Hamed had not requested any new credit cards.
    Still, he received three new credit cards this week.

    A   This week, Hamed received three new credit cards that he had not requested.

    B   Because Hamed had not requested any new credit cards, he received three new ones this week.

    C   Hamed, who had not requested anything this week, received three new credit cards.

    D   The three new credit cards that Hamed had still not requested arrived this week.

Read each paragraph. Then choose the sentence that best fills the blank.

24.   In 1969 treasure hunter Mel Fisher read about an old Spanish ship, filled with gold, that had sunk in a hurricane off the Florida Keys. He became determined to find it and salvage its precious cargo. _____. Finally, in 1985, they found the sunken ship, complete with gold bars and silver coins. Mel Fisher suddenly became wealthy.

   F The media swarmed around Fisher, who proudly showed off what he had found.

   G For years, he and his family and crew searched for the ship in various spots on the ocean floor, but were repeatedly disappointed.

   H Fisher became interested in treasure hunting when he was just a boy.

   J Today, some of Fisher's finds are on display in Key West.

25.   Margot works downtown and has to fight traffic every evening. She has made a study of the worst times to drive on the freeway. If she can get out of work by 4:10, she can beat the heaviest traffic. If she waits until 6:15, she can get home quickly because most of the cars are already off the road. However, if she leaves work between those times, she knows she will be stuck in traffic, which frustrates her. Today, Margot couldn't get out of work by 4:10. _____.

   A Nevertheless, she has decided to work a little later tonight and leave her office at 6:15.

   B In the same way, she will leave the office at 6:15 to save herself some frustration.

   C Therefore, she has decided to work a little later tonight and leave her office at 6:15.

   D For instance, 6:15 is a good time to leave the office, so Margot is working late tonight.

26.   _____. The crown jewels are stored in a secluded chamber with only one entrance. This entrance has seven different locks. The keys to these locks are distributed among seven Czech VIPs, including the president of the Czech Republic, the prime minister, and the archbishop of Prague.

   F The royal crown, scepter, and orb are removed from Prague Castle for inaugurations.

   G The crown jewels of Prague Castle are among the loveliest in the world.

   H Prague has been home to many important writers and artists over the years.

   J It would be extremely difficult to sneak a peak at Prague Castle's crown jewels.

27.   Many words that we English speakers use daily have come to us from other languages. _____. Familiar words such as *taco* and *plaza* are from the Spanish language. We can thank various Native American tribes for *squash*, *raccoon*, and *chipmunk*. The French contributed such words as *ballet*, *bouquet*, and *bureau*.

   A The word *pretzel*, however, was first used in Germany.

   B Therefore, we got the word *pretzel* from Germany.

   C Nevertheless, Germany is the source of the word *pretzel*.

   D For example, *pretzel* is a word that comes from the German language.

28. _____. In the first room, there were traditional landscape and cityscape paintings. In the second room were large abstract paintings with bright colors and bold lines. Further back stood a set of gigantic wooden sculptures, which were carved using only a chainsaw. The last room had a selection of toys and games spread across the floor. Visitors were encouraged to play with the toys and to watch themselves on the TV monitors that hung from the ceiling.

    F There were all kinds of artistic styles represented in the gallery last month.

    G Sebastian has a new job as an art curator; he is hoping to discover new talent.

    H Leonardo da Vinci was one of the greatest artists who ever lived.

    J The nonprofit art gallery is in dire need of funds this year.

29.   Sheila remembers the way that her glamorous mom used to put on makeup before an evening party. First, she would sit at the mirror and tie her hair back to keep it out of the way. She would apply an even coat of liquid foundation and then dust powder on top to set it. _____. When she was done, she would take her hair down, turn from the mirror, and give Sheila a big smile.

    A Manufacturing and marketing cosmetics is now a multibillion dollar industry.

    B She would gather all the cosmetics, brushes, and powder puffs she was likely to need in one place.

    C After her foundation was on, she would apply blush, eye shadow, mascara, and, finally, lipstick.

    D Sheila's mom used to attend several parties every year, especially during the holiday season.

Choose the answer that best develops each topic sentence.

30. In contrast to some decades that are quickly forgotten, the 1960s have a persistent hold on the national memory.

    F The wild, colorful clothes of the 1960s reappear regularly in the offerings of today's fashion designers. Sixties rock music is still heard on the radio every day.

    G George and Doris grew up in a different era, the 1930s, when jobs were hard to find and almost every family was suffering. They viewed the youth of the 1960s as selfish and pampered.

    H Each decade has its own character. Consider, for example, the 1980s with its polyester clothing and the "big hair" look for women.

    J It is tempting to guess what we will remember best when we recall the current decade in years to come. Which events, fashions, fads, and attitudes will characterize the years we are living through?

31. When an important event occurs in our lives, a recent poll says that most Americans celebrate in one of three ways.

    A Typical reasons to celebrate might be a wedding, an anniversary, or a promotion. Each family decides which reasons are likely to prompt major festivities.

    B The poll shows that about 50 percent of us like to celebrate at a restaurant, while 33 percent prefer to party at home. About 18 percent of the time, a friend or relative will throw a celebration party for us.

    C A poll is a time-honored way to keep track of changes in the way we think and act. Polls, for example, are widely used before national elections and have been shown to be quite accurate in predicting winners.

    D Are American habits of celebration different from those of people in other countries? Perhaps another poll is needed to compare American partying preferences with those of citizens of other nations.

Read each paragraph. Then choose the sentence that does <u>not</u> belong in the paragraph.

32.   **1.** Experts recommend using a different kind of lighting in each room of your house. **2.** A good reading lamp is absolutely necessary in the den or family room. **3.** Most houses built before 1950 did not have family rooms. **4.** Task lighting, that is, intense lighting that focuses on a limited area, is particularly useful in kitchens, where cooks need adequate light for cutting and slicing.

    F Sentence 1

    G Sentence 2

    H Sentence 3

    J Sentence 4

33.   **1.** It is becoming increasingly obvious that Don is an Internet addict. **2.** More and more homes are hooking up to the Internet and discovering all it has to offer. **3.** As soon as he gets up in the morning, he runs to his computer and checks the latest news. **4.** From the time he gets home after work until the time he goes to bed, he is either exploring the Net or sending and receiving e-mail messages.

    A Sentence 1

    B Sentence 2

    C Sentence 3

    D Sentence 4

Pretest continued

Read the following letter and paragraphs and look at the numbered, underlined parts. Choose the answer that is written correctly for each underlined part.

April 16, 2004

(34) Handy housewares, inc.

(35) 423, East wisconsin avenue
Milwaukee, WI 53202

(36) To whom it may concern,

(37)   Your company had a booth at the home and garden show in Lima my home

(38) town last weekend. Watching your salesman's cooking demonstration, your

pans were excellent! I would like more information about your line of cooking

(39) utensils. Would you please send me a catalog, thank you in advance.

(40) Sincerely yours:

Elise Abernathy
Elise Abernathy

---

34. F Handy Housewares, inc.

   G Handy Housewares, Inc.

   H Handy Housewares, Inc

   J Correct as it is

35. A 423 East wisconsin avenue

   B 423, East Wisconsin Avenue

   C 423 East Wisconsin Avenue

   D Correct as it is

36. F To Whom it May Concern:

   G To Whom It May Concern:

   H To whom it may concern;

   J Correct as it is

37. A Lima my home town,

   B Lima, my home town

   C Lima, my home town,

   D Correct as it is

38. F Your salesman's cooking demonstration with your pans were excellent!

   G Watching your salesman's cooking demonstration, I learned that your pans are excellent!

   H When I was watching your salesman's cooking demonstration, your pans were excellent!

   J Correct as it is

39. A a catalog? Thank

   B a Catalog. Thank

   C a catalog. Thank

   D Correct as it is

40. F Sincerely Yours,

   G Sincerely your's,

   H Sincerely yours,

   J Correct as it is

(41) To work from their homes is the wish of many people, like mothers with small children. Too many of these people are attracted by
(42) newspaper ads that promise "that they can earn $2,000 a week from home."
(43) The ads ask the reader to send cash sometimes quite a bit for instructions
(44) for making easy money. Unfortunately, theres no such thing as a free lunch.

41. A To work from their homes are

    B Working from their homes are

    C That they work from their homes are

    D Correct as it is

42. F promise that they can earn $2,000 a week from home.

    G promise, "that they can earn $2,000 a week from home."

    H promise: "that they can earn $2,000 a week from home."

    J Correct as it is

43. A cash, sometimes quite a bit

    B cash sometimes, quite a bit

    C cash, sometimes quite a bit,

    D Correct as it is

44. F Unfortunately, theres'

    G Unfortunately, there's

    H Unfortunately, theirs

    J Correct as it is

People who send money to the person running the ad are almost
(45) sure to get letters telling him or her to run the same kind of ad. In other
(46) words, the victims of the scam had been advised to cheat other people
(47) the same way they theirselves were cheated. The only sensible thing to
(48) do is ignore such ads. Why would anyone want to lose money and feeling insulted?

45. A him, or her,

    B them

    C he or she

    D Correct as it is

46. F the victims of the scam are advised

    G the victims of the scam is being advised

    H the victims of the scam are advising

    J Correct as it is

47. A themselves

    B themself

    C himself or herself

    D Correct as it is

48. F to lose money and having felt insulted?

    G to lose money and being insulted?

    H lose money and feel insulted?

    J Correct as it is

Pretest Answer Key and Evaluation Chart

This Evaluation Chart will help you find the language skills you need to study. Circle the questions you answered incorrectly and go to the practice pages covering those skills.

Key

1.	C	25.	C
2.	G	26.	J
3.	B	27.	D
4.	F	28.	F
5.	D	29.	C
6.	H	30.	F
7.	A	31.	B
8.	H	32.	H
9.	C	33.	B
10.	H	34.	G
11.	C	35.	C
12.	H	36.	G
13.	D	37.	C
14.	F	38.	G
15.	A	39.	A
16.	F	40.	H
17.	B	41.	D
18.	J	42.	F
19.	C	43.	C
20.	G	44.	G
21.	D	45.	B
22.	H	46.	F
23.	A	47.	A
24.	G	48.	H

Tested Skills	Question Numbers	Practice Pages
pronouns	15, 47	23–26, 27–30
antecedent agreement	8, 45	31–34
verbs	12	35–38, 39–40, 43–46
subject/verb agreement	19, 41, 46	47–50
easily confused verbs	11	51–54
adjectives and adverbs	9	55–58, 59–62, 63–66
use of negatives	10	67–70
sentence recognition	18, 39	75–78, 79–82
sentence combining	20, 21, 22, 23	83–86, 87–90, 91–94
sentence clarity	16, 38, 48	95–98, 99–102, 103–106
topic sentences	26, 28	111–114, 115–118
supporting sentences	30, 31	119–122
sequence	24, 29	123–126
unrelated sentences	32, 33	127–130
connectives and transitions	25, 27	131–134
proper nouns and proper adjectives	13, 34	139–142, 143–146
end marks	2	155–158
commas	4, 6, 7, 17, 37, 43	159–162, 163–166, 167–170, 171–174
semicolons and colons	1	175–178
quotations	3, 14, 42	183–186, 187–190
apostrophes	5, 44	191–194
letter parts	35, 36, 40	195–198

Correlation Chart

Correlations Between Contemporary's Instructional Materials and TABE® Language and Language Mechanics Tests

Test 4 Language

Subskill	TABE® Form 9	TABE® Form 10	TABE® Survey 9	TABE® Survey 10	Practice and Instruction Pages			
					Achieving TABE Success in Language, Level A	*GED Language Arts, Writing*	*Complete (Essential) GED**	*English Exercises (1–5)***
Usage								
pronouns	2, 4, 37, 42, 49, 55	12, 40, 49, 50	19, 25	6	23–26, 27–30	38–44, 71–73	91–95 (73–76)	1: 19–21
antecedent agreement	5	5, 55			31–34	159–165	95–101 (76–80)	1: 22 3: 9
verb tenses	1, 44	4, 6		2	35–38, 39–42, 43–46	51–57	73–83 (64–71)	1: 12–18 3: 5–6
subject/verb agreement	36				47–50	62–73	87–91 (71–74)	2: 8–18
adjectives	12, 51	9	21		55–58	145–146		1: 23, 25, 27–28
adverbs	43	13		7	59–62	145–146		1: 23, 24, 27–28
choosing between adjective/adverb	11	35, 39, 46 53		18, 23	63–66			
use of negatives	50, 52	3	20, 22		67–70			1: 26
Sentence Formation								
sentence recognition		42, 44, 54		21	75–78, 79–82	19–24, 96	65–67, 105–109 (61, 83–84)	2: 3–7, 23–26 4: 9–10
sentence combining	19, 20, 21, 22, 23, 24, 25, 26	16, 17, 18, 19 20, 21	8, 9, 10	10	83–86, 87–90, 91–94	83–98	110–118 (84–87)	2: 19–22
sentence clarity	6, 10, 40, 54	15, 37, 43	24	9, 20	95–98, 99–102, 103–106	147–158	126–131 (92–93)	3: 3–4, 10–11

*Complete GED pages are listed without parentheses. *Essential GED* pages are listed inside of parentheses.

** Numbers correspond to the following titles: 1 = *Mastering Parts of Speech;* 2 = *Using Correct Sentence Structure;* 3 = *Improving Writing Style and Paragraphing;* 4 = *Building Punctuation Skills;* 5 = *Improving Spelling and Capitalization*

TABE® Forms 9 and 10 are published by CTB/McGraw-Hill. TABE is a registered trademark of The McGraw-Hill Companies.

Subskill	TABE® Form 9	TABE® Form 10	TABE® Survey 9	TABE® Survey 10	Practice and Instruction Pages			
					Achieving TABE Success in Language, Level A	*GED Language Arts, Writing*	*Complete (Essential) GED**	*English Exercises (1–5)***
Paragraph Development								
topic sentences	28, 29	25, 26	12		111–114, 115–118	115–119	153–157 (99–101)	3: 15–16
supporting sentences	33	28, 29	13	13	119–122	115–116		3: 27–28
sequence	27, 30	22, 23	11	11	123–126	60–61, 101–102	84	3: 22
unrelated sentences	34, 35	30, 31	14	14	127–130	127–131	160–162 (104–105)	3: 17–18
connectives/ transitions	31, 32	24, 27		12	131–134	83, 90, 97–98	162–165 (105–106)	3: 19–20
Capitalization								
first words	14		5		147–150	29		5: 17, 22, 25
proper nouns	3, 9, 39, 48	7, 48	1, 3, 18	3, 25	139–142, 143–146	34–35, 177–178	135–138 (94–95)	5: 18–20, 23
titles of works		11, 14		5, 8	147–150			5: 17, 22, 25
Punctuation								
commas	7, 13, 15, 38, 41, 53	2, 10, 36, 38, 41, 45, 51, 52	2, 4, 6, 23	1, 4, 19, 22	159–162, 163–166, 167–170, 171–174	31, 87, 93, 183–195	111–112, 139–142 (96–97)	4: 5–8, 11
Writing Conventions								
quotation marks	8, 16, 18	1, 47		24	183–186, 187–190		143 (98)	4: 22–25
apostrophes	17	8	7		191–194	36–37, 43, 179–180	72–73, 94–95, 143 (98)	4: 17–19
business letter-parts	45, 46, 47	32, 33, 34	15, 16, 17	15, 16, 17	195–198	33, 61, 88	161 (104)	5: 24

Complete GED pages are listed without parentheses. *Essential GED* pages are listed inside of parentheses.

** Numbers correspond to the following titles: 1 = *Mastering Parts of Speech;* 2 = *Using Correct Sentence Structure;* 3 = *Improving Writing Style and Paragraphing;* 4 = *Building Punctuation Skills;* 5 = *Improving Spelling and Capitalization*

TABE® Forms 9 and 10 are published by CTB/McGraw-Hill. TABE is a registered trademark of The McGraw-Hill Companies.

Test 6 Language Mechanics

Subskill	TABE® Form 9	TABE® Form 10	TABE® Survey 9	TABE® Survey 10	Practice and Instruction Pages			
					Achieving TABE Success in Language, Level A	GED Language Arts, Writing	Complete (Essential) GED*	English Exercises (1–5)**
Sentences, Phrases, Clauses								
end marks		20		20	155–158	29		4: 3–4
quotation marks	5, 9, 14	1, 3, 13	5, 9, 14	1, 3, 13	183–186, 187–190		143 (98)	4: 22–25 5: 25
commas	1, 3, 8, 11, 12, 13, 16, 17	4, 6, 12, 14, 19	1, 3, 8, 11, 12, 13, 16, 17	2, 4, 6, 7, 12 14, 19	159–162, 163–166, 167–170, 171–174	31, 87, 93, 183–195	111–112, 139–142, (96–97)	4: 5–8, 11
semicolons	7	7, 9	7	9	175–178		143 (98)	4: 12–13
colons	10, 15	2, 8, 18	10, 15	8, 18	175–178		143 (98)	4: 16
Writing Conventions								
proper nouns		10		10	139–142, 143–146	34–35, 177–178	135–138 (94–95)	5: 18–20, 23
proper adjectives	19		19		143–146			5: 18, 20
capitalize titles	2	5, 11	2	5, 11	147–150			5: 17, 22, 25
apostrophes	4, 6	15	4, 6	15	191–194	36–37, 43, 179–180	72–73, 94–95, 143 (98)	4: 17–19
business letter-parts	18, 20	16, 17	18, 20	16, 17	195–198	33, 61, 88	161 (104)	5: 24

*Complete GED pages are listed without parentheses. Essential GED pages are listed inside of parentheses.

** Numbers correspond to the following titles: 1 = Mastering Parts of Speech; 2 = Using Correct Sentence Structure; 3 = Improving Writing Style and Paragraphing; 4 = Building Punctuation Skills; 5 = Improving Spelling and Capitalization

TABE® Forms 9 and 10 are published by CTB/McGraw-Hill. TABE is a registered trademark of The McGraw-Hill Companies.

Nouns

A **noun** is the name of a person, place, or thing. Some nouns name things that can be seen, heard, smelled, tasted, or touched; others name abstract ideas and emotions, such as *freedom* and *surprise*. The nouns in the following sentence are underlined.

> With great anticipation, people filed into the auditorium.

A **singular noun** names only one person, place, thing, or idea. A **plural noun** names more than one. Usually, plural nouns end in *s*. In the following sentence, the singular noun is underlined once and the plural nouns are underlined twice.

> The members of the orchestra lifted their instruments.

The plural forms of some nouns are formed in unusual ways. Memorize these and other unusual plural forms:

man—men	woman—women	child—children
mouse—mice	foot—feet	tooth—teeth

Every noun is either singular or plural. Similarly, every noun is either common or proper. A **common noun** is the general name of any person, place, or thing. A **proper noun** is the name of a particular person, place, or thing. Every important word in a proper noun should be capitalized.

> **Common:** A well-known singer performed with the orchestra.
>
> **Proper:** Maria Walker sang with the Medina Symphony.

Underline the nouns in each of the following sentences. Above each noun, write two sets of letters: *S* or *PL* (for singular or plural) and *C* or *PR* (for common or proper).

>   *S, C*   *PL, C*   *S, PR*
> **Example: Traffic is heavy on the freeways around Los Angeles.**

1. Artists displayed their paintings by the old cathedral.

2. Robert Frost read a poem at the inauguration of John F. Kennedy.

3. The cars revved their engines at the starting line.

4. Ben pleased his clients with his attention to details.

5. The Smiths hiked along the Appalachian Mountains.

6. The mechanic admitted that the previous repair had been done rather carelessly.

7. After the accident, traffic on the freeway came to a standstill.

Practice

Identify the nouns in each sentence. If the nouns are not capitalized correctly, rewrite the sentence correctly on the line. If the nouns are capitalized correctly, write *Correct* on the line.

1. Abraham lincoln was known for his honesty and compassion.

   _____

2. dolores will soon become a citizen of the united States.

   _____

3. The audience applauded as the actors took their bows.

   _____

4. Ms. Baxter called the Members of the Committee into her Office.

   _____

5. Ken and betsy ordered appetizers and sandwiches at the copper pot Restaurant.

   _____

6. Women and Children hastily boarded the lifeboats.

   _____

Each of the following sentences is missing one noun. Write a noun on the line to complete the sentence. The kind of noun that is needed is described in parentheses.

7. This tour is scheduled to stop at _____ (proper) tomorrow.

8. There are never enough _____ (plural) to please this hungry crowd.

9. _____ (proper) has written a new mystery featuring a wily private detective.

10. I felt a deep sense of _____ (common) when I read about the robberies.

11. The ingredients in this _____ (singular) are surprisingly expensive.

12. _____(plural) ran onto the field after the game ended.

13. When the _____ (common) arrives at Public Square, almost everyone gets off.

14. When I was young, I couldn't wait to get my first _____ (singular).

15. Drew hopes to land a job at _____ (proper).

Apply

Beside each common noun in the list below, write a matching proper noun. For example, to match the common noun *continent,* a proper noun might be *Africa.* Remember to capitalize the proper nouns.

1. relative or friend _____

2. celebrity _____

3. city _____

4. state _____

5. body of water _____

6. store _____

7. day _____

8. month _____

9. bank _____

10. pet _____

Now choose six of the proper nouns you wrote in the exercise above. On the lines below, write a paragraph using those nouns and underline them.

_____

_____

_____

_____

_____

_____

_____

_____

_____

_____

Check Up

Read each sentence and look at its underlined word. Choose the answer that best describes the underlined word.

1. <u>Passengers</u> on the flight to Houston were served light snacks and soft drinks.

    A   plural proper noun

    B   singular proper noun

    C   plural common noun

    D   None of these

2. The <u>manual</u> for this printer is difficult to understand.

    F   plural proper noun

    G   singular common noun

    H   plural common noun

    J   None of these

3. Into what body of water does the <u>Danube River</u> flow?

    A   singular common noun

    B   singular proper noun

    C   plural proper noun

    D   None of these

4. There are about 2,200 square <u>feet</u> of living space in Sally's new house.

    F   singular common noun

    G   singular proper noun

    H   plural common noun

    J   None of these

5. The <u>Atlas Mountains</u> are located in northern Africa.

    A   plural proper noun

    B   singular proper noun

    C   plural common noun

    D   None of these

6. The <u>guide</u> at the historic site wore a costume from the Colonial period.

    F   singular proper noun

    G   singular common noun

    H   plural common noun

    J   None of these

7. Striking workers <u>picketed</u> outside the factory.

    A   singular common noun

    B   plural proper noun

    C   plural common noun

    D   None of these

8. The <u>apples</u> that Aunt Betty uses in her famous pie are slightly sour.

    F   singular common noun

    G   singular proper noun

    H   plural common noun

    J   None of these

9. These tomatoes should be ripe by late <u>July</u> or early August.

    A   plural common noun

    B   singular proper noun

    C   singular common noun

    D   None of these

10. Jack's family doctor referred <u>him</u> to a specialist for his allergies.

    F   singular common noun

    G   singular proper noun

    H   plural common noun

    J   None of these

Personal Pronouns

Pronouns are words used in place of nouns. They eliminate the need to repeat a noun over and over. Instead of a sentence such as *Andre takes Andre's daughter to the tots' story hour when Andre goes to the library,* pronouns make this sentence possible: *Andre takes his daughter to the tots' story hour when he goes to the library.* Using the pronouns *his* and *he* in place of *Andre* improves the sentence.

In the sentence above, *his* and *he* are examples of one kind of pronoun, the personal pronoun. **Personal pronouns** are usually used in place of a person's name; however, a personal pronoun can also refer to a thing.

        Andre looked for his daughter's hat. It had fallen behind the desk. (*It* refers to *hat.*)

Pronouns are grouped in three ways: by number, by gender, and by person.

Number: *Singular* pronouns refer to one person, place, or thing. *Plural* pronouns refer to more than one.

Gender: *Masculine* pronouns refer to males (*he, him, his*). *Feminine* pronouns refer to females (*she, her, hers*). *Neuter* pronouns refer to things or animals (*it, its*). Only singular pronouns reflect gender.

Person: *First-person* pronouns refer to the person who is speaking. *Second-person* pronouns refer to the person who is spoken to. *Third-person* pronouns refer to other people, places, or things.

	Singular	Plural
First Person:	I, me, my, mine	we, us, our, ours
Second Person:	you, your, yours	you, your, yours
Third Person:	he, she, him, her, it his, hers, its	they, them, their, theirs

Circle the personal pronoun in each sentence. Draw an arrow from it to the noun it refers to.

1. Grandma waved to the children, and then she went back into the house.

2. The trees began to lose their leaves rapidly after Labor Day.

3. Greg said, "I always try to pay my entire credit card balance each month."

4. Deeane, why don't you make that suggestion at the next meeting?

5. The travelers waited in long lines to get their luggage X-rayed.

6. The play certainly lived up to its reviews.

Practice

Personal pronouns change form, depending upon how they are used in a sentence.

A **subject** names the person or thing the sentence or clause is about. These pronouns are used as subjects in sentences or clauses.

> I   we   you   he, she, it   they
>
> Isabel gave her dad a hug before she climbed into the car.

Objects complete the meaning of a verb or a preposition such as *by, of,* or *to*. These pronouns are used as objects of verbs or prepositions.

> me   us   you   him, her, it   them
>
> The librarian smiled at the children and helped them get dressed. (object of verb *helped*)
>
> Isabel's friend waved to her. (object of preposition *to*)

Often, a pronoun is used as part of a compound subject or a compound object. If you become confused about which pronoun to use, leave out the other part of the compound and try the sentence with the pronoun alone.

> Andre and she sang a song on the way home. (She sang a song.)
>
> A neighbor met Andre and her by the back door. (A neighbor met her by the door.)

For each sentence, decide whether the missing pronoun is used as a subject or an object. Write *subject* or *object* on the line. Then underline the correct pronoun(s) to complete the sentence. If the pronoun is used as an object, circle the verb or preposition it completes.

1. _____ Jan bought a new coat, but (she, her) returned it the next day.

2. _____ If you ask (he, him), Cal will give you his honest opinion.

3. _____ The hostess led (him, he) and (her, she) to a candlelit table.

4. _____ The Smiths just moved here, and (they, them) like the neighborhood.

5. _____ Whenever we visit the outlet mall, (we, us) buy too much.

6. _____ The car salesman rode with (we, us) on the test drive.

7. _____ It irritates me when you correct (I, me) in front of my friends.

8. _____ If Tom and (I, me) come to the party, we will bring a hot dish.

9. _____ Telephone (they, them) when you leave your house.

10. _____ If Teri doesn't get a raise soon, (her, she) will look for a new job.

Apply

Personal pronouns that show ownership, or possession, are called **possessive pronouns**.

> The artist called her latest painting *Untitled 281*. (The artist owns the painting. *Her* refers to *artist*.)

	Singular Possessive	**Plural Possessive**
First Person:	my, mine	our, ours
Second Person:	your, yours	your, yours
Third Person:	his, her, hers, its	their, theirs

Note that possessive pronouns, unlike possessive nouns, do not use apostrophes to indicate ownership. Also note the spelling of *their*. Do not confuse it with these words: *there, they're*.

Most possessive pronouns have two forms. One form is used with a noun (*my* car; *our* project; *your, her, their* record). The other form (*mine, ours, yours, hers, theirs*) is used alone, as in *Those skis are mine*. Two possessive pronouns, *his* and *its*, have only one form. These pronouns can be used either alone or with a noun.

Underline the possessive pronoun in each sentence. Then circle the correct number, gender, and person of that pronoun. (If the pronoun is plural, mark *No gender*.)

1. His friends met him at the airport.

   Number: S   P   Gender: M   F   N   No gender   Person: 1   2   3

2. They watched the butterfly flap its golden wings and fly away.

   Number: S   P   Gender: M   F   N   No gender   Person: 1   2   3

3. We all signed our names on the birthday card.

   Number: S   P   Gender: M   F   N   No gender   Person: 1   2   3

4. They argued that the accident wasn't their fault.

   Number: S   P   Gender: M   F   N   No gender   Person: 1   2   3

Underline the possessive pronoun that correctly completes each sentence.

5. I have been saving up for (mine, my) dream vacation for two years.

6. She insisted that the bill for the dinner was (her, hers) this time.

7. I hope I can see (there, they're, their, theirs) address in the dark.

8. We were certain that the black suitcase we picked up was (our, ours).

9. Both neighbors are convinced that the apple tree is (theirs, their's, their, they're).

Check Up

Choose the word or phrase that best completes each sentence.

1. The reporter refused to reveal the names of _____ sources.

   A she

   B her

   C they

   D hers

2. The governor told _____ that better times were just around the corner.

   F we

   G our

   H us

   J our's

3. When Bob and _____ arrive, we'll open the presents.

   A her

   B she

   C him

   D them

4. The shark sleeps with _____ eyes wide open.

   F its

   G it's

   H it

   J theirs

Read each set of sentences. Choose the sentence that is written correctly.

5. A Molly snuggled into hers warm, soft bed.

   B Roy and me like to watch the evening news before retiring.

   C My daughter Rita can't sleep without her teddy bear.

   D Would you like you're bedtime cocoa warmed up?

6. F The dentist gave Shannon and he new toothbrushes.

   G Owen and us sat in the waiting room and read magazines.

   H The doctor prescribed antibiotics for mine strep throat.

   J Joann took her son to the emergency room twice this month.

7. A Gary was shocked that the award was given to him.

   B If you send in your entry, this beautiful car might be your's.

   C Have your ever won a contest or a lottery?

   D After Brenda and him won the contest, they went out to dinner.

8. F Craig's brother gave he a reflective vest for jogging.

   G Julie and he swim twenty laps three times a week.

   H Just between you and I, I have to admit that I hardly ever exercise.

   J The boys left they're baseball equipment in my van.

More Pronouns

Demonstrative pronouns—*this, that, these,* and *those*—point out particular persons, places, or things. Demonstrative pronouns may modify nouns, or they may be used alone. Use *this* and *that* with singular nouns; use *these* and *those* with plural nouns. *This* and *these* point out people or things that are near, while *that* and *those* point out people or things that are farther away. (The pronoun *them* is not a demonstrative pronoun.)

> This meeting will come to order. This is an important meeting.
>
> These members are absent. Those are the candidates.

The **interrogative pronouns** *who, whom, whose, what,* and *which* are used to ask questions. In a question in which the pronoun stands for a person, use *who* as the subject and *whom* as an object.

> **Subject:** *Who* is recording the minutes?
>
> **Object:** By *whom* were the minutes recorded? (*Whom* is the object of the preposition *by*.)

The **relative pronouns** are *who, whom, whose, which,* and *that*. Relative pronouns introduce relative clauses and relate them to nouns or pronouns in the main part of the sentence. Although a relative clause has a subject and a predicate, it cannot stand on its own. Remember that *who* is used as the subject of a clause and *whom* as the object. *That* and *which* are used to relate the clause to a thing, not a person.

> The chairperson, *who was just elected*, ran the meeting. (*Who* refers to *chairperson*.)
>
> The pen *that I dropped on the floor* is red. (*That* refers to *pen*.)

Circle the demonstrative or interrogative pronoun in each sentence. On the line, write *D* for demonstrative or *I* for interrogative.

1. _____ Whom have you chosen as your running mate?

2. _____ This has been one of the most surprise-filled days of my life.

3. _____ Can you see the words written on those signs ahead?

4. _____ What would you say is the hardest part of your job?

Underline each relative clause and circle the relative pronoun that introduces it.

5. The movie that is currently at the top of the charts is a romantic comedy.

6. Give your evaluation form to the gentleman who is standing by the door.

7. The candidate for whom we voted is giving her acceptance speech.

Practice

When you want to refer to people, places, and things in a general way, you can use an **indefinite pronoun**. The indefinite pronouns are listed in the chart below. As you can see, some are always singular, some are always plural, and a few can be either singular or plural, depending on the way they are used. (If the pronoun refers to a single quantity, as in *all of the soup*, it is singular. If it refers to plural items, as in *all of the vegetables*, it is plural.)

Singular	Plural	Singular or Plural
anybody, anyone, each, either, everyone, everything, neither, nobody, no one, nothing, one, somebody	both, few, many, several	all, most, none, some

Reflexive pronouns end with *-self* (singular) or *-selves* (plural).

	Singular	Plural
First person:	myself	ourselves
Second person:	yourself	yourselves
Third person:	himself, herself, itself	themselves

A **reflexive pronoun** reflects an action to a noun or pronoun used earlier in the sentence or clause. Reflexive pronouns must be used after the noun or pronoun they refer to. They cannot be used alone.

> **Reflexive:** Bill reminded himself to set the alarm early.
>
> **Incorrect:** The invitation was for Anna and myself.

Underline the reflexive and indefinite pronouns in the following sentences. On the line write *REF* for reflexive or *IND* for indefinite. Draw an arrow from each reflexive pronoun to the noun or pronoun it refers to.

1. _____ Paula surprised herself by actually jumping from the plane.

2. _____ The artist himself will talk to customers at the show.

3. _____ The players challenged themselves to try harder.

4. _____ Anyone with a sense of humor would enjoy this comedian.

5. _____ Many of the cars had trouble starting on that cold morning.

6. _____ When Dana saw herself in the mirror, she decided to go on a diet.

7. _____ The film itself was not very scary, but the audience was intent.

8. _____ As a parent, you yourself are your child's best teacher.

Apply

Circle the indefinite pronoun in each sentence. On the line, write *S* if the pronoun is singular or *P* if it is plural.

1. _____ Many of the salmon could not get past the dam in the river.

2. _____ Everyone in the cast and crew did an excellent job.

3. _____ The captain was looking for someone who knew Morse code.

4. _____ If either of my sons calls, ask him to phone me at work.

5. _____ Several of the eyewitnesses claimed they saw a blue van drive away.

6. _____ All of the guests raised their glasses in a toast.

7. _____ For years, nothing was done about the problem of water pollution.

8. _____ The director ordered that none of the information be leaked to the press.

9. _____ The parents promised that neither of the boys would misbehave again.

10. _____ Most of the errors occurred because of an unclear memo.

Write a pronoun to complete each sentence. Supply the type of pronoun described in parentheses.

11. (reflexive) The hostess _____ led her guests to their seats.

12. (relative) The people _____ bought my house have three children.

13. (demonstrative) Please pick _____ flowers and bring them here.

14. (reflexive) The unhappy little boy cried _____ to sleep.

15. (relative) The neighbors _____ cat ran away have posted its picture all over the neighborhood.

16. (demonstrative) I'll give you a taste of _____ if you'll give me a taste of that.

17. (interrogative) To _____ is the package addressed?

18. (interrogative) _____ is the population of Zimbabwe?

19. (indefinite) _____ of my clothes got wrinkled in the suitcase.

Check Up

Read each set of sentences. Choose the sentence that is written correctly.

1. **A** The speaker which talked about the future was fascinating.

    B Probably some of them predictions will come true.

    C Whom did you hear at the conference?

    D I wish I could have heard himself talk about advances in communications.

2. **F** The reporter interviewed the witness who saw the accident.

    G The passenger whom was in one of the cars was slightly dazed.

    H The police officer asked whom car entered the intersection first.

    J Anyone that saw that accident should contact the police.

3. **A** I myself have been practicing for weeks for this dance contest.

    B I wonder what dance steps those judge is looking for.

    C That dancers certainly look exhausted.

    D My friends think the judges will choose myself as the winner.

4. **F** The chef which was at this restaurant before has quit.

    G The sauce that you poured on the beans is delicious.

    H We treat ourselfs to a meal at this restaurant once a year.

    J If you are not going to finish them cookies, let's take them home.

Choose the word that best completes each sentence.

5. _____ has a copy of the annual report to the stockholders?

    A Whom

    B Whose

    C Who

    D That

6. For a few seconds, the umpires _____ could not agree on the ruling.

    F themself

    G themselves

    H themself's

    J they

7. Unfortunately, _____ doughnuts are stale already.

    A themselves

    B that

    C those

    D them

8. Did you hear _____ singing in the shower?

    F me

    G myself

    H herself

    J I

Making Pronouns Agree with Their Antecedents

You know that a **pronoun** is a word that is used in place of a noun. The noun that the pronoun replaces is called its **antecedent**. Usually, an antecedent comes before the pronoun in the same sentence or in a previous sentence.

> Marcus washes his car every Saturday.

> (The antecedent of the pronoun *his* is *Marcus*.)

Pronouns and antecedents must match, or agree, in three ways: number, gender, and person.

Agreement in Number: Use singular pronouns to refer to singular antecedents and plural pronouns to refer to plural antecedents. If the antecedent is made up of one or more nouns or pronouns joined by *and*, the pronoun that refers to it must be plural. When the antecedent is an indefinite pronoun, the pronoun that refers to it can be either singular or plural, depending on the indefinite pronoun itself and how it is used in the sentence. The chart below may be used as a reference.

> Shontae is hoping that her car lasts through the winter. (singular)

> Customers enjoy the service they receive at that dealership. (plural)

> Ken and Ray advertise their great deals on the radio. (plural)

> Somebody forgot his or her umbrella. (singular)

> Many of the salespeople made their sales goals this month. (plural)

Singular	Plural	Singular or plural
anybody, anyone, anything, each, either, everybody, everyone, everything, much, neither, nobody, no one, nothing, one, somebody, someone, something	both, few, many, several	all, more, most, none, some (*singular when referring to a single quantity; plural when referring to multiple items*)

Underline the pronoun in each sentence. Circle its antecedent.

1. Mallory introduced her brother to the next-door neighbor.

2. The workers ate their lunches high on the girders of the new building.

3. When the hikers took a break, they feasted on fresh fruits and cool water.

4. Mr. Turner wants to expand the department, so he is interviewing candidates.

5. Everyone at the party received his or her own photo album.

Practice

Agreement in Gender: This type of agreement applies only to singular pronouns. The pronouns *he, him,* and *his* refer to masculine (male) antecedents; *she, her,* and *hers* refer to feminine (female) antecedents; and *it* and *its* refer to neuter (neither male nor female) antecedents. Because the gender associated with a singular indefinite pronoun such as *somebody* is unclear, a phrase such as *his or her* refers to it.

Correct: Somebody left his or her notebook on my desk.

Incorrect: Somebody left their notebook on my desk.

Agreement in Person: Pronouns must agree with their antecedents in person. Remember that first-person pronouns refer to the person who is speaking, second-person pronouns refer to the person who is spoken to, and third-person pronouns refer to other people, places, or things. The chart below shows the person of each pronoun.

	Singular	Plural
First Person:	I, me, my, mine	we, us, our, ours
Second Person:	you, your, yours	you, your, yours
Third Person:	he, she, him, her, it his, hers, its	they, them, their, theirs

Read each pair of sentences. Circle the letter of the sentence in which the pronoun agrees with its antecedent.

1. **A**   Most of the milk had leaked out of its carton and onto the table.

    B   Most of the milk had leaked out of their carton and onto the table.

2. **A**   The troop leader let one of the boys call their mother on the cell phone.

    B   The troop leader let one of the boys call his mother on the cell phone.

3. **A**   The climbers wanted to reach the summit, but we were exhausted.

    B   The climbers wanted to reach the summit, but they were exhausted.

4. **A**   Did each of the swimmers earn their lifesaving badge?

    B   Did each of the swimmers earn his or her lifesaving badge?

5. **A**   Fran needed apples for her pie, so she bought them at a roadside stand.

    B   Fran needed apples for her pie, so she bought it at a roadside stand.

6. **A**   The principal asked the students for their cooperation during the emergency.

    B   The principal asked the students for his cooperation during the emergency.

Apply

Underline the pronoun that completes each sentence correctly. Circle its antecedent.

1. The players had practiced the new plays, but they forgot (it, them) during the game.

2. Karen collects dolls from around the world, and she displays (it, them) in a case.

3. I'm afraid that neither of the debaters has proved (his, their) point to my satisfaction.

4. My sister who lives in Pittsburgh is taking (their, her) family on a camping vacation.

5. The sailor looked for the lighthouse, but (he, you) couldn't see through the thick fog.

Read each sentence. If it has a pronoun agreement error, rewrite it correctly on the line. If the sentence is correct, write *Correct*.

6. After everybody made their guess, the answer was revealed.

   _____

7. The doctor tells her patients to restrict his salt intake.

   _____

8. Both Ned and Van have his own pool tables.

   _____

9. Mrs. Parker put on her glasses because you couldn't read the fine print.

   _____

10. Did each of the children take home his or her party favor?

    _____

11. A few of the actors forgot his or her lines.

    _____

12. Did either of those Miss America finalists describe their home state?

    _____

13. Both Jason and Val brought his surfboards to the beach.

    _____

Check Up

Choose the pronoun that completes each sentence correctly.

1. Most of our employees are doing _____ best to serve the customers.

   A their

   B his or her

   C my

   D your

2. Did everyone remember to bring _____ passport?

   F their

   G your

   H his or her

   J its

3. Alan likes pancakes for breakfast; he always pours lots of syrup over _____.

   A itself

   B him

   C them

   D it

4. Your favorite show has many fans, but _____ got panned by the critics.

   F they

   G it

   H you

   J she

Read each set of sentences. Choose the sentence that is written correctly.

5. A The auctioneer held up the quilt and invited everyone to bid on them.

   B All of the cab drivers waited outside the airport in his cabs.

   C I loved cocoa; they always made me feel warm and secure.

   D The photo showed Joyce and Andy, but I could hardly see their expressions.

6. F Has either of the custodians introduced themselves to you?

   G Some of the popcorn fell out of its carton as I walked to my seat.

   H When some of the players protested the call, the coach didn't try to stop him.

   J Many of the fans held up signs to encourage his or her favorite players.

7. A After dinner, the men excused ourselves and went to the family room to watch the game.

   B If we ourselves don't follow the rules, how can we expect others to follow them?

   C My kitten was startled by their own reflection in the mirror.

   D I tried to get home on time, but because of the traffic tie-up, you couldn't move for hours.

8. F Many of the roads are still snow-covered because snowplows haven't reached it yet.

   G Nobody wants their children to be left behind.

   H The grocery store owner told their customers that the foods they sold were top quality.

   J After the water main break, citizens were advised to boil their water.

Verbs

A **verb** is a word that identifies an action or a state of being. A verb with more than one word is called a **verb phrase**. Every complete sentence has at least one verb or verb phrase.

> The music <u>was</u> loud, and the villagers <u>were dancing</u>.

Some verbs that show action may pass the action on to persons or things. Whatever receives the action is called the **object** of the verb. Below, the second verb now has an object.

> The music <u>was</u> loud, and the villagers <u>were dancing</u> a polka.

The verb *were dancing* did not change, but adding the object, *polka*, made our understanding of the action more complete.

A verb that shows a state of being, such as *was*, does not take an object. Instead, a state-of-being verb may link its subject to another noun or pronoun, or to an adjective. Such a verb is called a **linking verb**.

> The dance <u>was</u> a polka. (*Was* links *dance* and *polka*.)

> The dance <u>was</u> charming. (*Was* links *dance* and *charming*.)

> The dance <u>was</u> in a musical. (no link)

Some verbs, called **helping** or **auxiliary verbs**, are used before the base form of other verbs. They include *can, must, will, could,* and *should.*

> The dancers <u>*must*</u> <u>practice</u> regularly.

Underline every verb and verb phrase in each sentence. If an action verb has an object, write its object on the line. If a verb is a linking verb, write the two words that are linked.

1. Some of the cookies were stale, but none of the children objected. _____

2. Carmakers introduce new models every year. _____

3. If you arrive at the mall before I get there, please wait for me. _____

4. The marathon runner finished in fifth place even though she is blind. _____

5. Computers and printers have replaced typewriters almost completely. _____

6. Pete would like a dessert, but Mona is full. _____

7. I must finish this project before I leave for class. _____

Practice

Each verb has forms that are called **principal parts**. The chart below has examples of verbs in their present, past, and past participle forms.

Present Tense	Past Tense	Past Participle
call	called	(has) called
marry	married	(has) married
meet	met	(has) met
sing	sang	(has) sung

If the past tense and past participle of a verb are both formed by adding –ed or –d to the base form, that verb is **regular**. In the chart above, the verbs *call* and *marry* are examples of regular verbs. If the principal parts of a verb do not follow that pattern, the verb is **irregular**. In the chart, the verbs *meet* and *sing* are irregular verbs.

Three irregular verbs—*be, do,* and *have*—serve as both main verbs and helping verbs. Their principal parts are formed in irregular ways.

Present Tense	Past Tense	Past Participle
be	was, were	(has) been
do	did	(has) done
have	had	(has) had

Underline the verb or verb phrase in each sentence. Identify the principle part of the main verb. On the first line, write *P* for *past tense* or *PP* for *past participle*. On the second line, write *R* if the verb is regular or *I* if it is irregular.

1. Consumers have bought DVD players at a record pace. _____ _____

2. On his last birthday, Rudy was eight years old. _____ _____

3. Who played drums for the group during that tour? _____ _____

4. Before her heart attack, Gina had considered a nomination for mayor. _____ _____

5. Early motorists drove only during good weather. _____ _____

6. The new hair salon has sent coupons to all residents in the area. _____ _____

7. Only half of the staff reported for work during the blizzard. _____ _____

8. With a little overtime, Debra's team has completed the project on schedule. _____ _____

9. How many people have stood for such treatment? _____ _____

Apply

In a sentence where the subject names the person or thing performing the action and the object names the person or thing receiving the action, the verb is said to be in **active voice**.

> Test pilots <u>have flown</u> this experimental plane many times.

In a sentence where the subject names the person or thing receiving the action, the verb is said to be in **passive voice**. The person or thing that performs the action may be named elsewhere in the sentence or not mentioned at all.

> This experimental plane <u>was flown</u> by test pilots.

> This experimental plane <u>was flown</u>.

Every passive verb is made up of the past participle of the main verb and a helping verb that is a form of *be*.

> The pilots <u>*are* pleased</u> by the model's maneuverability.

> The plane <u>*will be* sold</u> to the public soon.

Underline the verb in each sentence. Above it, write *A* if it is in active voice or *P* if it is in passive voice.

1. How many patients were seen by Dr. Hogan today?

2. Lydia was promoted to supervisor.

3. Max prefers potatoes that are baked in a conventional oven over microwaved potatoes.

4. The light bulb was shattered when it was dropped.

5. That old, dead tree was felled after termites invaded it.

6. Grapes that are grown in this region are used in red wine.

For each item, write an original sentence in the voice requested. Choose the correct verb form.

7. Use active voice. Choose between *breaks* and *is broken.*

   _____

8. Use passive voice. Choose between *taught* and *have taught.*

   _____

9. Use active voice. Choose between *will choose* and *will be chosen.*

   _____

Check Up

Choose the verb or verb phrase that best completes each sentence.

1. Every Sunday, the Gomez family _____ in the park.

   A walking

   B walks

   C is walked

   D have walking

2. Wait till the dough _____ to twice its original size.

   F rises

   G rising

   H has rose

   J risen

3. For years, scientists _____ for a cure for Alzheimer's disease.

   A search

   B were searched

   C have search

   D have searched

4. The lobby of our building _____ for the holidays.

   F decorated

   G is decorated

   H has decorated

   J decorate

Read each set of sentences. Choose the sentence that is written correctly.

5. A Lu's youngest child will starting school.

   B Lu's youngest child starting school.

   C Lu's youngest child will start school.

   D Lu's youngest child will started school.

6. F Professor Quinn has teaching English for thirty years.

   G Professor Quinn teach English for thirty years.

   H Professor Quinn teaching English for thirty years.

   J Professor Quinn has taught English for thirty years.

7. A Leaf blowers been noisy to the point of damaging one's hearing.

   B Leaf blowers are noisy to the point of damaging one's hearing.

   C Leaf blowers be noisy to the point of damaging one's hearing.

   D Leaf blowers being noisy to the point of damaging one's hearing.

8. F Oddly enough, songs are wrote about principles of chemistry.

   G Oddly enough, songs have writing about principles of chemistry.

   H Oddly enough, songs are written about principles of chemistry.

   J Oddly enough, songs writing about principles of chemistry.

Verbs and Their Tenses

Every verb has forms called **tenses** that indicate the time of action. There are simple tenses, progressive tenses, and perfect tenses. Each group has three tenses. The three **simple tenses** are the present, past, and future tenses.

> **Present:** Raul talks with Katy every day. They talk for hours.
>
> **Past:** Last night they talked about engagement.
>
> **Future:** Soon they will talk about a wedding date.

Use the **present tense** to indicate action that happens now or on a regular basis, as in *Ministers and justices of the peace perform marriages.*

For almost all verbs, the present tense forms match the pattern shown below for *want*. The forms of *have* and *be* are different.

> **want**—I want, you want, she wants, we want, they want
>
> **have**—I have, you have, he has, we have, they have
>
> **be**—I am, you are, it is, we are, they are

Use the **past tense** to indicate action that happened in the past. This tense is the second principal part of a verb. Form the past tense of any regular verb by adding *-ed* or *-d* to the base form. Irregular verbs form their past tense in many different ways. If you do not know the past tense of an irregular verb, refer to a dictionary. The verb *be* has two past tense forms: *was* (singular) and *were* (plural).

Use the **future tense** to indicate action that will happen in the future. Form the future tense of both regular and irregular verbs by using a helping verb such as *will* or *shall* with the base form.

For each item, write *Present*, *Past*, or *Future* on the line to identify the simple tense of the underlined verb.

1. Without a shade on that lamp, the bulb really glares. _____

2. The movie misrepresented the facts of the case. _____

3. I can hardly wait until you open my present. _____

4. Despite years of searching, nobody found the lost ship until now. _____

5. They will present the first performance of the sonata on Sunday. _____

6. Racecar drivers depend on fast, knowledgeable pit crews. _____

7. If the account falls below the minimum, the bank shall impose a fee. _____

Practice

The **progressive tenses** indicate actions that continue for some time. Every verb in a progressive tense has at least two words: a form of *be* and the present participle of the main verb. The **present participle** is the present tense form of a verb that ends in *-ing*. In the progressive tenses, the following forms of *be* are used with the present participle: present progressive—*am, is, are*; past progressive—*was, were*; future progressive—*will be*.

> Who <u>is calling</u> at this hour? (present progressive)
>
> I <u>was sleeping</u> before this call. (past progressive)
>
> In a few minutes I <u>will be coming</u> to your aid. (future progressive)

Underline the verb form that correctly completes each sentence.

1. During the commercials, we (scanning, will scanning, were scanning) the other stations.

2. Next week, voters (will be casting, were casting, be casting) ballots in statewide races.

3. Whenever Jennifer (is tried, is trying, is try) to impress a date, she becomes stiff and unnatural.

4. Credit card holders who (are carrying, will carrying, carrying) a balance must pay interest.

5. According to the weather forecast, we (are enjoy, will enjoying, will be enjoying) sunshine for several days.

6. When Rocky hit the homer, most fans (were walked, were walking, walk) toward the exits.

Complete each sentence by filling in the correct progressive form (present, past, or future) of the verb in parentheses. (For some sentences, more than one answer may be correct.)

7. (plan) Right now, store managers _____ their decorations for the holidays.

8. (accept) The college _____ applications beginning next week until August.

9. (visit) During the week of the flood, the Kirks _____ Maine.

10. (run) Voter dissatisfaction with the administration's foreign policy _____ high.

11. (eat) Please don't hum while you _____ .

12. (swim) The coach watches critically as her athletes _____ practice laps.

13. (rake) Once the leaves begin to fall next month, we _____ the yard every day.

Apply

When you write a sentence that identifies two or more actions, make sure the tenses of the verbs correctly indicate the times of the different actions. For example, if you tell about two actions that happen about the same time, you should use verbs that are in the same tense—present, past, or future.

If both actions happen for a limited time, use the same simple tense for both verbs.

> **Example:** After Jim <u>parked</u> the car, he <u>went</u> into the restaurant. (both past)

If both actions continue for some time, use the same progressive tense for both verbs.

> **Example:** The diners <u>were talking</u> as they <u>were waiting</u> to be served. (both past progressive)

If one action continues and the other does not, use a progressive tense verb for the continuing action and a simple tense for the limited action.

> **Example:** The waitress <u>was pouring</u> coffee when someone <u>bumped</u> her. (past progressive and past)

Choose the verb or verb phrase that best completes each sentence.

1. Workers came upon these artifacts while they _____ a new sewer system.

   A are digging

   B were digging

   C will be digging

   D dug

2. We blow a fuse whenever we _____ three appliances.

   F are using

   G used

   H were using

   J will be using

3. When the cup hit the floor, it _____ into pieces.

   A was shattering

   B shatters

   C is shattering

   D shattered

4. While you are enjoying your vacation, the rest of us _____ as usual.

   F were working

   G work

   H will be working

   J will work

5. Lightning was flashing and the wind _____.

   A will be howling

   B was howling

   C is howling

   D howled

6. Time was running out, so the team _____ on an unusual play.

   F gambles

   G will gamble

   H was gambling

   J gambled

Check Up

Choose the verb or verb phrase that best completes each sentence.

1. Colonists _____ many letters to the king before the war.

   A send

   B sent

   C sending

   D are sending

2. At the moment, Troy _____ his homework.

   F does

   G did

   H is doing

   J will be doing

3. When the music stopped in the game of musical chairs, both Gail and Ferdie _____ over the same seat.

   A are hovering

   B hover

   C were hovering

   D hovered

4. The mayor announced that next year the city _____ a marathon.

   F will host

   G hosts

   H hosted

   J was hosting

Read each set of sentences. Choose the sentence that is written correctly.

5. A The pomegranate, a juicy fruit, is having many seeds.

   B People in ancient Greece love the taste of the pomegranate.

   C However, in one myth, they blamed pomegranate seeds for winter.

   D Emma learned the connection when she will read the story of Persephone.

6. F Uncle Sam is becoming a symbol of the United States almost two centuries ago.

   G Apparently people first use the nickname for our government during the War of 1812.

   H During that war, barrels of food supplied to the army will bear the initials "U.S."

   J In 1961 Congress gave credit for the nickname to one particular supplier, "Uncle Sam" Wilson.

7. A Last fall Nola took an art class and was making kites there.

   B Before she made her first kite, she will learn how kites fly.

   C For over 400 years, people in Japan are celebrating kites with an annual festival.

   D During the 1800s, scientists learned about winds and clouds from measuring devices that kites carried into the sky.

8. F Walter's hobby is fishing.

   G Whenever he was out in his boat, he is enjoying himself.

   H If your father catches fish on his fishing trip, we ate it tonight.

   J After he cleaned his catch, I will be cooking it.

Perfect Tenses of Verbs

Tenses that express action completed by a certain time are called **perfect tenses**. Each perfect tense verb is made up of at least two words: a simple tense form of *have* and the past participle of the main verb. The simple tense forms of *have* are the following: present—*has, have*; past—*had*; future—*will have.*

Use the **present perfect tense** to express action that began in the past. The action may be complete or continuing.

> A serious storm system <u>has entered</u> Channel 16's viewing area. (continuing)
>
> In the past year, tornadoes <u>have struck</u> the county twice. (complete)

Use the **past perfect tense** to express action that was completed before another action in the past.

> Winds <u>had blown</u> Dale's trailer over before <u>he heard about the tornado warning</u>.

Use the **future perfect tense** to express action that will be completed before a time or action in the future.

> The storm <u>will have damaged</u> many buildings <u>by the time it ends</u>.

Underline the perfect tense verbs in each sentence.

1. If everyone has seen this video, we can rent a different one.

2. Tina searched for her red sweater, but her younger sister had already borrowed it.

3. Dr. Thompson has advised me to cut down on salt.

4. Before the hero of this movie finds the treasure, he will have survived more disasters than viewers can count.

5. The judges gave a prize to the statue that Bernard had carved.

6. Edna will have used all her sick leave before she is released from the hospital.

7. Christopher has improved his times on short distances, but his results on longer races have not changed.

8. During the Middle Ages, builders rediscovered techniques that the Romans had used.

9. By the time we went out for our walk, the sun had disappeared.

10. Al cleaned out his refrigerator and threw out the food on which mold had developed.

Practice

Read each pair of sentences. Circle the letter of the sentence that uses verb tenses correctly.

1. **A** For years, the Barretts have dreamed of a vacation in Hawaii.

    B For years, the Barretts has dreamed of a vacation in Hawaii.

2. **A** The Allies had decoded messages between German headquarters and the field before their victory in World War II.

    B The Allies will have decoded messages between German headquarters and the field before their victory in World War II.

3. **A** By the time the last snow falls, I will have enjoyed cross-country skiing for months.

    B By the time the last snow falls, I have enjoyed cross-country skiing for months.

4. **A** Temperatures around the world have risen in recent years.

    B Temperatures around the world will have risen in recent years.

5. **A** Scientists will have discussed climate changes for years before governments recognized the problem.

    B Scientists had discussed climate changes for years before governments recognized the problem.

6. **A** The club will have operated for over 40 years before it burned down last Friday.

    B The club had operated for over 40 years before it burned down last Friday.

Complete the following chart by filling in each missing verb.

Verb	Present Perfect	Past Perfect	Future Perfect
fill	**7.**	had filled	**8.**
9.	has or have blown	**10.**	will have blown
11.	has or have spoken	had spoken	**12.**
tap	**13.**	**14.**	will have tapped
15.	**16.**	had written	will have written
sing	has or have sung	**17.**	**18.**
19.	has or have squeezed	**20.**	will have squeezed
see	has or have seen	**21.**	**22.**
skip	**23.**	**24.**	will have skipped
open	**25.**	had opened	**26.**

Apply

Choose the verb that correctly completes each sentence.

1. Dad complains that the rules of basketball _____ radically since he played.

   A change

   B are changing

   C have changed

   D will have changed

2. Whenever I come to visit Aunt Frances, she _____ something new.

   F knitted

   G is knitting

   H had knitted

   J have knitted

3. Signs warned of an undertow, yet Arnold _____ into the water.

   A went

   B is going

   C will have gone

   D had gone

4. Before I list this house with a realtor, I _____ to sell it myself.

   F try

   G was trying

   H will have tried

   J have tried

5. Josie _____ score for the bowling team before she became a member.

   A kept

   B was keeping

   C has kept

   D had kept

6. Dwayne _____ in the Army before he became a police officer.

   F serves

   G will be serving

   H has served

   J had served

Complete each sentence with a perfect tense of the verb in parentheses.

7. (cook) My mother points out that she _____ meals far longer than any of us have eaten them.

8. (buy) By the time Simmons left the circus, he _____ an elephant named Maisie.

9. (bark) By the time its owners came home, the dog in the next apartment _____ for more than three hours.

10. (startle) Each time that squirrel has leaped onto the porch roof, the noise _____ me.

Check Up

Choose the verb or verb phrase that best completes each sentence.

1. With two final exams scheduled for tomorrow, Abby _____ quite anxious.

   A has grown

   B had grew

   C will have grown

   D grown

2. Until he started to use a scheduling program, Morgan _____ his appointments in a pocket calendar.

   F have written

   G will have written

   H has written

   J had written

3. The cat carefully licked off every drop of milk that _____ onto its fur.

   A has fallen

   B had fallen

   C will have fallen

   D fallen

4. By the time we get home, Tony _____ his little sister.

   F has teased

   G will have teased

   H had teased

   J have teased

Read each set of sentences. Choose the sentence that is written correctly.

5. A Before the Revolutionary War, colonists in America have flown the British flag.

   B From 1775 to 1777, one popular flag has shown the British flag as part of its design.

   C However, on June 14, 1777, the Continental Congress adopted a flag with 13 red and white stripes and 13 stars on a blue field.

   D That is why we will have celebrated June 14 as Flag Day.

6. F Recently Karl has worked in a florist's shop.

   G Before he was getting that job, he is looking for a job for several months.

   H Currently Karl had spent most of his time delivering flowers.

   J He hopes that he will have kept the job because the pay is good.

7. A After my parents bought their house forty years ago, they had planted a small lilac next to it.

   B My father had dug up the lilac from his parents' yard.

   C The lilac will have grown in my parents' yard ever since.

   D When I buy a house, I will have found a young shoot on my parents' bush and transplant it in my yard.

8. F Joann had spent her summer vacation looking for fossils in Wyoming.

   G Fossils are the remains of plants or animals that have living tens of thousands of years ago.

   H Today the search for fossils had focused on the Northwest.

   J Scientists has determined a great deal about long-gone animals from found bones.

Agreement of Subjects and Verbs

Verbs in the present tense can be singular or plural. Choose the form that agrees with the subject. Use a singular verb with a singular subject; use a plural verb with a plural subject. Keep the same rule in mind when choosing among the helping verbs *am/is/are*, *was/were*, and *has/have*.

Usually, the plural form of a verb is its present tense form.

> Different drivers <u>change</u> the settings on the car radio.

Use the plural form of a verb with *I* and *you* as well as with plural nouns and pronouns.

> You <u>know</u> that I <u>listen</u> to the oldies station.

Almost always, the singular form of a verb is its base form plus *-s* or *-es*. This form is used only with a third-person singular subject. (Any subject that can be replaced with *he, she,* or *it* is third-person singular.)

> The traffic reporter <u>says</u> that fog <u>has</u> caused problems.

The important exceptions to the above rules are as follows:

- The singular form of the verb *have* is *has* (*he, she,* or *it has; they have*).
- *Be* has two singular forms in the present tense, *am* and *is*. Use *am* with *I* (*I am*). Use *is* with third-person singular subjects (*he is, she is, it is*).
- The present-tense plural form of *be* is *are* (*we are, you are, they are*).
- *Be* has two past-tense forms: the singular *was* (*I was, he/she/it was*) and the plural *were* (*we were, you were, they were*).

Read the following paragraph. Each numbered, underlined part has a verb in parentheses following the subject of that verb. On the answer line, first identify the number of the subject. Write *S* for singular or *P* for plural. Then write the correct form of the present-tense verb.

(1)   This <u>brochure (explain)</u> an inexpensive tour to England
(2) and France. The <u>plane (leave)</u> New York at 10:00 A.M. on
(3) Day 1. <u>It (arrive)</u> at London's Heathrow Airport at 9:30 P.M.
(4) local time, and tour <u>participants (go)</u> immediately to their
(5) hotel in the heart of the city. Early on Day 2, <u>buses (pick)</u> up
(6) the group for a tour of London. <u>Stops (include)</u> both historic
     sites and famous stores.

1. _____   4. _____

2. _____   5. _____

3. _____   6. _____

Practice

Frequently a subject and its verb are separated by a modifier or other phrase. The verb agrees with the subject, not the last word in the phrase.

> The price of these sweaters has been marked down. (The subject is *price*, a singular noun. The verb must be singular.)

> Special items—look for a red sticker—are at clearance prices. (The subject is *items*, a plural noun. The verb must be plural.)

When you need to choose the correct verb form in a sentence, first find the subject. Ignore the words between the subject and the verb. Then choose the verb form that matches the subject.

> **Problem:** Belts made of leather (cost, costs) more than these do.
>
> **Process:** The subject is *Belts*. Think of the sentence as *Belts (cost, costs) more than these do.*
>
> **Solution:** Belts made of leather cost more than these do.

Circle the subject in each sentence. Then underline the correct form of the verb.

1. The boys who were late to class yesterday (is, are) serving a detention.

2. In the past, girls who wanted careers in science (was, were) not taken seriously.

3. Every package on the supermarket's shelves (shakes, shake) with each aftershock.

4. The workers in the union (is, are) on strike.

5. The bells in the church tower (rings, ring) every hour.

6. Thirty letters, all contributed by one employee, (jams, jam) the Suggestion Box.

7. The girl with the tattoos on her arms (works, work) out at my gym.

8. The basketball players on the bench (waits, wait) for a chance to play in the game.

9. The cars that were blocking the entrance to the driveway (was, were) towed.

10. A house with four bedrooms (sells, sell) faster than a house with two or three bedrooms.

11. The puppy with the large paws (is, are) wagging its tail excitedly.

12. The Smiths, who live in the brick house down the street, (goes, go) running together every morning.

Apply

A **compound subject** has two or more parts. Use a plural verb for a compound subject whose parts are joined by *and*.

> Bryan and his dog are never far apart.

When the parts of a compound subject are joined by *or* or *nor*, use the verb form that agrees with the part closest to the verb.

> Gerbils or an iguana needs to be kept in a cage. (The singular subject *iguana* is closer to the verb, so the verb is singular.)

> Have the gerbils or the iguana escaped from their cages lately? (The plural subject *gerbils* is closer to the helping verb that changes form, so the helping verb is plural.)

In a few compound subjects, the two parts refer to one person or thing. For example, "macaroni and cheese" names a single dish. This type of compound subject takes a singular verb.

> The winner and still champion is Mabel's Siamese cat.

In each sentence, underline each part of the compound subject and circle the word (*and*, *or*, or *nor*) joining the parts. Then underline the correct verb form in parentheses.

1. Two family portraits and a mirror (hangs, hang) on the wall.

2. Either the brakes or the steering mechanism (am, is, are) the problem.

3. (Has, Have) the foreman or his assistants arrived on the site yet?

4. Neither Kendra nor her parents (eats, eat) meat.

5. (Was, Were) the mums or the rosebush still in bloom?

Complete each sentence by filling in the correct form of the verb in parentheses.

6. (resemble) Neither Gloria nor her sister Sheryl _____ Mrs. Compton.

7. (be) A cholesterol-fighting food and healthy breakfast _____ oatmeal.

8. (have) _____ the antique doll or Grandpa's old board games been found in the attic?

9. (need) At the moment, both the printer and the copier _____ new toner cartridges.

10. (do) _____ the flower pots or the potting soil belong in the storage shed?

11. (seem) Neither the board members nor the company president _____ willing to compromise.

Check Up

Choose the verb or verb phrase that best completes each sentence.

1. Those mountain peaks topped by snow
   _____ a memorable landscape.

   A create

   B creates

   C creating

   D is creating

2. My workouts at the gym _____ my arm
   muscles.

   F have strengthened

   G has strengthened

   H was strengthening

   J strengthens

3. In the next scene, Lili and Roger _____
   in a fast-paced duet.

   A joins

   B is joining

   C join

   D was joined

4. Either the cable cars or the Golden Gate
   Bridge _____ San Francisco to many
   people.

   F symbolizes

   G symbolize

   H have symbolized

   J symbolizing

Read each group of sentences. Choose the sentence in which the subject and verb agree.

5. A The prince, without his usual army of
   bodyguards, are touring the White
   House later today.

   B The golfers playing the entire course
   are taking too long to finish.

   C Either one large container or three of
   the smaller boxes weighs forty
   pounds.

   D Has the set designer and his
   apprentices completed their plans?

6. F It take years of practice to excel at an
   instrument.

   G Participants in the 10K race is
   warming up now.

   H The haddock and the lobster are both
   fresh, not frozen.

   J Neither Sandy nor Josh believe in
   Santa Claus any more.

7. A Neither the original movie nor its
   sequels have won any awards.

   B How much do a home in this area
   cost?

   C My annual visit to the antique stores
   bore my husband.

   D I is truly surprised by the warm
   greeting you have given me.

8. F The old man and his dog walks by
   my house every day.

   G The restaurant that I feel surpasses all
   others is Mercy's Poultry Palace.

   H Am Kitty or I among the finalists?

   J Has the girls or Jim been over to see
   you?

Easily Confused Verbs

Certain verbs are easily confused because they are close in meaning. In order to use these words correctly, you need to memorize their meanings. Since many of these verbs are irregular, you will also find it useful to memorize their principal parts.

***Raise* and *Rise*:** *Raise* means "to lift (something)" or "to grow (something)." It always takes an object. *Rise* is a verb meaning "to go up." It does not take an object.

Present	Past	Past Participle
raise	raised	(have) raised
rise	rose	(have) risen

The McHenrys raise sheep on their ranch. (*Sheep* is the object.)

Their day begins before the sun rises. (no object)

***Set* and *Sit*:** *Set* means "to place (something)." It usually takes an object. *Sit* means "to rest (in a chair)." It does not take an object.

Present	Past	Past Participle
set	set	(have) set
sit	sat	(have) sat

Janey sets the table. (*Table* is the object.)

The family sits down for breakfast. (no object)

***Teach* and *Learn*:** *Teach* means "to instruct." *Learn* means "to gain knowledge." You teach someone a body of knowledge or a skill, and that person learns what has been taught.

Present	Past	Past Prticiple
teach	taught	(have) taught
learn	learned	(have) learned

Last month, Paul taught Buddy how to shear.

Buddy learned to remove wool without hurting the sheep.

Read each pair of sentences. Circle the letter of the sentence in which the verb is used correctly.

1. **A** Before the storm arrived, Phil had raised early this morning to run three miles.

   B Before the storm arrived, Phil had risen early this morning to run three miles.

2. **A** My son likes to set in the back of the classroom with his friends.

   B My son likes to sit in the back of the classroom with his friends.

3. **A** Didn't your mother ever teach you not to speak with your mouth full?

   B Didn't your mother ever learn you not to speak with your mouth full?

Practice

Lay and *Lie*: *Lay* usually means "to place (something)." When the word has that meaning, it takes an object. *Lie* means "to rest or recline." It does not take an object.

Present	Past	Past Participle
lay	laid	(have) laid
lie	lay	(have) lain

After the test I laid my pencil on the desktop. (*Pencil* is the object.)

I lay down for a short nap earlier this afternoon. (no object)

Accept and *Except*: *Accept* means "to take or receive willingly." The principal parts of *accept* follow regular rules (*accept, accepted, accepted*). *Except*, when used as a preposition, means "other than" or "leaving out."

Lyle hoped that Jenny would accept his proposal.

All their friends except Sean were happy for the couple.

Complete each sentence by writing the principal part described in parentheses.

1. (past of *lie*) The missing newspaper _____ behind the bushes.

2. (past of *rise*) Silently, the ghost _____ and drifted through the wall.

3. (past participle of *sit*) Patti had _____ by the phone for hours, waiting for the call.

4. (past of *teach*) The ex-governor _____ a class at a prestigious university.

5. (past participle of *lay*) The senator thought she had _____ the rumors to rest.

6. (past of *accept*) The supervisor _____ full blame for the unfortunate mix-up.

Complete each sentence by circling the correct word in parentheses.

7. Gina believes that (rising, raising) her family is her most important job.

8. The waitress (set, sat) the heavy tray on the counter.

9. As a child, Dianne was (learned, taught) to speak respectfully to adults.

10. All my children (except, accept) Billy have had chicken pox already.

11. I'm afraid I will never (teach, learn) how to balance my checkbook!

12. The price of gas has (risen, raised) steadily for the past year.

Apply

Read each sentence. If you find a verb used incorrectly, rewrite the sentence correctly on the line. If the sentence is written correctly, write *Correct* on the line.

1. Alana quietly laid her baby in the crib and tiptoed away.

   _____

2. I hope that you except credit cards because I don't have enough cash on me.

   _____

3. Even though the temperature had raised, the weather was still chilly.

   _____

4. That clock has set on the mantle for more than twenty years.

   _____

5. I was learned the multiplication tables in third grade.

   _____

6. When Katie rises her voice, you know she is really angry.

   _____

Write an original sentence using each of the verbs whose present tense form is listed below. You may use any of the principal parts of the verb in your sentence.

7. teach

   _____

8. rise

   _____

9. accept

   _____

10. lay

    _____

11. learn

    _____

Check Up

Read each set of sentences. Choose the sentence that is written correctly.

1. **A** Everyone accept Iris knows how to play a musical instrument.

   B Dan learned himself how to play the accordion.

   C Brian's harmonica always laid in his pocket, just in case he ever needed it.

   D Warren was taught how to play the fiddle when he was a boy.

2. **F** The level of excitement in the stadium raised during the last, exciting seconds of the game.

   G Unfortunately, these errors have risen doubts about your competency.

   H The great bird raised its wings and lifted into the air.

   J The captain lay his charts on the desk and began to plot the ship's course.

3. **A** Rover laid by his owner's feet and dozed off.

   B The smoke from the campfire raised straight up into the night sky.

   C To make a fire, sit the logs on each other in a crisscross pattern.

   D If you want to get warm, sit close to the fire.

4. **F** Mrs. Miller has taught first grade for almost thirty years.

   G Her experience has learned her that each child is different.

   H She told the custodian to sit the books by the door.

   J Faithful studying and hard work are sure to make your grades raise.

5. **A** I had laid awake for hours before my alarm finally went off.

   B On warm summer evenings, we set on the porch and watched the fireflies.

   C The inquiry has raised new questions about the company's bookkeeping.

   D Justin is not quite ready to except the responsibility that comes with a driver's license.

6. **F** Owen is learning his son how to ride a bicycle.

   G The lowly serfs were not even allowed to raise their eyes to look at the king as he passed.

   H The disappointed child watched as his balloon raised slowly into the air.

   J Julie said, "I can't except a gift as expensive as this."

7. **A** We had sat in the exit row, where we needed to be capable of opening the door in an emergency.

   B The airplane set on the runway for twenty minutes before it took off.

   C As the plane raised, passengers could see the city below.

   D The pilot rose the landing gear soon after takeoff.

8. **F** The librarian has lain the best sellers on a special shelf.

   G At night Tom lowered the shades, and every morning he rose them.

   H The company plans to rise the price of all of its products.

   J Just lay your coats on the sofa in the family room.

Adjectives

To modify a word means to describe it or to limit its meaning in some way. **Adjectives** are words that modify nouns or pronouns. They may describe *which, what kind,* or *how many.*

The form of an adjective changes when the word it modifies is compared to another word. If the adjective is a short word of one or two syllables, add *-er* when comparing two objects. Use *-est* when comparing three or more objects.

> This salsa is <u>milder</u> than yours. (comparative form)
>
> This salsa is the <u>mildest</u> I've ever tasted. (superlative form)

If the adjective has two or more syllables, use *more* or *less* for the comparative form. Add *most* or *least* for the superlative form.

> Newer oscillating fans are <u>more efficient</u> than older models.
>
> Which company makes the <u>most efficient</u> model of all?

Never use more than one form of an adjective in a comparison.

> **Incorrect:** This is the <u>most dullest</u> show on television.
>
> **Correct:** This is the <u>dullest</u> show on television.

Circle all the adjectives in each sentence.

1. Six portraits in fancy wooden frames hung on the wall.

2. Choose a different pen with a finer point for the small lettering.

3. Young children often have an imaginary friend.

4. This pie is delicious but tastes unusual!

5. Farmland in Nebraska is more level than it is in West Virginia.

6. Were the reporter's questions inappropriate or invasive?

7. I'll wear the gaudiest outfit I own to the costume party.

8. Of all the people I know, Cecilia is the most likely to find the perfect birthday gift.

9. The least expensive hotel is also the nearest one to the convention center.

10. Does an eagle have keener eyesight than a hawk?

Practice

The following spelling rules apply when adding -er or -est to adjectives:

1. Double the final consonant for one syllable words with a short vowel followed by a single consonant.

    hot   hotter

2. Drop the final e in words that end in e.

    brave   bravest

3. Change the y to i in words that end with a consonant and y.

    easy   easier

Some adjectives have a completely different comparative and superlative form.

    good   better   best   bad   worse   worst
    many   more   most   little   less   least

In each sentence, the adjective is underlined. If there is a mistake in its form, write the correct form on the line. If there is no mistake, write Correct.

1. My apartment is <u>more cleaner</u> than my sister's. _____cleaner_____

2. Use the <u>larger</u> of all the saucepans to cook the spaghetti. _____largest_____

3. Which brand of facial tissues is the <u>most softest</u>? _____softest_____

4. Cocker spaniels have <u>fluffier</u> coats than beagles. _____

5. Steam the vegetables in the <u>least</u> amount of water possible. _____

For each adjective, write its comparative form on the first line and its superlative form on the second line.

6. high   _____   _____

7. lonely   _____   _____

8. graceful   _____   _____

9. many   _____   _____

10. wet   _____   _____

11. honest   _____   _____

12. gentle   _____   _____

56 Adjectives

Apply

Complete each sentence by adding an adjective.

1. Is *The Lord of the Rings* a _____ movie than *Star Wars*?

2. To cut that heavy material, use the _____ scissors you can find.

3. Keisha gave me some _____ advice.

4. Which of these three plums looks _____ to you?

5. Act Three is the _____ part of this play.

6. That was the _____ film I have ever seen!

7. A _____ noise startled everyone in the office.

8. These crackers are _____ than those.

Each of the following items lists a particular kind of adjective. Write a sentence using that kind of adjective to describe one of the subjects named in the box.

desert	leopard	waterfall	museum	storm
garden	ladder	frog	shoes	umbrella

9. (comparative form using *more*) _____

_____

10. (comparative form of a one-syllable adjective) _____

_____

11. (superlative form of an adjective) _____

_____

12. (superlative form of a one-syllable adjective) _____

_____

13. (superlative form using *most*) _____

_____

14. (comparative form of an adjective that changes form in comparisons) ____

_____

Check Up

Read each set of sentences. Choose the sentence in which the adjective is written correctly.

1. **A** The food is cheaper at the diner, but it is less tasty as well.

   B Who is the most richest person in America?

   C My diamond ring is my most valuablest possession.

   D Is basketball a most exciting sport than football?

2. **F** No one could decide which of the four stories was the funnier.

   G This shampoo makes my hair more shinier.

   H The sunshine grew brighter as the day progressed.

   J That is the most best suggestion I've heard this week!

3. **A** The more we tried to repair the plaster, the worser it looked.

   B She is the most talented artist of her generation.

   C This coat is designed for the more fuller figure.

   D The smaller of the two cats was the most friendliest.

4. **F** This cookie jar is emptier than it was the last time I checked.

   G Which contractor gave you a more better estimate?

   H Many unique creatures live in the more deeper parts of the ocean.

   J Is it true that Paris is the beautifulest city in the world?

Read each sentence and note the underlined part. Choose the answer that is written correctly for the underlined part.

5. Only a <u>little</u> amount of this soap cleans a regular load of laundry.

   A less

   B least

   C lesser

   D Correct as it is

6. This garden is even <u>most lovely</u> than I remembered.

   F more lovelier

   G most loveliest

   H lovelier

   J Correct as it is

7. Anton insists that his strudel is the <u>most best</u> in the world.

   A better

   B goodest

   C best

   D Correct as it is

8. The more it snowed, the <u>more slippery</u> the road became.

   F most slippery

   G more slipperier

   H slippery

   J Correct as it is

Adverbs

Adverbs are modifiers that give additional meaning to verbs, adjectives, or other adverbs. They may describe *how, when, where,* or *to what degree.* Many, but not all, adverbs end in *-ly.*

      <u>Certainly</u>, I did not expect any problems.

      A <u>highly</u> trained person <u>almost always</u> performs tasks <u>skillfully</u>.

Adverbs and adjectives follow the same rules for comparisons. When the adverb has one or two syllables, use *-er* for the comparative form (comparing two people or things) and *-est* for the superlative form (comparing three or more). For adverbs with two syllables or more, use *more* or *less* for the comparative form and *most* or *least* for the superlative form.

      Fran stood <u>nearer</u> to the entrance than anyone else in the group.

      Kevin ascended the peak the <u>most cautiously</u> of all the climbers.

Read each sentence. Write the adverb on the line. Circle the word it modifies.

1. _____ Kerry never thought she would be selected for the job.

2. _____ The goalie limped painfully off the soccer field.

3. _____ I'm sure that we passed this road sign twice!

4. _____ Who carves the turkey more expertly, Uncle Pete or Grandpa?

5. _____ Frau Blumenfeld teaches German superbly.

6. _____ I will arrive later than expected.

7. _____ We would work more efficiently if our equipment were in the same room as yours.

8. _____ Eleanor thoroughly enjoyed her day at the spa.

9. _____ Surely Perry remembered to bring the report!

10. _____ That gigantic furniture sale ended yesterday.

11. _____ He worked energetically for over an hour until he finished.

12. _____ Let's take this path since it ascends the hill more gradually than the others do.

Practice

In forming the comparative and superlative forms, the same spelling rules apply to both adverbs and adjectives.

> In springtime, daffodils bloom <u>early</u>, some tulips bloom <u>earlier</u>, and crocuses bloom <u>earliest</u> of all.

> early   earlier   earliest   close   closer   closest

The comparative and superlative forms of some adverbs are completely different words.

> well   better   best   badly   worse   worst

> much   more   most   little   less   least

Remember to use only one form of an adverb in a single comparison.

> **Incorrect:**   Labor and management resolved their differences <u>more better</u> this time than last time.

> **Correct:**   Labor and management resolved their differences <u>better</u> this time than last time.

Read each pair of sentences. Circle the letter of the sentence in which the adverb is used correctly.

1. **A**   Colin had traveled the most farthest of anyone at the school reunion.

   B   Colin had traveled the farthest of anyone at the school reunion.

2. **A**   The home team's fans cheered loudlier than the visiting team's supporters.

   B   The home team's fans cheered more loudly than the visiting team's supporters.

3. **A**   Who contributed least to the success of our venture?

   B   Who contributed most least to the success of our venture?

4. **A**   The more I hear that song, the better I like it.

   B   The more I hear that song, the more better I like it.

5. **A**   She responded enthusiastically to the challenge.

   B   She responded much enthusiastically to the challenge.

Write the comparative and superlative form of each adverb.

6. recently   _____   _____

7. badly   _____   _____

8. fast   _____   _____

9. late   _____   _____

Apply

Add an adverb to complete each sentence. Remember to use the proper form for any comparison.

1. A guide _____ counted each visitor that entered the museum.

2. Please go to the store _____.

3. The pan scorched because there was _____ any water in it.

4. Will this larger engine perform _____ than the smaller one?

5. With all the freeway construction, we _____ never get to work on time.

6. Ignoring the chatter around him, Ignatio worked _____ on his car.

7. Guide dogs are _____ trained animals.

8. The swimmer who dives _____ will win the gold medal.

9. Matthew begins his new job _____.

10. Tanya ran the marathon the _____ of all the women in her age group.

11. The bright sunshine _____ melted the snow on the ground.

12. Arlene's baby walked _____ than most babies do.

Underline the adverb in each sentence. If the adverb is incorrect, write the proper form on the line. If the adverb is used properly, write _Correct_.

13. The yard was entirely overgrown with weeds. _____

14. Leslie immediately sold her car and bought a new one. _____

15. Computer equipment becomes obsolete most quickly than televisions. _____

16. Which of the two candidates spoke more convincingly? _____

17. The falcon soared out of sight most rapidly than the sparrow. _____

18. Although Ian ran well in the preliminaries, he failed to make the finals. _____

19. There was hardly any traffic on the road last Friday. _____

20. Lois types the worsest of all the secretaries in the office. _____

Check Up

Read each sentence and look at the underlined part. Choose the answer that is written correctly for the underlined part.

1. Any experienced shopper moves much more swiftly down the aisles than I do.

    A more swiftlier

    B more swift

    C swiftlier

    D Correct as it is

2. This bulb shone more brighter a month ago than it does now.

    F more brightly

    G brightlier

    H most brightly

    J Correct as it is

3. Jennifer appeared the lesser likely of the dozen contestants to win the grand prize.

    A little

    B least

    C less

    D Correct as it is

4. Of all the workers, who drives the delivery truck more often?

    F more oftener

    G most oftenest

    H most often

    J Correct as it is

5. Does she cut hair skillfullier than the other barber in the shop?

    A most skillfully

    B skillfully

    C more skillfully

    D Correct as it is

6. Of all the voters, those in Ward 16 responded less favorably to the levy.

    F less favorable

    G least favorable

    H least favorably

    J Correct as it is

7. This raincoat fits more better than the leather jacket does.

    A better

    B gooder

    C best

    D Correct as it is

8. Nancy's clock chimes regularly on the hour and the half-hour.

    F regular

    G more regularly

    H most regularly

    J Correct as it is

9. Since Betty was napping, Paul cleaned the house most quietly than usual.

    A quietly

    B more quietly

    C more quiet

    D Correct as it is

10. After a month on a strict diet, his clothes hung more looser on him.

    F looselier

    G more loosely

    H loosest

    J Correct as it is

Adjective or Adverb?

Both adjectives and adverbs are modifiers. There are some words that can function as either type of modifier without changing form at all.

> He bought the <u>late</u> edition of the paper. (adjective, tells *what kind*)

> The bus arrived fifteen minutes <u>late</u>. (adverb, tells *when*)

The adjective *good* and the adverb *well* have identical comparative and superlative forms:

> **adjective:** good   better   best

> **adverb:**   well   better   best

The work a modifier does in a particular sentence determines whether it is an adjective or an adverb.

Adjectives

- Modify nouns or pronouns
- Describe *which one, what kind, or how many*

Adverbs

- Modify verbs, adjectives, or other adverbs
- Describe *how, when, where,* or *to what degree*
- May add a positive or negative meaning
- In many cases, end in *-ly*

Read each sentence. Circle the word modified by the underlined word. On the line, identify the modifier as an adjective or adverb by writing *ADJ* or *ADV*.

1. Who gave you the <u>best</u> advice about your problem? _____

2. All talking stopped <u>immediately</u> when the CEO entered the room. _____

3. Diamond is one of the <u>hardest</u> substances on the earth. _____

4. The deadline for all applications is <u>tomorrow</u>. _____

5. Amanda <u>never</u> remembered to order office supplies before she needed them. _____

6. On vacation we move at a <u>slower</u> pace than normal. _____

7. Great swarms of gnats were <u>everywhere</u>. _____

8. Copies of the financial report will be available <u>soon</u>. _____

9. Where is your <u>most</u> recent issue of *Time*? _____

10. Courtney stared at the <u>blank</u> screen in disbelief. _____

Practice

A descriptive adjective that explains *what kind* can often be changed to an adverb that describes *how*. Add *-ly* to make this change.

Adjective	Adverb
wise	wisely
ready	readily
bashful	bashfully

Notice how different the adjective and adverb forms are when they are used in comparisons:

Adjective	Adverb
wise, wiser, wisest	wisely, more wisely, most wisely
ready, readier, readiest	readily, more readily, most readily
bashful, more bashful, most bashful	bashfully, more bashfully, most bashfully

When making comparisons, first decide whether an adjective or an adverb is needed. Then determine the correct form to use.

Complete each sentence by using the adjective or adverb listed. If necessary, use the comparative or superlative form of the word.

heavy   heavily

1. Route 25 is the _____ traveled road in our state.

2. He seems to carry a _____ burden than most people.

3. Can you lift that _____ package by yourself?

clever   cleverly

4. The latch was _____ concealed within the carving.

5. How _____ of you to recycle those metal drums!

6. Jacob is the _____ mathematician in our group.

efficient   efficiently

7. My _____ office manager keeps everyone on task.

8. Our newer machines work _____ than the older ones.

9. This Z300 is the _____ business machine we own.

Apply

Underline the correct form of the adjective or adverb in each sentence.

1. The politician's slogan was "Vote for (Honest, Honestly) Joe."

2. Select the (softest, most softly) pillow you can find.

3. Palm trees swayed (graceful, gracefully) in the breeze.

4. Sasha (courageous, courageously) overcame her illness.

5. The tide is (lowest, most lowly) at midday.

6. Strive to become a (good, well) informed person.

7. She solved the dilemma (more imaginative, more imaginatively) than I could have.

8. Buy the mattress with the (firmest, most firmly) support.

9. My (sympathetic, sympathetically) neighbor listens to all my complaints.

10. Joshua behaved (bad, badly) in preschool yesterday.

11. At the end of the concert, the performer bowed (polite, politely) to the audience.

12. The patient looked (more robust, more robustly) after the surgery.

Write an adjective or adverb to complete each sentence. Use correct forms in comparisons.

13. Does the convenience store close _____ than the supermarket?

14. It is difficult to hear over the noise, so please speak _____.

15. According to the weather bureau, April was the _____ month on record.

16. This repair estimate is _____ than the other one.

17. We waited _____ for our guests to arrive.

18. Dr. Patel is the _____ doctor at the clinic.

19. Even with the lights on, Marilyn _____ could see the car in front of her.

20. Because of the holiday, the post office will be closed _____.

Check Up

Read each set of sentences. Choose the sentence in which adjectives and adverbs are used correctly.

1. A Eric made a futile attempt to catch his runaway dog.

   B Currants were exceptional sweet this year.

   C The usual talkative bus driver never uttered a word.

   D Enrique was unable to move free through the dense crowd in the marketplace.

2. F The picture quality on the new TV is crisply and brightly.

   G I just had the most strangest experience!

   H We listened attentively to the badly news.

   J Scientists believe the earliest humans appeared during the Cenozoic Period.

3. A My cat purrs most contented after she has been fed.

   B Jamie's picture hung precariously on the slender nail.

   C The wheat crop was more abundantly this year than last year.

   D Doris injured her back bad when she accidentally fell off the stepladder.

4. F In old movies, the family dog regular rescues someone.

   G My son wept uncontrollably when his pet fish died.

   H Find the clerk who is less busily, so we won't have to wait in line.

   J I think the darkly rug is prettier than the lighter one.

5. A Is it more better to trade the car or to sell it?

   B The aurora borealis provided a brilliantly display in the night sky.

   C My landlord never forgets to check my mail when I'm on vacation.

   D There's never been a product as well as this one!

6. F Melinda fondly remembered her old English teacher.

   G Cindy's boots were covered with a thickly coat of mud.

   H The more the silver dish was polished, the shiniest it became.

   J Mr. Gaithers exhibits the most positively attitude of anyone I know.

7. A Patrice wore the more heavier of her winter jackets.

   B The toothache throbbed worser during the night.

   C The wind is most strongest on the north side of the house.

   D A sudden movement in the bushes totally startled me.

8. F Benjamin appeared reluctantly to take on any more responsibilities.

   G Your photographer vividly captured your personality in this picture.

   H I'm so pleased that the children get along so good.

   J Maria most careful examined every aspect of the plan.

Using Negative Words

You should avoid sentences that contain double negatives. A speaker or writer commits a **double negative** error when he or she uses two or more negative words in the same sentence or clause. The following sentence contains a double negative.

| FROM: LEX KENNEDY |
| TO: SHIPPING DEPARTMENT |
| RE: DATE CHANGE |
| **MEMO** |
| WE NEED TO SHIP THE MATERIALS ON MARCH 3 RATHER THAN ON MARCH 20. |

Our department <u>didn't</u> get <u>no</u> memo about the date change.

Never use two of these common negative words in the same sentence or clause.

| no | nobody | not | nowhere |
| no one | none | nothing | never |

Other negative words include contractions that end in *n't* and the words *barely, hardly,* and *scarcely.*

To correct a double negative, remove all but one of the negative words from the sentence or clause.

Incorrect: We <u>can't hardly</u> be expected to meet the new deadline.

Correct: We <u>can't</u> be expected to meet the new deadline.

Correct: We can <u>hardly</u> be expected to meet the new deadline.

Circle every negative word in each sentence. If a sentence or clause contains two or more negative words, write *DN* for double negative on the line.

1. _____ The Jacksons didn't never regret their decision to buy the old house.

2. _____ There was plenty of popcorn left, but I didn't want none.

3. _____ Tonight's audience was nowhere near as big as last night's.

4. _____ Beth told me that she doesn't need no special class to learn the program.

5. _____ Because Renata didn't have no plans for the night, she went to bed early.

6. _____ No swimming is allowed when there isn't no lifeguard on duty.

7. _____ Most people don't know exactly how television works.

8. _____ The forecasters didn't never predict snow today, but here it is.

9. _____ The sun had barely risen when the rooster started crowing.

10. _____ Carlos was relieved to see that there wasn't nothing out of place in his apartment.

Practice

Each underlined sentence contains a double negative. Circle the letter of the sentence that corrects the double negative.

1. You don't pay no sales tax on clothing in this state.

   A   No one pays no sales tax on clothing in this state.

   B   You don't pay any sales tax on clothing in this state.

2. The real estate agent could hardly find no houses that pleased her clients.

   A   The real estate agent couldn't never find any houses that pleased her clients.

   B   The real estate agent could find no houses that pleased her clients.

3. There wasn't no one available to answer the phone during the lunch hour.

   A   There was no one available to answer the phone during the lunch hour.

   B   There wasn't scarcely anyone available to answer the phone during the lunch hour.

4. The accountants didn't find nothing improper about the company's books.

   A   The accountants found nothing improper about the company's books.

   B   The accountants never found nothing improper about the company's books.

5. Hardly anybody watches that TV comedy no more.

   A   Hardly nobody watches that TV comedy anymore.

   B   Hardly anybody watches that TV comedy anymore.

Read each sentence. If it contains a double negative, rewrite it correctly on the line. If it is written properly, write *Correct* on the line.

6. You can hardly find workmanship like this no more.

   _____

7. There wasn't barely enough room for two cars in the garage.

   _____

8. Sara hoped that nothing would go wrong on her vacation.

   _____

9. I'm sure that I didn't order no anchovies on my pizza.

   _____

Apply

Complete each sentence by circling the correct word in parentheses.

1. The detective didn't notice (nothing, anything) suspicious about the witness's story.

2. Luckily, on my last visit the dentist didn't find (any, no) cavities.

3. I thought I wouldn't (never, ever) forget the friends I made in high school.

4. Duane can't think of (anywhere, nowhere) else to look for his wallet.

5. Although rain was predicted all week, we didn't get (none, any).

6. Doesn't (anybody, nobody) at this table know how to order in French?

7. Even though she stood on her tiptoes, Amy (could, couldn't) scarcely reach the top shelf of the cabinet.

8. Although Wade tried to comfort his child, there didn't seem to be (anything, nothing) that could make Brian stop crying.

9. There (wasn't, was) hardly enough flour in the bin to make bread today.

Think of two different ways to correct the double negative in each sentence. Write the two sentences on the lines.

10. The ad didn't attract no one who was willing to buy our car.

    _____

    _____

11. Pam can't never find enough time to read the newspaper.

    _____

    _____

12. Surprisingly, the runner wasn't scarcely breathing hard after the race.

    _____

    _____

13. My teenage son's jacket doesn't hardly fit him this year.

    _____

    _____

Check Up

Read each set of sentences. Choose the sentence that uses negative words correctly.

1. A The crocuses and daffodils aren't blooming no more.

    B Brett won't use no chemical fertilizers in his garden.

    C Julie didn't expect to get no bouquet on her birthday.

    D The florist didn't have any yellow roses available.

2. F I don't have no strong opinions about the candidates.

    G I'm afraid I didn't learn nothing about the issues that concern me.

    H No one has ever asked me to be part of a poll.

    J The crowd couldn't hardly wait to learn the election results.

Read the paragraph and look at the numbered, underlined parts. Choose the answer that is written correctly for each underlined part.

Advertisers are inventing new ways to reach their customers these days.
(3) They fear that hardly nobody is paying attention to the commercials on the
(4) television. Indeed, in some homes, viewers armed with remote controls can't
never stop themselves from channel surfing as soon as the commercials begin.
Frustrated advertisers are resorting to undercover tactics such as paying to have
their products featured in the background in movies and TV shows. In this new
(5) world, viewers don't have no idea that advertisers are manipulating them.
Reportedly, guests on talk shows are being paid to recommend products, even
(6) though they haven't admitted to anyone that they are collecting fees for the
seemingly spontaneous endorsements. Could it be that all is fair in the pursuit of
the customer's money?

3. A hardly nobody isn't

    B hardly anybody isn't

    C nobody is

    D Correct as it is

4. F can't ever

    G can hardly never

    H won't never

    J Correct as it is

5. A never have no idea that

    B don't have any idea that

    C aren't scarcely aware of when

    D Correct as it is

6. F haven't admitted to no one

    G have never admitted to no one

    H haven't let nobody know

    J Correct as it is

Review

Nouns

A **noun** is a word that names a person, place, or thing. **Singular nouns** name one, and **plural nouns** name more than one. **Common nouns** are general names of any persons, places, or things; **proper nouns** are the names of particular persons, places, or things. Every important word in a proper noun begins with a capital letter.

Pronouns

A **pronoun** is a word that stands for a noun. The word the pronoun replaces is its **antecedent**. Pronouns must agree with their antecedents in **number**, **gender**, and **person**. Pronouns are categorized as **personal**, **demonstrative**, **interrogative**, **relative**, **reflexive**, or **indefinite**. The form of a pronoun may change depending upon how it is used.

Verbs

A **verb** identifies an action or a state of being. They may be **active** or **passive**. A **linking verb** links its subject to another noun or pronoun or to an adjective. A **helping verb** is used along with the base form of a verb to make a verb phrase.

Each verb has forms that are called **principal parts:** the present tense form, past tense, and past participle. The form, or tense, of a verb indicates when an action happens. Verbs and their subjects must agree, or match, in number.

Many people use certain pairs of verbs incorrectly because the words sound alike or are close in meaning to one another. Careful speakers and writers must memorize the meanings of those confusing pairs.

Adjectives and Adverbs

An **adjective** is a word that modifies a noun or a pronoun. Adjectives answer the questions *which one, what kind,* and *how many.* An **adverb** modifies a verb, an adjective, or another adverb. Adverbs answer the questions *how, when, where,* and *to what degree.* Some, but not all, adverbs end in *-ly.* When they are used in comparisons, adjectives and adverbs change their forms.

Negative Words

The following words are classified as negative: *no, not, never, hardly, scarcely, barely,* and all contractions made using the word *not.* Avoid using two negative words in the same clause or sentence; such an error is called a **double negative.**

Assessment

Choose the word or phrase that correctly completes each sentence.

1. Next week, I _____ in the blue waters of the Caribbean Sea.

   A swam

   B had swum

   C will be swimming

   D swum

2. At his birthday party, Aaron made a wish and _____ out the candles.

   F will blow

   G is blowing

   H blows

   J blew

3. When the clerk was ready, I gave _____ my credit card number.

   A she

   B her

   C hers

   D herself

4. What could be _____ than a big bowl of oatmeal for breakfast?

   F more healthier

   G healthier

   H most healthiest

   J healthiest

5. Gayle can hear _____ when she wears her hearing aid.

   A better

   B more better

   C more good

   D more gooder

6. By the end of the first class, Mr. Frost _____ all his students' names.

   F learning

   G was learned

   H had learned

   J learn

7. The workers packed away _____ tools before they left the work site.

   A they're

   B there

   C their

   D them

8. This crossword puzzle is _____ than the one in yesterday's newspaper.

   F easier

   G easily

   H more easily

   J easilier

9. The hiker wearing blue sunglasses _____ at a steady pace.

   A were walking

   B walk

   C have walked

   D walks

10. If the applicant wants the job, _____ will have to make a good first impression.

    F her

    G she

    H hers

    J they

Read each set of sentences. Choose the sentence that is written correctly.

11. **A** The player with the fewest points win the game.

    B Children on the parade float was waving at the crowd.

    C My bouquet of roses and carnations are wilting.

    D The cars on this lot are all available at sale prices.

12. **F** The family was unusually quiet at the dinner table that night.

    G Thelma made a specially effort to be friendly to the newcomers.

    H Darryl is real particular about his morning coffee.

    J The boys were terrible hungry after the swim meet.

13. **A** You have risen an interesting question.

    B My grandmother rarely needs to raise her voice to get our attention.

    C Could you please rise the left side of picture a little?

    D When the temperature raises above ninety degrees, I start feeling sick.

14. **F** Most of the drivers in the traffic jam gave up on his or her plans of getting home on time.

    G Did either of the truck drivers honk their horn at us?

    H One of the passengers left his or her magazine on the seat.

    J The driver was glad to see the police officers and told her how the accident happened.

15. **A** Julie and Sam is going to pick you up from school today.

    B Either the treadmill or the elliptical trainer are a machine that you might enjoy.

    C The dogs that have short tails are the cutest.

    D The man answering the phones are the receptionist.

16. **F** Jillian can't never get up in time to make herself a full breakfast.

    G Can't nobody convince Howard to stop smoking?

    H I don't hardly know how to explain the situation to you.

    J No one expected such a violent storm on such a beautiful spring day.

17. **A** Both boys and I are eager to see the new blockbuster movie.

    B Neither the president nor his aides has arrived at the party yet.

    C Sandwiches, chips, and chocolate cake is on the menu for the picnic.

    D Do either of the customers want to pay by credit card?

18. **F** To who did you wish to speak?

    G Gliding silently through the ocean, the shark never closes its eyes.

    H I wish them telephone solicitors would stop calling me at suppertime!

    J The head mechanics theirselves supervised the repair of the mayor's limousine.

Read the passages and look at the numbered, underlined parts. Choose the answer that is written correctly for each underlined part.

(19)   Everybody has their own way of learning. For example, some people learn best by using their eyes. These folks are most likely to remember things they
(20) see or read. Other people depends more on their ears than their eyes. To teach
(21) these people something new, it may be most efficient to speak clear and repeat
(22) needed information often. Some learners learn by doing. They can't scarely learn except by touching and manipulating objects. They have to be physically involved in the subject in order to kickstart their brains and their ability to remember. In which way do you learn best?

19. **A** our own way

    B his or her own way

    C its own way

    D Correct as it is

21. **A** clearly

    B more clear

    C most clearest

    D Correct as it is

20. **F** depend

    G is dependent

    H depending

    J Correct as it is

22. **F** can hardly learn nothing

    G can't learn nothing

    H can't learn

    J Correct as it is

       Van fidgeted while waiting in the room outside the personnel office at Blake
(23) Industries. Over and over, he told himself that whether he got this job really
(24) didn't make no difference. After all, he had a perfectly good job already. He
(25) realized that the current pay for his services were not impressive, and there was
(26) almost no hope for advancement, but a job is a job. Suddenly, he was wished that he had not begun this job search. He could picture his familiar office and his friends in the lunchroom. However, when the receptionist said it was time to meet Mrs. Blake, he found himself thinking, "I hope I get this job!"

23. **A** themselves

    B he

    C hisself

    D Correct as it is

25. **A** was

    B are

    C have been

    D Correct as it is

24. **F** made hardly no difference

    G didn't make any difference

    H didn't matter none

    J Correct as it is

26. **F** will be wishing

    G had wished

    H wished

    J Correct as it is

Complete Sentences and Fragments

It is necessary to have both a subject and a predicate to make a complete sentence. The **subject** names the person or thing that the sentence is about. The **predicate**, which always includes a verb, tells what the subject is doing.

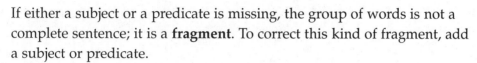

Mrs. Barresi | is waiting at the door.

subject   predicate (The verb is underlined.)

If either a subject or a predicate is missing, the group of words is not a complete sentence; it is a **fragment**. To correct this kind of fragment, add a subject or predicate.

Fragment: Our local radio station.

Correct: Our local radio station won a prestigious award. (Add a predicate.)

Fragment: Fed the tigers this morning.

Correct: The new zookeeper fed the tigers this morning. (Add a subject.)

Write _F_ beside each fragment. Write _Correct_ beside each complete sentence. Underline the subject of each complete sentence and circle the predicate.

1. _____ Alyssa just got a promotion at work.

2. _____ The smallest kitten in the litter.

3. _____ Arrived at nine o'clock on the dot.

4. _____ Won the pie-eating contest last year.

5. _____ The art museum is free on Thursdays.

6. _____ Dan swims five miles every day.

Complete each sentence by following the instructions in parentheses.

7. The famous ballet dancer _____. (Add a predicate.)

8. _____ made blueberry pancakes for breakfast. (Add a subject.)

9. _____ learned how to drive when she was seventy years old. (Add a subject.)

10. All twenty of Alma's grandchildren _____. (Add a predicate.)

Practice

There are two more types of fragments.

Sometimes a fragment has neither a subject nor a predicate.

    Fragment: Into thin air.

    Correct: <u>The magician's rabbit disappeared</u> into thin air. (Add a subject and a predicate.)

Sometimes a fragment contains both a subject and a predicate. Then it is called a **dependent clause.** A dependent clause has a subject and a predicate but cannot stand on its own. Dependent clauses begin with words such as *after, although, as, because, if, since, though, unless, when, where,* and *while.*

    Fragment: Since he turned sixteen.

    Correct: Since he turned sixteen, <u>Max has grown at least four inches.</u> (Add a complete sentence.)

Correct each fragment and write the new sentence on the line. If the item is a complete sentence, write *Correct* on the line.

1. On League Street, above the Italian market. _____

    _____

2. An enormous selection of fruits and vegetables. _____

    _____

3. While she was making coffee. _____

    _____

4. The desserts at this restaurant are spectacular. _____

    _____

5. Ben bought a puppy for his son. _____

    _____

6. By the fountain in the park. _____

    _____

7. Because Eliza was doing so well in school. _____

    _____

Apply

Correct each fragment or pair of fragments and write the complete sentence on the line.

1. After these customers leave. I'll close up for the night.

   _____

2. Wants to have a big family someday.

   _____

3. Illustrating a comic book about a boy from outer space.

   _____

4. As Kevin picked up the grocery bag. He noticed that his eggs had been crushed.

   _____

5. The biggest pumpkin at the county fair.

   _____

6. Since construction began on the highway.

   _____

7. Can recite the alphabet in six different languages.

   _____

8. I asked Sherry for help. Because she's good with numbers.

   _____

9. On the way to the theater.

   _____

10. Is having a going-out-of-business sale.

    _____

11. The winner of the watermelon seed spitting contest.

    _____

12. Next to the portrait of Harry Houdini.

    _____

Check Up

Read the following passage and look at the numbered, underlined parts. Choose the answer that is written correctly for each underlined part.

(1)   Bram Stoker, a theater manager in London. Began writing his famous novel, *Dracula*, after waking from a terrifying nightmare about a vampire. When the novel was published seven years later, it received mixed reviews from the critics.

(2) In the hundred years since then. *Dracula* has inspired countless stage productions and more than 200 film adaptations. Few other literary works have been so warmly embraced by popular culture.

1. **A** Bram Stoker, a theater manager in London, began writing his famous novel, *Dracula*. After waking from a terrifying nightmare about a vampire.

   B Bram Stoker, a theater manager in London, began writing his famous novel, *Dracula*, after waking from a terrifying nightmare about a vampire.

   C Bram Stoker, a theater manager in London began writing. His famous novel, *Dracula*, after waking from a terrifying nightmare about a vampire.

   D Correct as it is

2. **F** In the hundred years since then, *Dracula* has inspired countless stage productions and more than 200 film adaptations.

   G In the hundred years since then, *Dracula* has inspired countless stage productions. And more than 200 film adaptations.

   H In the hundred years since then, *Dracula* has inspired. Countless stage productions and more than 200 film adaptations.

   J Correct as it is

Read each set of sentences. Choose the sentence that is written correctly.

3. **A** Drank a cold glass of apple cider and sighed contentedly.

   B The soft, pink petals of the peony flower.

   C A squirrel has moved into my attic.

   D Below the murky surface of the pond.

4. **F** Got a really bad haircut this time.

   G Lincoln and his wife, Ann.

   H I left my book on the train.

   J Since the new pizza place opened on 9th Street.

5. **A** After Ingrid left the restaurant.

   B The best apple pie I've ever eaten.

   C Laughing until her sides ached.

   D Nobody ate the rice pudding.

6. **F** The garbage workers are on strike again.

   G All of the traffic lights on this road.

   H In the mayor's filing cabinet.

   J Playing hopscotch in the driveway.

Run-On Sentences

In a **run-on sentence,** two or more complete sentences are joined without the correct punctuation. Run-on sentences can be confusing for readers. To insure that your writing is clear, avoid run-on sentences.

One type of run-on joins two sentences with no punctuation between them. In the following example, the first sentence is underlined.

> Rachel broke her leg she can't run the marathon next week.

In another kind of run-on, two complete sentences are joined with just a comma.

> Rachel broke her leg, she can't run the marathon next week.

The following items are run-on sentences. Draw a vertical line between where the first sentence ends and the second sentence begins.

1. Marty and Kris had a quiet night at home they cooked dinner and watched a movie.

2. It's chilly out tonight take your jacket.

3. I'm not familiar with computers can anyone help me?

4. Genevieve is going to Greece for the summer her family lives near Athens.

5. Ryan was my best friend in grade school I haven't seen him in thirty years.

Write _C_ beside each complete sentence and _RO_ beside each run-on sentence.

6. _____ The pumpkin that you carved looks like my Aunt Helena.

7. _____ I bought this antique desk at the yard sale down the street.

8. _____ Nancy won't wait past seven o'clock, she'll leave without us.

9. _____ These headphones don't work I'm going to return them.

10. _____ Esther, who used to hate cooking, is studying to be a chef.

11. _____ Terrence is building a shed it will be done by October.

12. _____ San Francisco has always been a wonderful place to raise a family.

13. _____ Thirty dollars is too much, I'll give you twenty-five.

Practice

The following is a list of several ways to correct run-ons

1. Divide the run-on into two sentences by inserting an end mark (period, exclamation point, question mark) after the first statement. Begin the second statement with a capital letter.

   Rachel broke her leg. She can't run the marathon next week.

2. Insert a semicolon after the first statement. Do not capitalize the first word of the second statement. This is a good solution if the statements are closely related.

   Rachel broke her leg; she can't run the marathon next week.

3. Insert a comma after the first statement. After the comma, use a conjunction such as *and, but,* or *or.*

   Rachel broke her leg, and she can't run the marathon next week.

4. After the first statement, insert a semicolon and a transition word such as *however, nevertheless,* or *therefore* followed by a comma.

   Rachel broke her leg; therefore, she can't run the marathon next week.

Read each of the following run-on sentences. Choose the sentence that best corrects the run-on.

1. Amber and Vinicio were married on Saturday it was a beautiful ceremony.
   - **A** Amber and Vinicio were married on Saturday; it was a beautiful ceremony.
   - **B** Amber and Vinicio were married on Saturday, it was a beautiful ceremony.
   - **C** Amber and Vinicio were married on Saturday; nevertheless, it was a beautiful ceremony.

2. John wanted to pitch the coach put him in the outfield.
   - **F** John wanted to pitch, the coach put him in the outfield.
   - **G** John wanted to pitch the coach, and put him in the outfield.
   - **H** John wanted to pitch, but the coach put him in the outfield.

3. I don't know where my lucky socks are I can't perform without them.
   - **A** I don't know, where my lucky socks are I can't perform without them.
   - **B** I don't know where my lucky socks are. I can't perform without them.
   - **C** I don't know; where my lucky socks are I can't perform without them.

4. Fifty people called about the job we only have one opening.
   - **F** Fifty people called about the job, we only have one opening.
   - **G** Fifty people called about the job; however, we only have one opening.
   - **H** Fifty people called about the job, therefore, we only have one opening.

Apply

Read each item. If it is a run-on, rewrite it correctly on the line. If the item is a complete sentence, write *Correct* on the line.

1. Auditions were held yesterday, Al tried out for the part of the shopkeeper.

   _____

2. I don't think that I would enjoy seeing the bullfight.

   _____

3. Oliver isn't feeling well his stomach hurts.

   _____

4. When my father was a boy, his family had bottles of milk delivered every morning.

   _____

5. Hiram loves burgers and fries, but his wife is a vegetarian.

   _____

6. This street used to be quiet, these days, car alarms go off all night long.

   _____

7. Twenty blocks is too far to walk in this weather, therefore I'll take the bus.

   _____

8. I'd like to go to the party on Friday; however, I have to work that night.

   _____

9. It rained all morning the sun came out around lunchtime.

   _____

10. Randall will have to build more shelves to accommodate all of these books.

    _____

11. Mike's dog has a passion for shoes he chewed up two pairs last weekend.

    _____

12. Frank and Adriana are going away; they've asked me to water their plants.

    _____

Check Up

Read the following paragraph and look at the numbered, underlined parts. Choose the answer that is written correctly for each underlined part.

(1)   The "slow food" movement officially began in Italy it also has roots in France. "Slow food" is a response to the effects that the "fast food" culture may be having on the quality of our lives. Slow food advocates believe that it is more important that foods be fresh and wholesome than that they be ready instantly. They recommend eating locally grown fruits and vegetables that have ripened

(2) naturally. They believe that meat and dairy products should be produced without the use of hormones or antibiotics.

1. A The "slow food" movement officially began in Italy, it also has roots in France.

   B The "slow food" movement officially began in Italy, nevertheless it also has roots in France.

   C The "slow food" movement officially began in Italy, although it also has roots in France.

   D Correct as it is

2. F They believe that meat and dairy products should be produced. Without the use of hormones or antibiotics.

   G They believe that meat and dairy products should be produced; without the use of hormones or antibiotics.

   H They believe that meat and dairy products should be produced, or without the use of hormones or antibiotics.

   J Correct as it is

Read each set of sentences. Then choose the sentence that is written correctly.

3. A My cousin is coming from Italy, she plans on staying for a month.

   B If you throw a penny in the fountain, your wish will come true.

   C Andy baked brownies for the first time they were delicious.

   D I usually like shrimp, however those don't look very good.

4. F The shed is crammed full of junk, I'm afraid to open the door.

   G I tried to catch Paul after the play, but he had already left.

   H Mina can't keep a secret she told me that Joan was quitting.

   J I hope that you can visit it's been so long since we've seen you.

5. A Kyle broke the teapot he feels very embarrassed about it.

   B Smith is the best candidate therefore she will get my vote.

   C Mabel moved to Las Vegas; she got a job in a casino.

   D Lucy's sweater is cashmere; and must be very expensive.

6. F Bethany hates the country she doesn't even like the fresh air.

   G I would love to go to Paris, it seems like such a romantic place.

   H Joachim has never had chicken pox, he's also never had the measles.

   J I'll buy the hammock; however, I'll have to get permission to hang it from the trees.

Sentence Combining: Compound Sentence Parts

When two or more sentences have subjects that are identical or nearly identical, combine them by using a **compound predicate.**

> The fireworks exploded. They lit up the sky.
>
> The fireworks exploded and lit up the sky.

The two actions of the fireworks are joined in a compound predicate, so only one subject, *fireworks*, is needed.

When two or more sentences have predicates that are identical or nearly identical, combine them by using a **compound subject.**

> Candice loves crossword puzzles. Rich loves crossword puzzles.
>
> Candice and Rich love crossword puzzles.

Compound predicates and subjects are usually joined by the conjunctions *and, but, or,* and *nor.* Choose the conjunction that is appropriate for the sentence.

> Troy sent the letter. He did not expect a reply.
>
> Troy sent the letter but did not expect a reply.

Combine each pair of sentences by forming a compound subject or a compound predicate.

1. The team is on a winning streak. The team will probably win the championship.

   _____

2. My husband planned a surprise party for me. My friends planned a surprise party for me.

   _____

3. We listened carefully to the speech. We didn't understand it.

   _____

4. My brother works for the family business. My two sisters work for the family business.

   _____

5. Brian may keep score today. Mandy may keep score today.

   _____

6. The kangaroo is an animal native to Australia. The koala is an animal native to Australia.

   _____

Practice

Sentences with the same predicate or subject are not the only sentences that can be combined. When two or more sentences have common words, it may be possible to combine them into one sentence.

Jake plants tomatoes in his garden. He plants carrots in his garden.

Jake plants tomatoes and carrots in his garden.

This station broadcasts football games. It broadcasts soccer games.

This station broadcasts football and soccer games.

When two or more sentences have related topics, you may be able to combine them into one **compound sentence.** When they are combined in a compound sentence, the original sentences are called **independent clauses.** They may be joined by conjunctions such as *and, but, or, yet, so,* and *for,* or by a semicolon.

I tried to buy a ticket. The concert was sold out.

I tried to buy a ticket, but the concert was sold out.

Read each pair of sentences. Circle the letter of the sentence that combines them correctly.

1. The librarian noticed that the book was overdue. She noticed that the book was damaged.

   A The librarian noticed that the book was overdue and damaged.

   B The librarian noticed that the book was overdue and, also, she noticed it was damaged.

2. Ms. Ames offered Chloe several suggestions. Ms. Ames offered me several suggestions.

   A Ms. Ames offered Chloe several suggestions, and she offered some to me, too.

   B Ms. Ames offered Chloe and me several suggestions.

3. The talent show contestant sang well. The talent show contestant danced well.

   A The talent show contestant sang as well as she danced.

   B The talent show contestant sang and danced well.

4. Fill the tank with premium gas. Check the oil.

   A Fill and check the tank with premium gas and oil.

   B Fill the tank with premium gas and check the oil.

5. It snowed heavily yesterday. All the ski resorts are packed.

   A It snowed heavily yesterday, and all the ski resorts are packed.

   B It snowed heavily yesterday, or all the ski resorts are packed.

Apply

Read each sentence. Then choose the answer that describes the compound element in the sentence.

1. Not enough players showed up for the game, so we had to forfeit.

   A compound subject

   B compound predicate

   C other compound part

   D compound sentence

2. Ilya and Stefan are learning English.

   F compound subject

   G compound predicate

   H other compound part

   J compound sentence

3. Jesse has experience selling DVD players and other video equipment.

   A compound subject

   B compound predicate

   C other compound part

   D compound sentence

4. The boy was pushed and fell down.

   F compound subject

   G compound predicate

   H other compound part

   J compound sentence

For each item, read the first two underlined sentences. Then read the third sentence. Decide whether this sentence combines the first two sentences correctly. If it does, write *Correct*. If it does not, rewrite the sentence correctly.

5. The Valley Photography Shop sells cameras.
   The Valley Photography Shop repairs cameras.

   The Valley Photography Shop sells cameras, and it repairs them, too.

   _____

6. My new car is very expensive.
   My new car is worth every penny.

   My new car is very expensive but worth every penny.

   _____

7. My grandmother's apple pie tastes delicious.
   My grandmother's homemade ice cream tastes delicious.

   My grandmother's apple pie tastes delicious and her homemade ice cream, too.

   _____

8. Sherlock Holmes is a famous fictional detective.
   Hercule Poirot is a famous fictional detective.

   Sherlock Holmes is famous and Hercule Poirot is famous for being a fictional detective.

   _____

Check Up

Read each pair of sentences. Then choose the sentence that best combines the underlined sentences.

1. The *Titanic* was the largest ship of its time.
   The *Titanic* was the most luxurious ship of its time.

   A The *Titanic* was the largest ship, and it was the most luxurious of its time.

   B Of its time, the *Titanic* was the largest ship and the most luxurious ship.

   C The *Titanic* was the largest and most luxurious ship of its time.

   D The *Titanic* was the largest ship of its time, and it was the most luxurious, too.

2. Mumps used to be a common disease among children.
   Measles used to be a common disease among children.

   F Mumps used to be common among children, and measles was a common disease.

   G Mumps and measles used to be common diseases among children.

   H Mumps and measles used to be among children who had common diseases.

   J One common disease among children used to be mumps, and another was measles.

3. Noelle was sick.
   She insisted on singing in the show on opening night.

   A Noelle was sick on opening night or sang in the show.

   B Noelle was sick but insisted on singing in the show on opening night.

   C Noelle was sick, so she insisted on singing in the show, for it was opening night.

   D Noelle insisted on singing sickly in the show and on opening night.

4. Drew invited Connor to go trout fishing with him.
   Connor prefers deep-sea fishing.

   F Drew invited Connor to go trout fishing and deep-sea fishing with him.

   G Drew invited Connor to go either trout fishing or deep-sea fishing with him.

   H Drew invited Connor with him to go trout fishing but prefers deep-sea fishing.

   J Drew invited Connor to go trout fishing with him, but Connor prefers deep-sea fishing.

5. Mr. Olson was in an accident last night.
   Mr. Olson will not be coming to work today.

   A Mr. Olson was in an accident last night to work but will not be in today.

   B Mr. Olson, who was in an accident last night, said he will not come to work today.

   C Mr. Olson was in an accident last night or will not be coming to work today.

   D Mr. Olson was in an accident last night and will not be coming to work today.

Sentence Combining: Subordinate Clauses

When you combine two sentences that have equally important ideas, you form a compound sentence. Each independent clause in a compound sentence can stand by itself.

If the idea in one sentence seems more important than the idea in the other sentence, or you wish to make it so, form a complex sentence. **Complex sentences** contain one independent clause and one or more dependent clauses. A **dependent clause** has a subject and a predicate, but it cannot stand by itself.

The person who won the lottery has not claimed the prize.

She explained why the procedures had to be changed.

Because the snow was deep, I shoveled the driveway.

Look at the underlined clause in each sentence. Write _I_ on the line if the underlined clause is independent or _D_ if it is dependent.

1. Since dinner would be late, Arnie ate a light snack. _____

2. We frequently dine at The Poplars, which serves inexpensive but delicious food. _____

3. Send in the reservation by next week, or the price increases by fifty dollars. _____

4. The fire chief credited whoever had sounded the alarm with saving many lives. _____

5. Unless the order is shipped quickly, it will not arrive on the scheduled date. _____

6. Mugs lined the shelves, and the aroma of freshly brewed coffee hung in the air. _____

7. David's strong desire to help people is what motivates him. _____

8. The woman who ran the old hardware store could always find what I needed. _____

9. When the order is processed, you will receive a notice by e-mail. _____

10. Please tell me where to find the director's office. _____

11. If the main road is under construction, try using a secondary route. _____

12. A needlepoint sampler, which we found in the attic, was sewn by my grandmother. _____

13. Dad put up the holiday lights, and Mom started to prepare the dinner. _____

14. The set is designed, but now it needs to be constructed. _____

Practice

There is often more than one way to combine sentences. The following is an example.

>Garrett Morgan invented the traffic light. This light regulates the flow of traffic.
>
>1. Garrett Morgan invented the traffic light that regulates the flow of traffic.
>2. The traffic light, which Garrett Morgan invented, regulates the flow of traffic.

When you combine certain sentences, the order of events may be important. Study the example below.

>Maggie prepared the soil. Then she planted flower seeds.
>
>1. Maggie prepared the soil before she planted flower seeds.
>2. After Maggie prepared the soil, she planted flower seeds.

The following words are often used to combine two sentences into one complex sentence: *who, which, what, that, whoever, whatever, how, when, where, why, after, although, as, because, before, if, since, unless, until,* and *while.* Remember that these connecting words are used to begin the dependent clause.

Read each pair of underlined sentences. Circle the letter of the complex sentence that correctly combines them.

1. Vernon worked two jobs.
   He paid off his auto loan.

   A Vernon worked two jobs until he paid off his auto loan.

   B Until Vernon worked two jobs, he paid off his auto loan.

2. An understudy acted in the leading role.
   Everyone marveled at her performance.

   A When an understudy acted in the leading role, everyone marveled at her performance.

   B When everyone marveled at her performance, an understudy acted in the leading role.

3. The computers suddenly crashed.
   Everyone lost data.

   A The computers suddenly crashed because everyone lost data.

   B Because the computers suddenly crashed, everyone lost data.

4. Sydney studied for several weeks.
   Then he took the civil service test.

   A Before Sydney studied for several weeks, he took the civil service test.

   B Before Sydney took the civil service test, he studied for several weeks.

Apply

Read each pair of underlined sentences. Then read the following complex sentence. If the complex sentence combines the underlined sentences correctly, write *Correct* on the line. If it does not, rewrite the sentence correctly.

1. Tammy was tired of listening to the concert.
   She quietly left her seat.

   Where Tammy was tired of listening to the concert, she quietly left her seat.

   _____

2. Grandfather told us about his uncle Horace.
   Uncle Horace was a farmer in Nebraska.

   Grandfather told us about his uncle Horace, who was a farmer in Nebraska.

   _____

3. Stanley went hiking in the dark.
   He fell and broke his leg.

   When Stanley fell and broke his leg, he went hiking in the dark.

   _____

4. Sarah opened a small bookstore.
   The store specialized in English literature.

   Sarah opened a small bookstore, who specialized in English literature.

   _____

5. A man was adrift in his disabled boat for a month.
   He was rescued by a passing ship.

   After a man was adrift in his disabled boat for a month, he was rescued by a passing ship.

   _____

6. The weather was perfect this year.
   We had an abundance of corn and soybeans.

   Since we had an abundance of corn and soybeans, the weather was perfect this year.

   _____

Check Up

Read each pair of underlined sentences. Then choose the sentence that correctly combines the underlined sentences.

1. Myron heard about an accident on the freeway.
   He drove another route home.

   A Although Myron heard about an accident on the freeway, he drove another route home.

   B When Myron drove another route home, he heard about an accident on the freeway.

   C When Myron heard about an accident on the freeway, he drove another route home.

   D Myron heard about an accident on the freeway, or he drove another route home.

2. My van was difficult to steer.
   The tires were out of alignment.

   F My van was difficult to steer, and the tires were out of alignment.

   G Because the tires were out of alignment, my van was difficult to steer.

   H Until my van was difficult to steer, the tires were out of alignment.

   J Because my van was difficult to steer, the tires were out of alignment.

3. Clevon designs Web pages.
   The Web pages describe sports equipment.

   A Clevon designs Web pages that describe sports equipment.

   B The Web pages that describe sports equipment Clevon designs them.

   C Clevon designs Web pages, and the Web pages describe sports equipment.

   D After Clevon designs Web pages, they describe sports equipment.

4. Memorial Forest is a charred ruin.
   A fire ravaged the area last summer.

   F Since Memorial Forest has been a charred ruin, a fire ravaged the area last summer.

   G Memorial Forest is a charred ruin while a fire ravaged the area last summer.

   H A fire ravaged the area last summer, but Memorial Forest is a charred ruin.

   J Memorial Forest has been a charred ruin since a fire ravaged the area last summer.

5. Dorothea is a librarian.
   She leads book discussions every month.

   A Dorothea is a librarian, yet she leads book discussions every month.

   B Dorothea is a librarian who leads book discussions every month.

   C While Dorothea is a librarian, she leads book discussions every month.

   D Although Dorothea is a librarian, she leads book discussions every month.

Sentence Combining: Adding Modifiers

Add variety to your writing by using adjectives and adjective phrases that give details about persons, places, and things. However, you do not need to write a whole sentence just to add a detail. You can combine short sentences into a single sentence that includes a modifier.

An adjective that is moved from one sentence into another is usually placed before the word it modifies. An adjective phrase is placed after the word it modifies.

Adding an adjective:

Adele ordered carpeting for her office.

The carpeting was gray.

Adele ordered gray carpeting for her office.

Adding an adjective phrase:

The ingredients are not difficult to find.

The ingredients are for the pie.

The ingredients for the pie are not difficult to find.

Read each pair of sentences. Then combine the sentences by correctly adding the modifier in the second sentence to the first sentence.

1. That umbrella has a broken handle. The umbrella is in the closet.

   _____

2. Melissa ordered a table for the dining room. The table was mahogany.

   _____

3. Hiking in the Rockies, we spotted mountain goats. The goats were on rocky ledges.

   _____

4. The scarf irritated my neck and chin. The scarf was woolen.

   _____

5. Students participated in the science fair. The students were from Harding School.

   _____

6. Our old chair needs a slipcover. The chair is near the fireplace.

   _____

Practice

You can add information about *how, when, where,* and *why* an action occurs when you use adverbs and adverb phrases to modify verbs. Adverbs and adverb phrases also modify adjectives and other adverbs. Try to put modifiers near the words they modify. However, adverbs that modify verbs usually make sense in various parts of a sentence.

> **Adding an adverb:**
>
> Jean defended her client.
>
> She spoke vigorously.
>
> Jean vigorously defended her client. *or*
>
> Jean defended her client vigorously. *or*
>
> Vigorously, Jean defended her client.

Each sentence in Column B combines one of the sentence pairs in Column A. Write the letter of the sentence in Column B on the line next to its match in Column A.

Column A

1. _____ Larry pored over the parts catalogue. He stared intently at it.

2. _____ Flo packs gift baskets. She works during her lunch hour.

3. _____ We installed a sprinkler system. We put it on our property.

4. _____ Bud collects papers for recycling. He does this daily.

5. _____ Heavy waves battered the seawall. They battered relentlessly.

Column B

A Bud collects papers daily for recycling.

B We installed a sprinkler system on our property.

C Flo packs gift baskets during her lunch hour.

D Heavy waves relentlessly battered the seawall.

E Intently, Larry pored over the parts catalogue.

Combine each pair of sentences. Add the modifier from the second sentence to the first sentence.

6. An artisan shaped the clay on the potter's wheel. She worked deftly.

   _____

7. Jake and Russ paddled the canoe. They went across the lake.

   _____

8. An officer arrived to assist us. The officer came within a few minutes.

   _____

Apply

Read each set of underlined sentences. Then read the following sentence. If it combines the underlined sentences correctly, write *Correct* on the line. If it does not, rewrite the sentence properly.

1. We received tickets to the game.
   The tickets were free.

   We received tickets to the game, and they were free tickets.

   _____

2. Maple trees are tapped for their sap.
   This happens in the spring.

   In the spring, maple trees are tapped for their sap.

   _____

3. The actor stepped into the spotlight.
   He moved slowly.
   He moved majestically.

   The actor stepped slowly into the spotlight, and he moved majestically.

   _____

4. During halftime, the high school band marched.
   They marched around the football field.

   During halftime, the high school band marched and marched around the football field.

   _____

5. Schools of fish darted through the water.
   The fish were colorful.
   The water was crystal clear.

   Schools of fish darted through the water, colorful and crystal clear.

   _____

6. Chef Pierre sliced the vegetables with a sharp knife.
   He cut precisely.
   He cut rapidly.

   Rapidly, Chef Pierre sliced the vegetables with a sharp knife and precisely, too.

   _____

Check Up

Read each set of underlined sentences. Then choose the sentence that best combines the underlined sentences.

1. A small brook trickled through the meadow.
   It flowed slowly.

   A A small brook trickled slowly through the meadow.

   B A small and slow brook trickled through the meadow.

   C A small brook trickled through the meadow, and it flowed slowly.

   D A small brook that trickled through the meadow trickled slowly, too.

2. Benny washed the dog's paw prints off the floor.
   He did it immediately.
   The paw prints were muddy.

   F Benny washed the dog's muddy paw prints off the floor, and he did it immediately.

   G Immediately, Benny washed the dog's paw prints off the floor, and they were muddy.

   H Benny immediately washed the dog's muddy paw prints off the floor.

   J Benny washed the dog's immediate and muddy paw prints off the floor.

3. Monte repaired a faulty gasket.
   The gasket was on the autoclave.

   A On the autoclave is a gasket, and Monte repaired it.

   B Monte repaired a faulty gasket on the autoclave.

   C Monte repaired a faulty gasket, and it was on the autoclave.

   D A gasket that Monte repaired was faulty and was on the autoclave.

4. Carpenter ants drilled several tunnels.
   They drilled inside the old tree.

   F Carpenter ants drilled several tunnels, and they were inside the old tree.

   G Inside the old tree, there were carpenter ants that drilled and made several tunnels.

   H Carpenter ants drilled inside the old tree and drilled several tunnels, too.

   J Carpenter ants drilled several tunnels inside the old tree.

5. The large cauldron of soup boiled on the hearth.
   It boiled cheerfully.

   A The large cauldron of soup, which boiled cheerfully, was on the hearth.

   B Boiling cheerfully, the large cauldron of soup was on the hearth.

   C The large cauldron of soup boiled on the cheerful hearth.

   D The large cauldron of soup boiled cheerfully on the hearth.

Sentence Clarity: Misplaced Modifiers

A writer who adds a descriptive word or phrase to a sentence usually helps the reader understand an idea or visualize a scene more easily. However, placing a description in the wrong part of a sentence can lead to confusion. For example, read this sentence:

A girl stopped to pet a little dog <u>with a backpack full of books</u>.

Because of its position in the sentence, the underlined phrase about the backpack seems to describe the dog. The phrase is a **misplaced modifier,** that is, a modifier placed in a sentence in such a way that it describes the wrong person or thing. Avoid confusion by placing every descriptive phrase as close as possible to the word being modified.

A girl <u>with a backpack full of books</u> stopped to pet a little dog.

Each of the following sentences contains a misplaced modifier. Rewrite each sentence correctly.

1. The children showed off for Grandma jumping on the trampoline.

   _____

2. Milton unplugged the lamp from the outlet on the wall that was wobbly.

   _____

3. Leaving the office early, the elevator was packed with eight of us.

   _____

4. Someone could get hurt tripping over that cat with his glasses off.

   _____

5. Lost in the attic for years, I finally found my class picture from first grade.

   _____

6. Everyone heard a loud boom who was at the restaurant.

   _____

7. Asleep on the couch, Lea tiptoed past Harold.

   _____

8. Maxine found a moldy orange looking through the refrigerator for a snack.

   _____

Practice

A **dangling modifier** is a modifying phrase that does not modify any word in its sentence. The following sentence is an example.

Hurrying past the window, nothing could be seen inside.

The underlined phrase seems to modify the word *nothing*, but that makes no sense. Actually, there is no word in the sentence that is modified by the phrase.

Avoid dangling modifiers by making sure that every modifier in a sentence relates to a specific word. Correct a dangling modifier by rewriting the sentence to include the word that is modified.

Hurrying past the window, I could see nothing inside.

Each of the following sentences has a misplaced or dangling modifier. Underline the modifier in each sentence and write *M* for misplaced or *D* for dangling on the line.

1. Before getting to bed, the alarm clock took some time to set. _____

2. After leaving those scissors outside in the rain, they rusted. _____

3. Rusty after being left out in the rain, Alexandra tried to use the scissors. _____

4. Losing your temper as easily as you do, this job will be difficult. _____

5. Save the leftover pizza for Joe with mushrooms in the oven. _____

6. Sliding downhill on a toboggan, his wrist was broken. _____

7. The job for the client finally got finished, working far into the night. _____

8. Avi finally finished the job for the client, who worked far into the night. _____

9. Losing many plants to a late frost, any profit from this year's crop will probably be small.

   _____

10. After clearing the table, the sink was full of dirty dishes. _____

Choose any two of the above sentences. Then rewrite them, correcting the misplaced or dangling modifiers.

11. _____

12. _____

Apply

Read each set of underlined sentences. Then choose the sentence that combines the underlined sentences correctly.

1. The musical is full of laughs.
    It has great music and a moving plot.
    Call the Palace Theater for tickets to the musical.

    A Full of laughs, great music, and a moving plot, call the Palace Theater for tickets.

    B Full of laughs, great music, and a moving plot, call the Palace Theater for tickets to the musical.

    C For tickets to a musical that is full of laughs, great music, and a moving plot, call the Palace Theater.

2. Rake your leaves and leave them in the street.
    City workers will pick up the leaves.

    F City workers will pick up raked leaves left in the street.

    G Left in the street, city workers will pick up raked leaves.

    H Raked into the street and left there, city workers will take care of the pickup.

3. Chad has been bothered by arthritis for months.
    Now he takes aspirin.
    The aspirin relieves the pain.

    A Bothered by arthritis for months, aspirin taken now relieves the pain.

    B Bothered by arthritis for months, aspirin that Chad takes now relieves the pain.

    C Bothered by arthritis for months, Chad now takes aspirin, which relieves the pain.

Read each set of underlined sentences. If the final sentence combines the underlined ones correctly, write _Correct_ on the line. If it does not, rewrite the sentence properly.

4. Eloise greeted her visitors.
    They were unexpected.
    She wished she had cleaned her apartment.

    Unexpectedly, Eloise greeted her visitors and wished she had cleaned her apartment.

    _____

5. Mr. and Mrs. Vance were walking across an intersection.
    A car almost ran them over.

    Mr. and Mrs. Vance were almost run over by a car walking across an intersection.

    _____

Check Up

Read each set of sentences. Choose the sentence that has no misplaced or dangling modifiers.

1. **A** Browsing through the bookstore, an excellent vegetarian cookbook is on sale.

    B Having received everything I want, Santa Claus won't get a letter from me this year.

    C The mail carrier dropped off a flyer about the July 4th celebration in my mailbox.

    D Chasing her puppy down the street, Lara slid on ice and fell.

2. **F** Gina recalled reading a scary story written by Edgar Allan Poe in her high school English class.

    G Growing more cloudy and threatening by the minute, the lifeguards urged everyone to get out of the pool.

    H Bringing her favorite casserole, Mattie strolled to the block party.

    J The first firefighters saved three residents who arrived at the fire.

3. **A** Every year, this award goes to an employee who volunteers time and effort to a local charity.

    B Named after the Kansa tribe, we moved to Kansas City five years ago.

    C The ice on the pond is not safe for the children melting in the spring sunshine.

    D After sending out 100 résumés, this is the only response that came in.

4. **F** Who is responsible for watering the office plants on the staff?

    G After spending the day at the beach, my clothes are full of sand.

    H The short forward with red hair is the most talented player in this gym class.

    J Charged with shoplifting, friends of the young man insisted he was innocent.

5. **A** This morning six people were shocked to see a deer, waiting for a bus at Fourth and Main.

    B The calendar with pictures of fish is the one on which I've entered all my appointments.

    C After donating blood once a month for a year, the company honors you as a caring citizen.

    D Parking in the street overnight, a foot of snow covered Leo's car by morning.

6. **F** Camisha invited everyone to her wedding in the office.

    G After sitting in the waiting room for an hour, the doctor finally examined Homer's eyes.

    H Packages of food are being stacked on empty desks that employees are donating to the hunger center.

    J Forgotten in the car's trunk, the bowling ball rolled out of its bag and over the groceries.

Sentence Clarity: Parallel Structure

The term **parallel structure** refers to the use of balanced, or similar, elements, usually in compound sentence parts. Look, for example, at the underlined compound parts in the following two sentences.

> Both your words and your behavior disturb your mother and me.
>
> We may have to restrict your cell phone privileges and your television viewing.

Both sentences have parallel structure. In the first sentence, both subjects, *words* and *behavior*, are nouns modified by the pronoun *your*. In the second sentence, both objects, *privileges* and *viewing*, are modified by the adjective *your*.

Similarity in word patterns helps a reader recognize which parts of a sentence are meant to work together. Therefore, use of parallel structure makes writing easier to understand.

Read each sentence and look at the underlined parts. Decide whether the underlined parts are examples of parallel structure or nonparallel structure. Circle the appropriate letter.

1. The airline snack and when I took a short, dreamless nap took up some time on the long flight.

   A parallel structure   **B** nonparallel structure

2. Addie filled out the application and filed it promptly.

   A parallel structure   **B** nonparallel structure

3. The detective proved his client's innocence and that her co-worker stole the plans.

   A parallel structure   **B** nonparallel structure

4. Aaron bought the print with strong colors and to hang in his cubicle.

   A parallel structure   **B** nonparallel structure

5. The soothing voice of the all-night deejay on my favorite radio station and that I was dreaming merged.

   A parallel structure   **B** nonparallel structure

6. Lulu's supervisor commented favorably on how quickly she finished her own assignments and how often she helped her coworkers.

   A parallel structure   **B** nonparallel structure

Practice

All the verbs in a compound verb or a compound predicate should be in the same tense.

> Before heckling interrupted his speech, Eduard had hesitated but had continued. (past perfect verb)

> The would-be comedians are practicing their material and looking forward to their stage debuts. (present progressive verbs)

A **gerund** is a verb in its present tense form that ends in -*ing*. It is always used as a noun.

> Winning is fun.

An **infinitive** is a verb in its present-tense form preceded by the word *to*. Infinitives and infinitive phrases are often used as nouns.

> To hear one voice in this crowd is difficult.

Parallel structure also applies to infinitives and gerunds.

> **Parallel:**   I prefer to walk rather than to run.
>
> Walking causes less pain than running does.
>
> **Nonparallel:** I prefer to walk rather than running.

Read each sentence and look at the underlined part. Choose the answer that is written correctly for the underlined part.

1. The stranger knocked on the door and disappears when Eve answered it.

   A has disappeared

   B disappeared

   C to disappear

2. Didi told the children a story to keep them busy and makes them laugh.

   F making them laugh

   G made them laugh

   H to make them laugh

3. Sawing the wood and to paint it will not be difficult.

   A painting it

   B if you paint it

   C having painted it

4. Preparing the dinner took all day, but the eating took only a few minutes.

   F when we eat it

   G to eat it

   H eating it

5. Running along the lake and to swim at the pool are my favorite forms of exercise.

   A having swum

   B to go swimming

   C swimming

6. Whenever he gives a speech, the president stumbled over words and avoids eye contact.

   F will stumble

   G stumbles

   H having stumbled

Apply

Read each set of sentences. Choose the sentence that uses parallel structure correctly.

1. **A** Around our house, having the children choose their chores works better than assigning jobs.

   B Doing the dishes and to vacuum the rugs were Terry's choices.

   C Brett volunteered to walk the dog, watch his baby brother, and weeding the flowerbed, too.

   D We change jobs every week to avoid boredom and when they claim the other person's jobs are easier.

2. **F** The position of receptionist demands someone who can deal well with the public and to be friendly.

   G When she saw the ad, Marian promptly wrote a customized cover letter, attached her résumé, and was sending them in.

   H A few phone calls and two visits to the office for interviews followed.

   J Marian opens the mail, sorts it, and had delivered it to the sales reps.

3. **A** After debating where to go on vacation, coming to a decision, and we coordinated vacation days, we are ready to go on our trip.

   B We will fly to Mexico City, spend two days in the city, and then going on to the beach.

   C Taking a cab to the airport and to get on the plane are the first stages of our vacation.

   D Don't forget to close the blinds, turn off the light, and lock the door.

4. **F** Memorizing lines and to speak loudly are easy for Jack.

   G It's only natural, then, that he has joined a community theater group and had been trying out for the upcoming play.

   H If he doesn't get a part, he will help by working on scenery and publicizing the play.

   J The friendships he makes, the thrills he has onstage, and to have fun keep Jack active in theater groups.

Rewrite each sentence and correct its parallel structure.

5. Martin would prefer to fish or to hike or canoeing down the river.

   _____

   _____

6. Abby's whistling of old songs, her humming of a single note, and how she taps her fingers are signs that she is nervous.

   _____

   _____

Check Up

Read the passage and look at the numbered, underlined parts. Choose the answer that is written correctly for each underlined part. Make sure that each sentence with compound parts has parallel structure.

Which is the oldest amusement park ride still in use? This ride does
(1) not careen down steep hills nor turn its riders upside down <u>nor giving its riders whiplash</u>. It is the merry-go-round. Perhaps it does not top the list
(2) of favorites among teens and <u>when people want a thrill</u>, but the merry-go-round has many steady customers. There are the little children for whom the ride is exciting, the romantics who enjoy sharing a tranquil moment,
(3) and <u>recalling merry-go-rounds of the past by older riders</u>.

The first known merry-go-round, or carousel, in America was already operating in Salem, Massachusetts, in 1799. As people left farming to take
(4) jobs in factories and stores, they got more free time and <u>choosing to spend</u> some of that time in amusement parks. Therefore, amusement parks—and merry-go-rounds—became more and more popular. When new carousels were built, craftsmen made each one different, brightening horses' saddles with patriotic symbols, painting central panels with seascapes, and
(5) <u>added both wild animals and cherubs</u> to the decorations. Today, the carousels that survive reflect our cultural heritage. To see merry-go-rounds
(6) <u>is to be touched by the past</u>.

1. A nor to give its riders whiplash

   B nor give its riders whiplash

   C and its riders don't get whiplash

   D Correct as it is

2. F giving people a thrill

   G every time a person wants a thrill

   H thrill-seekers

   J Correct as it is

3. A older riders to recall merry-go-rounds of the past

   B older riders who recall merry-go-rounds of the past

   C if older riders recall merry-go-rounds of the past

   D Correct as it is

4. F chose to spend

   G were choosing to spend

   H to choose spending

   J Correct as it is

5. A both wild animals and cherubs were being added

   B to add both wild animals and cherubs

   C adding both wild animals and cherubs

   D Correct as it is

6. F having touched the past

   G having the past touch you

   H that you are touched by the past

   J Correct as it is

Sentence Clarity: Verbosity and Repetition

Using more words than needed to express an idea is called wordiness, or **verbosity.** Writing that is verbose repeats itself and introduces unnecessary information.

Verbose: Marathon is the name of a race that people run, and if you've ever wondered how the race got its name, marathon, there's a really interesting story about how it got its name, which starts back in ancient history when ancient Greeks fought a battle at a place called Marathon, which became famous, and that's where the name comes from.

Concise: The racing event called the marathon gets its name from the site of a famous battleground in ancient Greece.

Read each verbose sentence. Then choose the sentence that shortens the verbose sentence but does not change its meaning.

1. People who work in my office are always complaining about the temperature in the office because some people are hot, other people are cold, and everyone agrees that the heat isn't the same across the whole floor.

   A People who work in my office are always complaining.

   B People who work in my office always complain about the heat because it isn't the same across the whole floor.

   C When people in my office complain about the heat, which is just about always, it's because the heat isn't the same across the whole floor.

2. Last week the city held hearings for two whole days about the problem of noise near the airport, and some people who live near the airport said the noise level was much too high, while other people who live near the airport said that the noise wasn't that bad.

   F During the hearings that the city held last week, people who lived nearby said the noise level at the airport was too high and not that bad for two whole days.

   G Last week the city held hearings about the problem of noise near the airport, and some people who lived near the airport expressed their opinions.

   H During two days of hearings held by the city last week, people who lived near the airport expressed opposite opinions about the level of noise in the area.

Practice

Read each pair of sentences. Circle the letter of the sentence that is concise.

1. **A** Every week on Saturday, the Garcia children have to clean their rooms, and on that day, they do other chores, too, besides cleaning their own rooms.

   B Every Saturday, the Garcia children clean their rooms and do other chores.

2. **A** Because I see my neighbor's dog roaming the neighborhood almost every day, I think that she doesn't take good care of the dog.

   B I think that my neighbor doesn't take good care of her dog, and I say that because whenever I look I see her dog roaming the neighborhood almost every day.

3. **A** Usually, Verna begins a typical day by listening to the news and weather.

   B Usually, Verna begins the day by listening to the news and weather.

4. **A** At this restaurant, you create your own personal stir-fry by choosing among the ingredients and selecting just the ones you want.

   B At this restaurant, you personalize your stir-fry by choosing your own ingredients.

Read each sentence and look at the underlined part. Choose the answer that is written correctly for the underlined part.

5. The peasants wore drab, dull, and very monotonous clothing.

   A drab, dull, and monotonous clothing

   B drab clothing that was dull, too

   C drab clothing

   D Correct as it is

6. When you complete and finish this job, I have another one waiting for you.

   F you complete this job

   G you complete this job and it's finished

   H finish this complete job

   J Correct as it is

7. Except in unusual cases, the clerk ordinarily fills out this form.

   A Usually, the clerk

   B The clerk

   C In most cases, the clerk he

   D Correct as it is

8. The directions for assembling the toy were confusing.

   F directions that told how to assemble the toy

   G directions for assembling the parts that make up the toy

   H directions for putting together and assembling the toy

   J Correct as it is

Apply

Read each sentence. Choose the words or phrases that may not be dropped from the sentence without losing some meaning.

1. On a frigid day like this, the cold, freezing air makes the children's cheeks red.

    A frigid

    B cold,

    C red

2. After she burned it, Adele threw out the burned pie crust that she blackened by accident.

    F After she burned it

    G pie crust

    H that she blackened by accident

3. When Bert helped clean his grandfather's attic, he found some old, antique roller skates while he was there.

    A When Bert helped clean his grandfather's attic,

    B old,

    C while he was there

4. On most tests in chemistry class, Rudy gets the highest score, above everyone else, but not every time.

    F in chemistry class

    G above everyone else,

    H but not every time

Rewrite each of the following verbose sentences to make them concise. Be careful not to change the meaning of the sentences.

5. The family enjoyed a nice, pleasant day at the beach.

    _____

6. Wild with excitement, the over-enthusiastic fans eagerly pushed towards the stage, shoving, elbowing, and shouldering others aside in their drive forward.

    _____

    _____

7. Whenever Carrie watered the plants, she usually used a plastic bottle of the kind that milk comes in.

    _____

    _____

8. As soon as you have some free time, please call me when you can.

    _____

Check Up

Read each set of sentences. Choose the sentence that is written concisely.

1. **A** Ilona, who before now has never yet paid attention to fashion, wants to make herself over and become a smart, stylish, sharp dresser.

   B In the past, when she used to go shopping at the stores, she immediately bought the first outfit she tried on that fit.

   C Now, however, she prepares for shopping by examining recent fashion magazines and newspaper photos of well-dressed celebrities.

   D Probably, in the near future, she may soon try out new hairstyles as well as new styles in clothes.

2. **F** Frequently, very persuasive people who can talk other people into almost anything are often said to have kissed the Blarney Stone.

   G The Blarney Stone is a block of limestone that is part of a tower in Blarney Castle in Ireland; legend says that whoever kisses it will get the gift of speaking persuasively.

   H According to one story, the stone supposedly got its power from a spell that allegedly was cast by an old woman.

   J In another story, the tale says that an owner of the castle was very good at talking himself out of the duties that he was supposed to perform, and the stone in his tower was given credit for giving him that skill.

3. **A** The word *spelunking* is the name that we have given to the hobby of exploring caves, and the word *spelunker* is the name given to a person who takes part in the hobby of exploring caves.

   B This hobby is risky and very dangerous for any careless spelunker who does not follow the safety rules for exploring caves cautiously.

   C One of the rules is never to go into a cave alone and to always have a partner with you when you go spelunking.

   D Other rules are to take flashlights and other safety equipment with you and to let others know where you are going.

4. **F** Do you consider yourself a cat person, a dog person, or an independent?

   G Many cat owners typically worry about their cats being lonely and want to give their cats company.

   H A home that has a cat in it is very likely to have two cats or three cats or even more cats, although this is not always true.

   J Even a small apartment with not much space may have more than one cat in the apartment.

Review

Complete Sentences, Fragments, and Run-Ons

Every **complete sentence** has a subject and a predicate. The subject names who or what is doing something. The predicate tells what the subject is doing. The predicate always includes a verb.

> The owners of that house | are moving to another state.
>
>   subject   predicate (verb is underlined)

A **fragment** lacks either a subject or a predicate. A **run-on sentence** combines two or more sentences without correct punctuation.

Sentence Combining

Sentences that tell about closely related topics often can be combined.

In a **compound sentence,** each clause can stand alone.

> Beets grow underground. Beans grow on bushes.
>
> Beets grow underground, and beans grow on bushes.

In a **complex sentence,** only one of the clauses can stand alone.

> Will you drive us? Then we can get to practice on time.
>
> If you will drive us, we can get to practice on time.

When two sentences tell about the same object or action, modifiers from one can be moved to the other. They must be placed correctly.

> The man spoke to us. He was ill. He spoke softly.
>
> The ill man spoke softly to us.

Sentence Clarity

A **misplaced modifier** is placed in a sentence so that it describes the wrong word. A **dangling modifier** describes something not named in the sentence.

> **Misplaced:** In an aqua glass vase, the shopper bought flowers.
>
> **Dangling:** Waiting in the lobby, it will be easy to see you.

A sentence with **nonparallel structure** uses different types of words or phrases to do the same job.

> **Nonparallel:** To go on a diet and losing weight demand effort.
>
> **Parallel:** Going on a diet and losing weight demand effort.

Verbosity means using unnecessary words in a sentence.

> **Verbose:** At the beginning of the story, it starts when the heroine is a new baby.
>
> **Concise:** The story starts when the heroine is a baby.

Assessment

Read each set of sentences. Choose the sentence that is written correctly.

1. **A** Penny is always afraid of catching a cold and to get infected with germs of any kind.

   B Every day she takes two daily vitamin pills, morning and night.

   C Wiping off the phone receiver whenever she uses it.

   D Penny will probably make herself sick by taking unneeded medicine!

2. **F** You might expect that gardeners have nothing to do during winter.

   G That view would be mistaken because it doesn't match the facts and is quite wrong!

   H Gardeners are busy planning their next gardens and to review catalogs for seeds and plants.

   J With researchers always coming up with new varieties.

3. **A** Roy paints houses, he gets most of his business from referrals.

   B People who like the job he does and have friends with houses.

   C He tries to start each job on schedule and to finish it as quickly as possible.

   D Recommending him to other people, it's important that Roy do a good job.

4. **F** A traffic reporter gets news about traffic problems and to share it with various radio stations.

   G During the average rush hour, a reporter is usually speaking on one station while the announcer of another station is introducing him or her, typically.

   H When all goes well, the reporter completes one report and turns to the second station in time.

   J While keeping track of incoming reports about traffic conditions at the same time as speaking on air!

5. **A** Gayle and Verne have been searching for a new carpet it's not easy to find the right one.

   B They want a carpet that won't easily show dirt and wear.

   C With an abstract pattern in the right colors, they found one carpet they really liked.

   D Unfortunately, the price was too high, and they decided the carpet was too expensive because they didn't want to spend that much.

Read each set of underlined sentences. Then choose the sentence that correctly combines the underlined sentences.

6. Shane has seen a cardinal at his bird feeder.
   He has seen an oriole at his bird feeder.

   F Shane has seen a cardinal at his bird feeder and an oriole.

   G Shane, who has seen a cardinal at his bird feeder, has also seen an oriole there.

   H A cardinal has been seen at Shane's bird feeder, where an oriole has been seen, too.

   J Shane has seen a cardinal and an oriole at his bird feeder.

7. Deidra went to see some new condos last Sunday.
   The condos were expensive.

   A The condos were expensive and what Deidra went to see last Sunday.

   B The condos that Deidra went to see were expensive last Sunday.

   C Deidra went to see some expensive new condos last Sunday.

   D Last Sunday, when Deidra went to see some new condos, they were expensive.

8. Neither Kaylee nor Jonathan can swim.
   Kaylee cannot skate, either.

   F Neither Kaylee nor Jonathan can swim, and Kaylee cannot skate, either.

   G Kaylee can neither swim nor skate, and Jonathan can't, either.

   H Neither Jonathan can swim, nor Kaylee cannot swim or skate.

   J Together, Kaylee and Jonathan can't swim, and, by herself, Kaylee can't skate.

9. The tall plant leaned toward one side.
   The plant was in a large red pot.
   The plant was leaning dangerously.

   A The dangerously tall plant was leaning toward one side of a large red pot.

   B The tall plant in a large red pot was leaning dangerously toward one side.

   C The tall plant was in a large red pot leaning dangerously toward one side.

   D Although the tall plant was in a large red pot, it leaned dangerously toward one side.

10. Jeremy swam slowly through the waves.
    The waves were high.
    He swam to one of the docks.

    F Jeremy swam slowly through the waves to one of the docks, which were high.

    G When Jeremy was swimming slowly through the waves, they were high, and he swam to one of the docks.

    H Jeremy swam slowly through high waves to one of the docks.

    J Jeremy swam to one of the docks through slow waves that were high.

11. The roads were icy.
    Beth drove on them, anyway.
    She went to a party.

    A Beth drove on icy roads to a party.

    B Although Beth drove to a party, the roads were icy.

    C Although the roads were icy, Beth drove on them and, anyway, she went to a party.

    D Beth went to a party, driving on roads, anyway, that were icy.

Read the passage and look at the numbered, underlined parts. Choose the answer that is written correctly for each underlined part.

(12)   One of the greatest musical geniuses ever. Wolfgang Amadeus Mozart lived from 1756 to 1791, about the time of the American

(13) Revolution. He died when he was only 35 years old, but, despite his early death, he had already written more than 600 works when he died before his 36th birthday.

(14)   Born in Austria in 1756, Mozart's father was a composer and violinist. Little Wolfgang began to play the harpsichord at the age of

(15) four and writing music at five. He played for the empress of Austria

(16) when he was only six. His older sister was Nannerl. She was also an excellent keyboard player. She joined Wolfgang on concert tours of Europe, with the children's father as manager. Wolfgang enjoyed performing, meeting other musicians, and playing practical jokes.

12. **F** Wolfgang Amadeus Mozart, he was one of the greatest musical geniuses ever

    G One of the world's greatest musical geniuses ever, Wolfgang Amadeus Mozart, lived

    H Wolfgang Amadeus Mozart lived

    J Correct as it is

13. **A** He died when he was only 35 years old, but, despite his early death, he had already written more than 600 works.

    B He died when he was only 35 years old, but he had already written more than 600 works.

    C He died when he was only 35, but he had already written more than 600 works when he died before his 36th birthday.

    D Correct as it is

14. **F** Mozart was born in Austria in 1756. His father

    G Because Mozart was born in Austria in 1756, his father

    H Mozart was born in Austria in 1756, and that is where Mozart's father

    J Correct as it is

15. **A** and music was written by him when he was five

    B and the writing of music at five

    C and to write music at five

    D Correct as it is

16. **F** His older sister, who was Nannerl and also an excellent keyboard player, joined

    G His older sister Nannerl, also an excellent keyboard player, joined

    H His sister Nannerl, who was also older than him, was an excellent keyboard player. She joined

    J Correct as it is

The Main Idea of a Paragraph

Sentences in a paragraph work together to communicate a single idea, called the **main idea.** You can find the main idea by reading the paragraph and deciding what it is about.

What is the main idea of the following paragraph?

> The new subway cars will have many technological advantages. Each new car will have a handy electronic display panel that flashes the destination, the next station, and the time of day. Each car will also be equipped with an emergency intercom so that passengers can communicate with the conductor. The doors of the new cars will be four inches wider, to make getting on and off the cars easier. The doors will have sensors to detect any object that might be in their way as they close. All new cars will have an enhanced suspension system to cushion the ride, making subway travel more comfortable for everyone.

The first sentence in this paragraph does a good job of stating the main idea—the technological advantages of the new subway cars. This sentence is called the **topic sentence** because it sums up the main idea. The remaining sentences in the paragraph describe the advantages mentioned in the topic sentence.

Read each paragraph. Then choose the sentence that best states the main idea.

1.   The Yukon Territory in Canada has a coat of arms that represents its natural characteristics. The coat of arms has wavy white lines on a blue background, standing for the icy rivers of the Yukon. It has red triangles representing mountains and golden circles showing the precious metals found there. Standing at the top is a malamute dog, symbolic of courage, loyalty, and stamina.

   A The wavy white lines on the Yukon coat of arms represent its icy rivers.

   B In the Yukon, the malamute dog symbolizes courage, loyalty, and stamina.

   C Canada's Yukon Territory has a coat of arms that represents its natural characteristics.

   D The Yukon's flag has red triangles representing mountains.

2.   The stage actress Sarah Bernhardt was as famous for her unconventional ways as she was for her acting. She is said to have been the first actress to ever wear pants in public. She would accept her pay only in gold, which she carried everywhere in a beat-up old bag. When she lost her leg, she unashamedly made appearances with a wooden one. She purchased a coffin while she was still very much alive and occasionally used it as a bed.

   F When she lost her leg, actress Sarah Bernhardt made appearances with a wooden one.

   G Bernhardt may have been the first actress to wear pants in public.

   H Bernhardt purchased a coffin and occasionally used it as a bed.

   J Sarah Bernhardt was as famous for her unconventional ways as she was for her acting.

Practice

Each of the following paragraphs is missing a topic sentence that states the main idea. Read each paragraph. Then choose the topic sentence that would fit in the blank.

A   Dinner at Aunt Sophie's house is always an adventure for the taste buds.

B   Aunt Sophie has always been very politically active.

C   When my brother and I were kids, Aunt Sophie always brought us unusual gifts from her world travels.

D   Aunt Sophie enjoys her job as an elementary schoolteacher.

E   The Halloween costumes worn by Aunt Sophie are the most creative costumes I've ever seen.

1.   _____. When she came back from India, she gave us brightly colored stuffed elephants. One year, she gave my brother a grinning papier-mache skeleton from Mexico. From Spain, she brought me a pair of castanets so that I could pretend to be a flamenco dancer. When I was a little older, she gave me a beautiful wooden necklace from her West African trip; I still wear it all the time.

2.   _____. She's fond of her coworkers, all of whom are as committed to quality education as she is. She loves her students and takes pride in their success. She has fun doing all kinds of activities with the children, from reading aloud to going on field trips. And she certainly doesn't mind having summers off for her world travels.

3.   _____. Every time there is a presidential election in the United States, she volunteers for the Get Out the Vote drive. She reads up on various issues and writes letters to her representatives. In the Philippines one year, she served as an international monitor to ensure the fairness of the election. Recently she marched for the rights of Mexican migrant farm workers.

4.   _____. One year she dressed up as the ghost of beheaded queen Anne Boleyn; she looked so convincing that kids were screaming and running away. After visiting England a few years ago, she dressed up as Buckingham Palace. Her costume was so heavy that she could barely move. Last year she dressed as Paul Revere, riding up and down the street on a real horse. I can't wait to see what she dreams up this year.

5.   _____. One night she served us chicken tikka masala, a type of Indian dish. Another time she made Greek baklavah for dessert. The most unusual dinner occurred after a trip to Tibet, when she served us yak stew.

Apply

Write a topic sentence that states the main idea for each of the following paragraphs.

1. _____. Generally, butterflies are brightly colored while the colors of moths are dull. Butterflies tend to fly in the day, unlike moths, which fly mainly at night. Moths have feathery or straight antennae, while most butterflies have knobbed antennae. Also, a butterfly rests with its wings held together over its back, while a moth holds its wings either flat or curled around its body.

_____

_____

2. _____. She has hung beaded curtains in every doorway. Glowing lava lamps light the hallway in her apartment. A few weeks ago, she painted swirling vines with bright, gigantic flowers on the ceiling. In the kitchen and bathroom, she has covered the walls with posters of singers such as Bob Dylan and Jimi Hendrix. As a finishing touch, she usually has several sticks of incense burning in the living room.

_____

_____

3. _____. It can be diced and added to sauces and stir-fry dishes. Pickled and shaved into thin strips, ginger often accompanies a plate of sushi. It can be boiled in water to make a simple tea or digestive tonic. It can be sliced, coated in sugar, and candied for a sweet treat. And of course, extract of ginger is the essential ingredient in a true ginger ale.

_____

_____

4. _____. The dress was silky white with an overlay of antique lace. The waist was gathered in back with a lovely, simple bow. Tiny pearls were stitched all around the neck and at the cuffs. The dress had a seven-foot long train, which moved gracefully behind her as she walked down the aisle toward her groom.

_____

_____

5. _____. Red meat is our number-one protein source, but poultry, pork and fish are also high in protein. Soybeans and soy products such as tofu are excellent vegetarian sources of protein. Some vegetables, like avocados, can add a few extra grams of protein to your diet. Ounce for ounce, though, insects are the most protein-rich things you can eat.

_____

_____

Check Up

Read each paragraph. Then choose the best topic sentence for the paragraph.

1. _____. When you come through the front door, a host or hostess in a flight attendant's uniform greets you. He or she gives you a ticket and directs you to your seat. Before you are served, you must buckle your seatbelt and pull down your tray table. Your meal is served in shrink-wrapped containers, but it tastes much better than you might expect.

   A My friends and I go out to eat at least once a week.

   B The newest restaurant in town is designed to make you feel like you're on an airplane.

   C Food tastes better when it is served in plastic containers.

   D I've always been afraid of flying; I can't seem to get over it.

2. _____. During Victorian times, it was illegal in some parts of the United States to drink soda water on Sundays. Because of this, no one could order ice cream sodas on Sundays. A druggist who was upset with the loss of business decided to serve ice cream with syrup on top as a replacement for ice cream sodas. He named the dish after the day on which he served it.

   F The ice cream sundae was invented due to a strange Victorian-era law.

   G Vanilla was the most popular flavor of ice cream during the Victorian era.

   H Drug stores rarely have ice cream counters or soda fountains anymore.

   J The House of Representatives is voting on a bill to limit ice cream consumption.

3. _____. Its original name, Manhattan, was given by the Native Americans of the region. The early Dutch settlers decided to call the place New Amsterdam. In 1664 the name New York was first used by the British colonists. In the 1920s local actors and musicians gave the city its famous nickname, The Big Apple.

   A Frank Sinatra sang of New York City, "If I can make it there, I'll make it anywhere."

   B Dutch settlers purchased the island of Manhattan from a group of Native Americans.

   C New York City has gone by many names over the years.

   D New York City is made up of five boroughs.

4. _____. After she saw the film *Hoop Dreams*, she wanted to play basketball. Upon seeing the movie *Speed*, she decided to become a bus driver. After she saw the latest James Bond movie, she was determined to become a secret agent. Luckily, she's only twelve and has plenty of time to make up her mind.

   F My daughter Miranda is trying to get a job at the movie theater.

   G Miranda's career goals are easily influenced by what she sees in the movies.

   H This year's crop of movies looks like a good one.

   J Most movie directors began their careers doing something completely different.

Finding the Topic Sentence

The main idea of a paragraph is often explained in a **topic sentence.** Placed at the beginning of a paragraph, a topic sentence leads readers into the paragraph, as in the following example:

> Although there are many versions of the game of poker, the value of the hands remains the same. The highest hand is a straight flush, which occurs when all five cards are the same suit, and they are all in numerical sequence. Next highest is four-of-a-kind, followed by a full house, which is a combination of a pair and three-of-a-kind. Next comes a flush (all five cards of the same suit) and then a straight (five cards in numerical sequence). After a straight, the best hand is three-of-a-kind, followed by two pairs, followed by one pair. If you have none of these, then your highest card will have to stand alone.

After reading the topic sentence, readers are ready to learn details about the value of different poker hands.

Sometimes a topic sentence is placed elsewhere in the paragraph. In the middle or at the end, a topic sentence summarizes the details that the reader has already learned.

> If you're prepared to spend the big bucks, you can see big-name movie stars in large-scale productions on Broadway. Off-Broadway, you can find productions of a smaller scale and price. The quality of off-Broadway shows is usually just as good as, if not better than, that of Broadway shows. For a theater experience that is inexpensive, innovative, and exciting, if sometimes a bit cramped, try seeing a show "off-off-Broadway." You'll find that New York's theaters offer productions for nearly every visitor's taste and budget.

Wherever it is placed, a topic sentence helps the reader focus on the writer's message.

Read the following paragraph. Choose its topic sentence.

1. Fruits such as raspberries or Granny Smith apples can add a refreshing, tart flavor to your salad. Blueberries, pears, and raisins add a nice sweetness. Salad doesn't ever have to be boring. You can put in walnuts, almonds, pumpkin seeds, or sunflower seeds for a nutty crunch. Try adding cheeses like grated Parmesan or crumbled Greek feta for flavor and substance.

    A Fruits such as raspberries or Granny Smith apples can add a refreshing, tart flavor to your salad.

    B Blueberries, pears, and raisins add a nice sweetness.

    C Salad doesn't ever have to be boring.

    D Try adding cheeses like grated Parmesan or crumbled Greek feta for flavor and substance.

Practice

Read each paragraph. Then underline the topic sentence in the paragraph.

1. It is important to get enough calcium in your diet. Calcium is essential to the health of bones and teeth. It is necessary throughout life for bone structure and strength, nerve function, muscles, and blood clotting. A lack of calcium can lead to osteoporosis, in which the bones are weak and easily broken.

2. The legendary Ella Fitzgerald became a singer almost by accident. When Fitzgerald was sixteen, two girlfriends dared her to perform in amateur night at the Apollo Theater in Harlem. Fitzgerald then thought of herself as a dancer and planned to perform a dance number. But the Edwards Sisters, who danced before Fitzgerald went on, were so good that she lost her nerve. Standing onstage nervously in her dancing outfit, she sang instead. She was so good that the audience cried for an encore.

3. When Uncle Angelo goes out walking, he always picks up litter and deposits it into trash cans. When he stops into a restaurant or store, he is so nice to everyone that they are still smiling after he has left. He even donates to local charities to improve life for everyone in the neighborhood. More than anyone else I know, Uncle Angelo lives by the motto "Always leave things a little better than you found them."

4. Lester's first job when he was in high school was working as a clerk in a record store. Although he doesn't play an instrument, Lester's life has always revolved around music. By the time he was twenty, he'd gotten so skilled at fixing the store's stereo equipment that he opened up his own audio fix-it shop. Later on, he started managing a local rock band. Under Lester's wing, they gained a national following. Now Lester owns a nightclub, which features top-of-the-line jazz, blues, and rock acts.

5. The winter of 1977 was an unusual one all across the United States. Ski resorts in Colorado were forced to close due to lack of snow. Bears at the zoo in Anchorage, Alaska, were confused for months since it never got cold enough for them to go into hibernation. Miami, Florida, on the other hand, saw its first snowfall in recorded history.

6. Natalia has been offered a job at another publishing house. The job carries the same title as her current job, but the pay would be better. The new job would demand a further commute, but a monthly train pass comes as part of the salary package. The hours would probably be longer than those at her current job, at least for the first six months or so, which is a point against it. She would hate to say good-bye to the coworkers she's been with for nearly eight years, but the prospect of meeting new people is exciting. Natalia has been weighing all of the pros and cons but can't decide what to do.

Apply

Read each paragraph. Then write a topic sentence that would fit in the blank.

1. _____. She bought a matching sweatshirt and pair of sweatpants with a special lining to keep her body dry. She also picked up a pair of fancy running sneakers with high-traction soles and extra cushioning. Soon after, she came home with terrycloth sweatbands for her head and wrists. Then she bought several pairs of designer sweat socks with pink pom-poms at the ankles. Yesterday she got an expensive sports CD player with headphones.

   _____

   _____

2. My four year-old nephew, Christopher, sleeps in frog pajamas and has a frog mobile hanging above his bed. His favorite television star is Kermit the Frog. He loves to leapfrog around the house yelling out "Ribbit! Ribbit!" When he sees a real frog by the pond in the park, he shrieks with excitement. _____.

   _____

   _____

3. _____. We tried holding the couch horizontally, and then we tried holding it vertically. We tried pivoting and angling it every which way, but we still couldn't get it in through the door. We took the tiny legs off the bottom of the couch; we took the door off its hinges. As a last-ditch attempt, we even tried undoing the upholstery to see if there was anything to unscrew or pry off underneath. In the end, we gave the couch to a neighbor with a bigger doorway.

   _____

   _____

4. Traffic jams abound in the city, and finding a parking space is always difficult. If you get a good space near your apartment and want to leave your car there for a while, you still have to move it now and then for street cleaning. There is a high number of break-ins, especially involving cars with nice radios. Because of the higher rate of accidents and thefts, insurance costs are high in the city. _____.

   _____

   _____

Check Up

Read each paragraph. Then choose a topic sentence that would fit in the blank.

1. _____. One part of the rating is a measure of how quickly the tread will wear down, which shows how long it will be before you'll need to buy new tires. Another part of the rating has to do with traction; it lets you know how well the tires stop the car on wet pavement. The third part measures how well the tire will handle the build-up of heat.

   A   The tires on your car should be rotated regularly.

   B   The tires that are being manufactured these days can stop on a dime.

   C   A good mechanic will let you know when it is time to rotate your tires.

   D   All passenger car tires have a rating that gives the owner important information.

2. Some French friends of mine say that a glass of red wine a day keeps the doctor away. _____. To insure good health, my grandmother has stood on her head for ten minutes every day since she was twenty. My grandfather swears by a tonic made with Siberian ginseng and catnip. Strangest of all, I just learned that my brother-in-law soaks his feet in a warm vinegar bath every night.

   F   Everybody seems to have his or her own daily prescription for long life and health.

   G   There are many household uses for vinegar.

   H   Wine, like any alcoholic beverage, should only be drunk in moderation.

   J   Home remedies are often more effective than prescription medication.

3. Jean's sister, Rosemary, could not be seated next to their cousin, Sid, because she had never forgiven him for pushing her down the stairs when they were kids. Sid could not be seated anywhere near his sister-in-law, Bella, because she had broken his heart by marrying his brother. Even the bride's own parents, who loved each other very much, were having one of their famous fights over politics and had to sit at separate tables. _____.

   A   The wedding was to be catered by Estrella Family Catering.

   B   Jean, who is getting married this Saturday, comes from a big family.

   C   The bride-to-be didn't know how to seat her family.

   D   Sid was a really troubled kid, but he turned out just fine.

4. _____.The first good oil well spouted in Bartlesville, Oklahoma, in 1897, ten years before the state entered the Union. Members of the Osage tribe made a good deal of money by leasing land to the arriving oilmen. Before long, Oklahoma City was booming, and Tulsa began calling itself the Oil Capital of the World.

   F   Oil has been found in nearly every single one of Oklahoma's seventy-seven counties.

   G   The state of Oklahoma was built on oil.

   H   Unfortunately, some Native Americans had their oil-rich land stolen from them.

   J   Oklahoma has a "panhandle" that sticks out to the west, north of Texas.

Supporting Sentences

While a topic sentence states the main idea, the **supporting sentences** give the details that complete the picture. Writers use different types of supporting sentences, depending on what they wish to communicate.

The main idea in some paragraphs is supported with **examples.**

> On a trip to Italy, you can see many artistic masterpieces of the Renaissance. Michelangelo's famous statue of David stands, in all its glory, in the city of Florence. Also in Florence, you can see the works of master painters such as Botticelli and Raphael. A visit to the city of Milan will let you view Leonardo da Vinci's well-known *Last Supper* painting. In Rome, you can marvel at the dome of St. Peter's Basilica and gaze up in awe of Michelangelo's ceiling fresco in the Sistine Chapel.

Sometimes, a writer wants to persuade the reader to agree with his or her opinion. In this case, the supporting sentences might give **reasons** why the writer feels as he or she does about an issue.

> We must all go to the polls and cast our votes on Election Day. Many of our ancestors, denied the right to vote, fought and died so that we could have it. Other people in the world today would give almost anything to have this right that we take for granted. Staying home from the polls is not a protest. If we don't like either major-party candidate, we can vote for a third-party candidate or write a name in. Our vote is our voice.

Read each paragraph. Then circle the answer that completes the sentence that follows.

1. As a very mature fourteen year old, I should be allowed to go on a camping trip alone with my friends. I would learn wilderness survival skills, such as building a fire and putting up a tent. I would learn responsibility because no adults would be around to help. It would be healthy to be in the cool, fresh forest air. My friends and I would have time to bond, which is important for people of any age.

   This paragraph was developed using (examples, reasons).

2. Each neighborhood in lower Manhattan has its own personality. Greenwich Village has long been home to famous authors and artists, who can often be found in the Village's lively cafes and bars. Chelsea, named after its counterpart in London, is full of great restaurants, theaters, and shops. SoHo, meaning the neighborhood south of Houston Street, is world-famous for its art galleries. Little Italy was populated by Italian immigrants in the late 1800s; old-world influences can still be felt in its restaurants and bakeries.

   This paragraph was developed using (examples, reasons).

Practice

Sometimes a writer wants to explain the ways two things are alike and different. In this case, the supporting sentences may **compare and contrast** the things being discussed.

> I am considering moving to either San Francisco or Seattle. Both are West Coast cities and are known for their natural beauty. Both are known for their lively arts and music scenes. San Francisco is a much sunnier city, having twice the number of sunny days per year than Seattle has. But then again, San Francisco is more likely to experience an earthquake than Seattle.

Sometimes, a writer needs his supporting sentences to give **facts and figures.**

> While U.S. consumers continue to pay high prices for coffee, farmers receive less and less money for their coffee crops. Ten years ago, the world coffee economy was worth $30 billion, and farmers received $12 billion in total. Today, the world economy is worth $50 billion, and the farmers' share has dropped to $8 billion. Many of the 60,000 coffee farmers in Nicaragua are losing their land because of debts. In El Salvador, over 30,000 jobs have been lost due to the high prices taken by middlemen.

Read each paragraph. Circle the answer that completes the sentence that follows. Then choose the sentence that best fills the blank.

1. I'm amazed that both of these paintings were done by the same artist. _____. The details are crisp, clean, and very realistic. The other painting, also wonderful, is a large portrait of an elderly woman. It was made with thick, expressionistic brushstrokes. There is a blurred effect to the features; up close, you can't quite tell what you're looking at. This artist has amazing range!

    This paragraph is developed using (compare and contrast, facts and figures).

    A Pablo Picasso is my favorite artist because of his range.

    B One is a small portrait of a young woman in a flowered kimono.

    C You can see a wide range of styles at the Museum of Modern Art.

2. Greater Seattle, Washington, today has a population of 3,554,760. (The city itself has a population of 537,747.) Just over 49 percent of Greater Seattle's residents are male, while over 50 percent are female. _____. The average number of members in a Seattle family is 3.06. It is a predominantly white metropolitan area with 79.31 percent of residents being of European ancestry. The next highest racial group is Asian, at 7.90 percent.

    This paragraph is developed using (compare and contrast, facts and figures).

    F The median age of all residents is 35.3 years old.

    G The cool waters of Puget Sound lap the shores of Seattle.

    H Geoff has lived in Seattle since he was five years old.

Apply

Read each paragraph. Write one more supporting sentence for the paragraph, following the directions in parentheses.

1.   Ms. Garcia seems like the right person for this job. Her letter shows that she's been interested in social work for a long time. She may not have a lot of experience yet, but she has a willingness to learn. The fact that she's been taking night classes while working full-time shows a lot of motivation. _____. (Add a reason.)

_____

_____

2.   Recently, students at the local high school conducted a poll about issues facing Americans today. Almost 60 percent of the boys said that the state of the economy was the most important issue, while only 52 percent of the girls felt the same way. _____. (Add a sentence with an imaginary fact or figure.)

_____

_____

3.   Sometimes it's hard to believe that Joseph and his brother Isaac are even related. Joseph is short and muscular, while Isaac is tall and lanky. Isaac dresses and grooms himself carefully, while Joseph won't go out without his love beads and a big, wild hairdo. _____. (Add a sentence comparing or contrasting.)

_____

_____

4.   Good luck just seems to come Julianne's way. A conversation with the woman seated next to her on a train turned into a great job offer. When she bought a swingset for her kids, her name was entered into a drawing for a family vacation to Orlando. She didn't even realize that she'd been entered until they called to tell her that she'd won. _____. (Add a sentence with an example.)

_____

_____

5.   A set of identical twins who were separated at birth wound up living very similar lives. Each of them went by childhood nicknames; they are known as Jimmy and Johnny instead of James and John. Each married a tall, dark-haired woman who works as a cook. Each coaches a softball team in his city. _____. (Add a sentence comparing or contrasting.)

_____

_____

Check Up

Read each topic sentence. Choose the answer that best develops the topic sentence.

1. With so many telephone services offered now, it's easy to get confused.

   A   Many people are using cellular phones these days. Since the advent of cell phones, I have noticed a decline in the number of pay telephones on the street.

   B   As a child, I used to play the game of "telephone" with my friends.

   C   My telephone bill is getting larger and larger, and I don't make any more calls than I used to. I'm thinking about unplugging the phone and communicating by postcards.

   D   You can have caller ID so that you know who is calling before you answer. At the same time, you can have caller ID block, so that others won't know that you're calling.

2. I believe that good communication is the key to making a relationship work.

   F   About 64 percent of women say that they are or would like to be in a romantic relationship. Just over 61 percent of men say the same.

   G   Listening carefully to your partner shows that you value his or her opinions and feelings. If you talk about problems while they are small, they might never grow too big to handle.

   H   My brother just began a relationship with someone from work. He is worried because workplace relationships can have bad results if they don't work out.

   J   State University offers a communications major. Such a major is broad enough to allow a graduate to seek many kinds of communications-related jobs.

3. I am going to join either the gym on Fifth Street or the one on Eighth Street.

   A   I've been meaning to start a workout regimen for a long time now.

   B   Exercises such as the bench-press work muscle groups in the arms as well as muscles in the chest. Hammer-curls, done with dumbbells, work on the biceps.

   C   The gym on Fifth has a large free-weight room, while the gym on Eighth has state-of-the-art weight machines. With membership at the gym on Fifth comes two free sessions with a personal trainer, which the gym on Eighth does not offer.

   D   Eighth Street is a one-way street running east-west between Broad Street and the river. The gym is located on the southwest corner of Eighth and Pine.

4. The Eiffel Tower was built to seem light and airy in spite of its great size.

   F   The tower is now owned by the Parisian government.

   G   Aunt Helene visited Paris recently. She rode to the top of the Eiffel Tower and was amazed by the view.

   H   There were arguments about the Eiffel Tower when it was first built. Most people felt that it was far too ugly to stand in such a beautiful city.

   J   The tower was made using a crossbar system of 18,038 pieces of iron, fixed with 2,500,000 rivets. It stands 324 meters high and weighs only 7,300 tons.

Recognizing Sequence

When reading, it is important to understand how one event leads to the next. Therefore, writers often help readers by presenting events in time order, or **sequence.**

As Hansel and Gretel were led deep into the forest by their father and stepmother, Hansel scattered white pebbles along the path. When the moon rose, the children were able to find their way home by the shining pebbles. But the next day, Hansel was not able to gather any pebbles before they left home. As his father and stepmother led him and Gretel even further into the forest, he crumbled his bread and scattered the bits along the path. When the moon rose, he and Gretel searched for the white crumbs to guide them home. But they could find none. Birds had eaten them.

Sometimes, a writer will include key words to make the order of events clear. Words such as *first, initially, second, next, then, after that, last,* and *finally* help to show the time order of the events described.

Harry kept everyone in suspense around the poker table. The other players looked at him nervously and asked him to show his hand. First, with a grin, he pulled the jack of hearts from his hand and laid it down. Next, he laid down the nine of spades and sighed sadly at it. After that, he put down the queen of spades and glanced around the table. Then, with a sparkle in his eye, he lay down the king of clubs. There was muttering around the table. Finally, Harry let his last card fall out of his hand. Everybody watched. The card was the ten of diamonds, completing the straight.

Read the following paragraph. Then answer each of the questions.

Susan Anderson was diagnosed with a mild case of tuberculosis before graduating from medical school in 1897. A few years later, she moved by herself to Fraser, Colorado, correctly believing that its very dry, cold climate would help her beat the disease. Before long, a man heard that Susan had been to medical school. He brought his sick horse to her door, and she treated the horse successfully. After that, the man spread the word that there was a great woman doctor in town. People began coming to Susan for all of their illnesses; she became known in the region as Doc Susie. Eventually, she was recognized by the medical community of Colorado and given the job of county coroner.

1. What happened before Doc Susie graduated from medical school?

   _____

2. What happened right after Doc Susie treated one man's sick horse?

   _____

Practice

Some paragraphs describe the steps in a process. These paragraphs, like those that tell a story, must be presented in an order that shows which event happens first, next, and so on.

> Whenever the temperature dips below forty degrees, Richard bundles up his daughter, Julia, in so many layers that Julia can hardly move. First, in addition to her regular underwear, he dresses her in a layer of thermal underwear. On top of that, he puts her in a turtleneck, a sweater, and a pair of corduroy pants. Then he has her hold out each foot so that he can put on a thick pair of socks. After that, he bundles her into her down coat and wraps a scarf around her neck. Then on go the hat and mittens. Finally, as Julia waits patiently, Richard stuffs her feet into waterproof boots.

Read the following paragraph. Then answer each of the questions.

> Chef Jason plans to serve his famous Indian carrot soup to his customers tonight. In preparation for making the soup, he assembles all the ingredients he will need. Then he chops the carrots and onions and sautés them in butter. Next he adds the herbs—curry powder, cumin, and coriander. After adding water, salt, and pepper, he brings the mixture to a boil and then simmers it, covered, for fifteen minutes. Then he purees the mixture in a blender. After pouring the puree back into the pot, he blends cottage cheese, milk, and lemon juice in the blender and combines that mixture with the carrot puree. The soup is nearly ready to eat. All that needs to be done now is to heat the mixture over low heat. Finally, before Jason serves the soup, he puts a sprig of parsley on it.

1. What does Jason do just before putting the carrot and onion mixture in the blender?

   _____

2. What does Jason do just after heating the soup over low heat?

   _____

Read the topic sentence of the paragraph. Then read the four sentences below it. Fill in the blank spaces with the letters of the sentences to form the correct sequence.

3.   Everybody loves root beer, and it's easy to make your own. First, _____.

   Next, _____. Then, _____. Last, _____.

   A wait about fifteen minutes, releasing the pressure from the lid every now and then.

   B mix a bottle of root beer extract with sugar and water in a clean bucket.

   C add three pounds of dry ice to the mixture, and fit a lid tightly on the bucket.

   D take the lid off completely, and enjoy your super-fizzy root beer!

Apply

Read each topic sentence. Then read the four sentences below it. Number the sentences from 1 to 4 in time order.

1. Many people who travel to India take the sightseeing route known as the "golden triangle."

   _____ In Delhi, they visit museums, government buildings, and the historically important Red Fort.

   _____ They drive from Delhi to the city of Agra, where they visit the beautiful, world-famous Taj Mahal.

   _____ They complete the triangle with a trip to Jaipur, a lovely city with many textiles and crafts for sale.

   _____ From their home countries, they fly into the capital city of Delhi.

2. My friend Emmanuelle showed me how to cook an omelet the French way.

   _____ Wait until the egg mixture has solidified somewhat before sprinkling in a filling, such as spinach and brie cheese.

   _____ When the butter has melted, pour the egg mixture into the pan.

   _____ Fold the omelet over its filling, flip it, and slide it onto a plate.

   _____ Begin by whisking the eggs and milk in a bowl while melting a little butter in a nonstick pan.

3. Gregor, the magician's assistant, stepped onto the stage alongside the Great Mikmak.

   _____ The Great Mikmak opened a plain pine box, and Gregor lay down inside.

   _____ At last, he yanked the cloak off and lifted the box's lid; Gregor jumped out to much applause.

   _____ The Great Mikmak spun the box around three times, took out a saw, and sawed the box in half.

   _____ He pulled the two halves of the box apart, pushed them back together, and covered them with his velvet cloak.

4. Although I don't practice it often, I know how to do a perfect push-up.

   _____ Keeping your back straight, push yourself up until your arms are straight.

   _____ Lower your chest to the floor, take a breath, and push up again.

   _____ Place your hands, palms down, on the floor under your shoulders.

   _____ Lie on the floor, face down, with your feet flexed and the pads of your toes touching the floor.

Check Up

Read each paragraph. Then choose the sentence that fits correctly in the blank.

1.   A priceless jeweled cup was stolen from the art museum. The police arrived at the museum and taped off the crime scene. They searched for clues, dusted for fingerprints, and interviewed museum employees. One employee recalled that a man at a café had asked him a lot of questions about the jeweled cup. _____. A café cashier remembered that the man in the sketch said he worked at the computer software company around the corner. When the police arrived at the company office, they were told that the man had suddenly quit. But with all of the information they were able to gather at his workplace, the police tracked the man down and found the stolen cup.

A   The police handcuffed the suspect and brought him to the station.

B   The thief was sure to wear gloves so as not to leave fingerprints.

C   From the employee's description of the man, the police made a sketch and took it to the café.

D   The police completed their reports about the case back at the station.

2.   Marie Curie was born in Warsaw, Poland, in 1867. As a student, she became involved in a revolutionary organization and had to leave Warsaw. She moved to Paris, where she studied the sciences and met Pierre Curie, a professor of physics. _____. Together with her husband, she developed methods to study the element radium. When Pierre Curie died in 1906, Marie took his place as Professor of Physics; this was the first time that a woman had held such a position.

F   She and Pierre were married in 1895.

G   She received a general education in local schools, as well as some scientific training from her father.

H   Marie promoted the medical use of radium during World War I.

J   Today, Marie Curie is celebrated as one of the world's great scientists.

3.   John dreamed up the idea for his comic book while walking through the city one night. He went home and spent the night writing down the story. The next day, he revised the story and broke it up to fit in many little panels. Over the next few weeks, whenever he got the chance, he sketched drawings for the panels, throwing out many more ideas than he kept. _____. Having finished that, he inked in the colors and black lines. At last, he printed the words to his story in the bubbles and blank spaces of the panels.

A   He made several appointments with comic-book publishers.

B   With only six panels to a page, and about thirty pages to a book, he needed to tell his story in as few words as possible.

C   His friends and colleagues came over to see the finished product.

D   When he had the sketches he wanted, he carefully transferred them to panels on good paper.

Identifying an Unrelated Sentence

All the sentences in a paragraph must relate to the paragraph's main idea. Every sentence in a paragraph has a role to play—a topic sentence states the main idea; other sentences should support the main idea. Any sentence that does neither of these jobs does not belong in the paragraph.

All the sentences in a paragraph should explain or describe the main idea more fully. After you finish writing, take the time to read what you have written. Look for sentences that don't belong and remove them.

Read the following paragraph. The sentence that should be deleted has been underlined.

> Vivienne has a routine to get ready for winter. She gives her furnace a check-up to make sure it is working properly. She puts up her storm windows, hoping that her airtight home will conserve energy. She takes her car into the garage and asks her mechanic to give it a tune-up. <u>Some newer cars may not need tune-ups every year.</u> Only then does she feel ready for whatever winter may send her way.

Read each paragraph. Then answer the questions that follow.

> Wall color is an important feature in any room. Cool colors such as greens, blues, and violets seem to move away from the viewer. When painted on the walls, such colors can make a room seem calm and spacious. Darlene's living room is painted an elegant light green. Warm colors such as reds, oranges, and yellows seem to move towards the viewer. When painted on walls, they make a room seem warm and cozy.

1. What is the main idea of this paragraph?

   _____

2. Which sentence does not support the main idea?

   _____

> The whole Turner clan got together over the holidays. Paul drove in from Denver with his family. Ned and his wife flew home and arrived just in time for the holiday feast. It's annoying when planes are delayed during the holiday season. Even Melissa stopped in to introduce her new boyfriend to the rest of the family.

3. What is the main idea of this paragraph?

   _____

4. Which sentence does not support the main idea?

   _____

Practice

Read each paragraph. Then follow the directions.

Body language, specifically, the way you stand, can communicate your state of mind. If you stand with your hands on your hips, you may be expressing anger. Standing with arms folded across your chest may be a sign that you don't trust or believe what you are hearing. Standing with arms behind your back may be your way of communicating that you feel you are in charge. When you take a relaxed stance with your arms at your sides, you may send a message of confidence and good humor.

1. Choose the main idea of this paragraph.

   A   The way you stand may communicate your thoughts or emotions.

   B   Everyone should try harder to communicate his or her true feelings.

2. Choose the sentence that could be a supporting sentence in the paragraph.

   A   The way you shake hands is also important in revealing your feelings.

   B   Standing hunched over with your head down and your eyes downcast communicates a feeling of discomfort or guilt.

After Rob moved into his new house, he decided that the house was against him. The first problem Rob noticed was a slight leak in his bedroom. It took a crew of three men two days and $2,000 to fix the "slight" leak in the roof. One month later, the furnace stopped working on a cold night. After an emergency repair visit, the furnace was replaced for another few thousand dollars. The hot water tank went next and was followed by major problems with the bathroom plumbing.

3. Choose the main idea of this paragraph.

   A   Whenever anyone buys a new house, he or she should be ready for plenty of problems and repair bills.

   B   Rob's house has needed a great deal of repair.

4. Choose the sentence that could be a supporting sentence in the paragraph.

   A   When the washing machine started spraying hot water all over the basement floor, Rob began to wonder why he had ever dreamed that owning a home would be fun.

   B   Rob's new home is on a street filled with young families.

Apply

Read each paragraph. If all the sentences are related to the main idea, write _Correct_ on the line. If one sentence is unrelated, cross it out.

1. Every fall and winter, thousands of people around the world are affected by a condition known as Seasonal Affective Disorder. For most people, the disorder begins in September and is caused by a decreased amount of sunlight. The sun didn't rise this morning until eight o'clock. One of the symptoms of the disorder is a tiredness that no amount of sleep can overcome. Some SAD sufferers find themselves hungry all the time. Others have physical symptoms such as stomach or joint pain. One serious symptom is depression.

   _____

2. Are you cut out to run your own business? Small-business owners must possess certain personal qualities. For example, they must be willing to accept a great deal of uncertainty. Especially during the first few years of their businesses, statistics show that the chances are good that their business will fail. Small business owners must also be "self starters." In other words, they must feel enthusiasm and determination enough to keep going in spite of setbacks. Finally, they must be organized when it comes to budgets and expenses. Many unhappy employees long to start their own businesses.

   _____

3. There's always time for you to exercise, no matter how busy your schedule is. If you can't fit in a brisk walk, jog, or run, try these mini-exercises. Whenever possible, take the stairs instead of the elevator. Don't park near your destination; instead, find a parking place in the farthest lot. While you watch the television, do biceps curls holding books or other objects. During the commercials, get up and do a few quick jumping jacks. When you stand in line or even when you are sitting down reading, tighten your abdominal muscles. Although these exercises can't take the place of a long workout, they all add up to keep you on the road to physical fitness.

   _____

4. A good manager can make a major difference in the attitudes of his or her employees. Effective managers are good communicators. They let employees know what is expected of them and what they are responsible for. Good managers are neither too controlling nor too casual. Overcontrolling can make employees feel they are not trusted, while unclear directions often cause employees to feel uncertain and fearful. For example, I am never quite sure of what my manager expects of me. Finally, good managers listen to their employees and give them support in solving their on-the-job problems.

   _____

Check Up

Read each paragraph. Then choose the sentence that does <u>not</u> belong in the paragraph.

1. **1.** The dangers that are part of the sport of climbing high mountains are many.
    2. When climbers reach an altitude of around 20,000 feet, they may find that they can't take in enough oxygen to think or act normally. **3.** In addition, the highest mountains are notorious for having terrible weather, including below-zero temperatures and sudden blizzards. **4.** The highest mountain in the world, at 29,028 feet, is Mount Everest in Tibet.

    A Sentence 1

    B Sentence 2

    C Sentence 3

    D Sentence 4

2. **1.** Ted is hooked on word games. **2.** He never goes anywhere without his book of *The New York Times* crossword puzzles. **3.** To complete crossword puzzles quickly, you need to have a large vocabulary and to be familiar with the clues that are commonly featured in such puzzles. **4.** He feels that his day has not begun properly until he completes the word scramble and the word find in the local newspaper.

    F Sentence 1

    G Sentence 2

    H Sentence 3

    J Sentence 4

3. **1.** It is easy to find bed-and-breakfast inns if you search for them on the Internet.
    2. Unlike cookie-cutter motels, each B & B offers a unique experience. **3.** Your room may be furnished in almost any style, from Victorian antiques to log cabin chic. **4.** The breakfasts may be five-course gourmet meals or simple buffets with coffee, juice, and rolls.

    A Sentence 1

    B Sentence 2

    C Sentence 3

    D Sentence 4

4. **1.** A number of diets advertised today promise to help you lose weight. **2.** Chris has been on one diet or another for several years. **3.** One diet recommends that you avoid fats and eat plenty of vegetables. **4.** Another popular diet emphasizes limiting the number and kinds of carbohydrates that you eat.

    F Sentence 1

    G Sentence 2

    H Sentence 3

    J Sentence 4

Transition and Connective Words and Phrases

A well-written paragraph leads the reader from one idea to the next. One way a writer can connect related ideas is by using transition words and phrases.

In the following paragraph, the transitional words and phrases have been underlined.

> Derek and Nicole were concerned about the safety of their neighborhood <u>because</u> several break-ins had recently taken place on their street. <u>Therefore</u>, they organized a neighborhood watch committee. <u>Immediately</u>, neighbors started noticing who came and went on their street. <u>As a result</u>, residents of the neighborhood now feel safer.

Beside each category in the list below is a list of commonly used transition words and phrases.

Time: after, as soon as, at first, before, finally, first, last, immediately, meanwhile, often, next, when

Place: around, at the top, below, beside, beyond, in front of, inside, nearby, opposite, outside, over, there, within

Cause and Effect: as a result, because, consequently, for that reason, so, therefore

Comparison: besides, likewise, similarly

Contrast: even so, however, in spite of, nevertheless, on the other hand, still

Example: for example, for instance

Order of Importance: first, more important, primarily

Conclusion: finally, in conclusion

Underline the transition word or phrase in each item. Then choose the word that describes the relationship the transition makes clear.

1. Black clothes often seem to drain the color from a person's face. On the other hand, they also make the person look slim.

   A example   **B** contrast   **C** cause and effect

2. The excited girls climbed into the roller coaster car. When they reached the top of the first hill, they took a deep breath and then screamed as the car streaked downwards.

   F time   **G** conclusion   **H** place

3. Ken has learned more about car repair than he ever wanted to know. For instance, he has now mastered the technique of replacing worn-out disk brakes on a ten-year-old car.

   A example   **B** time   **C** comparison

Practice

Read each paragraph. Then choose the transition that correctly fills in the blank.

1.   The family reunion picnic was coming up soon. Each family was to bring a favorite dish to share. Pearl remembered the last reunion picnic, when seven people brought potato salads and no one brought any main dishes. She didn't want to repeat that strange menu. _____, Pearl asked each family to sign up ahead of time to bring a particular dish. A little planning, she believed, would bring a delicious variety of foods to the picnic.

   A For example   **B** For that reason   **C** On the other hand   **D** Primarily

2.   Anyone can walk all the way from Georgia to Maine on a long-distance trail called the Appalachian Trail. Really determined hikers can cover the distance in a single summer if they begin in early spring and hike straight through until October. The well-marked Appalachian Trail has been enjoyed by serious hikers for decades. _____, the newer, but even more spectacular Pacific Crest Trail attracts hikers on the West Coast. It also runs for thousands of miles and offers a remarkable outdoor experience for hardy walkers.

   F Similarly   **G** Nevertheless   **H** For example   **J** Nearby

3.   Alex took his sons to this year's school fundraiser, a bazaar. When they got to the school gym, they saw that at least twenty booths had been set up. First, Alex took his boys to the fish pond, where they lowered hooks into a fake pond in hopes of snagging a good prize. Then he bought some popcorn balls for them at a food booth. He bought tickets to give the boys a chance to toss coins into a cup and win a prize. Over the course of the night, the family tried their hands at about a dozen games of chance. Excited and proud, Matt won a live goldfish, and Mark won a stuffed bear. _____, Alex and his sons had a great time at the bazaar.

   A Likewise   **B** However   **C** All in all   **D** In contrast

4.   The temperature is a chilly 32 degrees, the wind is blowing, and a light snow is falling. _____, Lee is walking to school dressed in a lightweight summer jacket, a pair of jeans, and a pair of canvas tennis shoes. He is wearing no hat and no gloves. Why is he dressed as if it were late summer and not early winter? It's because that's the way his friends are dressing. The need for peer approval is strong in teenagers. No one wants to look different, even if it means almost freezing.

   F Therefore   **G** Nevertheless   **H** Immediately   **J** For instance

5.   It was an almost perfect day at the park. The sun was shining and a light breeze rustled through the branches of the trees. Marie sat under a tree and watched a man and his daughter flying a kite. _____, a vendor was setting up a hot dog booth.

   A As a result   **B** For example   **C** Often   **D** Nearby

Apply

Read each sentence and the directions in parentheses. On the line, write a sentence that relates to the first sentence and has an appropriate transitional word or phrase. Underline the transitional word or phrase in your sentence. Here is an example:

Example: A colorful, abstract painting hung on the wall. (Add a sentence that describes the location of something else in the room.)

<u>Beside</u> the painting was a small sign on which its title was printed.

1. Olivia had never held a newborn baby before. (Add a sentence that describes a contrast.)

   _____

2. James was hurrying to get home before the storm broke. (Add a sentence that describes the time of another, related event.)

   _____

3. Will had forgotten his house keys, and no one came to the door when he rang the bell. (Add a sentence about an event related to this one by cause and effect.)

   _____

4. Beatrice is learning how to speak Italian from tapes and library books. (Add a sentence that describes a comparison or similarity.)

   _____

5. The friends stood in a long line to buy tickets to the popular movie. (Add a sentence that describes the location of someone or something else.)

   _____

6. Recycling is a simple way for communities to address the problem of finding a place for their trash. The voters in our city have decided that they wish to begin a recycling program. (Add a sentence that states a conclusion.)

   _____

7. Young people should be encouraged to play team sports because sports are fun. (Add a sentence that contains an even more important fact.)

   _____

8. There are several jobs that I think would be exciting. (Add a sentence that gives an example.)

   _____

Check Up

Read each paragraph. Then choose the sentence that best fills the blank.

1.   Bridgit loves driving; nothing makes her happier than going for long road trips in her convertible. _____. That is why the sisters went on a cross-county trip from Boston to San Diego last summer. If they have their way, they will someday drive to every state in the nation.

  A Still, her sister Colleen is happiest when behind the wheel.

  B Similarly, her sister Colleen is happiest when behind the wheel.

  C Consequently, her sister Colleen is happiest when behind the wheel.

  D On the other hand, her sister Colleen is happiest when behind the wheel.

2.   Every television show has a limited lifespan. In the beginning of its run, a good show may be overlooked by the public, but soon the audience grows. For a while, the show enjoys a period of remarkable energy and popularity. _____. After that point, nothing can save it. Audiences become bored and stop watching, and inevitably, the show that had once been so popular is sent to the TV trash heap.

  F Soon, however, the show begins to seem tired and repetitive.

  G For example, the show starts repeating itself and begins to seem tired.

  H Likewise, the show seems tired and repetitive.

  J For that reason, the show changes, becoming tired and repetitive.

3.   Gavin's father was always too busy to spend much time with his family. His work as a salesman took him on one business trip after the other and forced him to miss out on many of the special moments in his children's lives. Gavin was determined not to repeat his father's mistakes. _____. It may not pay as much as another job would, but he knows that his job won't keep him from being there when his family needs him.

  A Nevertheless, Gavin's job never requires him to be away overnight.

  B Likewise, Gavin has found a job that never requires any overnight travel.

  C However, Gavin's job never requires any overnight travel.

  D Consequently, Gavin has taken a job that never requires any overnight travel.

4.   Irene knows that she made the right decision. Sensible people don't quit perfectly good jobs to try their luck at acting in Los Angeles. She tells herself that she couldn't have overcome the competition and that she is much better off working in a pleasant office. _____.

  F Similarly, she knows her life would have been different if she had followed her dream.

  G As a result, she wonders what would have happened if she had followed her dream.

  H Still, she often wonders how life would have been if she had followed her dream.

  J For example, she wonders how her life would have been different if she had followed her dream.

Main Idea and Topic Sentence

All the sentences in a paragraph work together to communicate a single idea called a **main idea.** In many paragraphs, the writer includes a **topic sentence,** which states the main idea of the paragraph. When it appears at the beginning of the paragraph, the topic sentence introduces the main idea; in the middle, it focuses the reader's attention on the main idea; and at the end, it summarizes the main idea.

Supporting Sentences

To develop the paragraph's main idea, writers use **supporting sentences.** Writers choose the most effective way to develop their ideas, depending on the message they are trying to communicate. The most commonly used ways of developing paragraphs include the following: *examples, comparison and contrast, reasons,* and *facts and figures.*

Sequence

When telling stories or describing processes, writers usually present events in time order, or in **sequence**. When you read, look for key words such as *first, before, second, next, then, after that, last,* and *finally* to keep track of the order of events or steps.

Unrelated Sentences

All the sentences in a paragraph must relate clearly to the paragraph's main idea. After you write a paragraph, read it over. Make sure all of the sentences support the main idea or explain it more fully. If any sentence does not, it should be removed from the paragraph.

Transition and Connective Words and Phrases

Every sentence in a paragraph should be connected to the sentences before and after it and should lead the reader from one idea to the next. One way a writer can show the connection between related ideas is by using transition words and phrases. The following are common transition words and phrases: *meanwhile, often, therefore, on the other hand, nevertheless, however, finally,* and *in conclusion.*

Assessment

Read each paragraph. Choose the sentence that best fills in the blank.

1. _____. Each hive is made up of 90 percent worker bees; these bees are all females. Tasks such as gathering nectar, building the honeycomb, and tending to the queen are divided up among the workers. The other bees in the hive are drones; they are all male, and their only job is to impregnate the queen. The queen lives longer than the other bees but must stay in the hive, breeding new workers, drones, and queens.

    A Queen bees are raised on a diet of royal jelly.

    B Before beekeepers reach inside a hive, they fill it with smoke to confuse the bees.

    C Bees have a very ordered society.

    D Bee stings can be very painful.

2. Peanuts can be roasted, boiled, or eaten right out of their shells. They can be crushed for peanut oil, which is used for frying and flavoring. They can be turned into peanut butter, a favorite sandwich filling. The peanut vine can be used as hay for livestock. Even the shells can be powdered and used in building materials. _____.

    F As the peanut plant grows, it puts nitrogen into the soil.

    G When people think of peanuts, they often think of Georgia.

    H Peanuts are not nuts at all; they are peas, a type of legume.

    J The peanut can be used for an amazing number of things!

3. The waitstaff at Chez Louis have their setup routine down pat. They arrive at the restaurant around 4:30 P.M.; they vacuum and dust the dining room and make sure that the bathrooms are tidy. They set each table, except for one, with tablecloths, napkins, glasses, and silverware. _____. After their meal they set the last table, change their clothes, and unlock the front door.

    A Sitting at the empty table, they quickly eat while discussing the specials for the night.

    B Then they greet each other and catch up on the previous night's happenings.

    C They decide which tablecloths to use each night.

    D They go over their receipts for the night, say good-bye to the cleaning staff, and leave.

4. We arrived at the old silver mine for our tour. As we entered the mine, we felt the darkness grow all around us. _____. When we stepped out of the elevator, we noticed how cold it was so far underground. Our guide described the practices used to mine minerals from the walls. Then she turned her light off to show us what true darkness was like. Then she turned her light back on and led us to the elevator.

    F We rode back up to ground level and made our way out of the cave.

    G The silver mine has not been operational since the 1950s.

    H Our guide directed us into an elevator, which took us down five levels into the earth.

    J Our guide pointed out an underground plaster saint that a miner had created.

Assessment continued

5.   Stargazing is a hobby that requires little, if any, special equipment. On a clear night, using only the naked eye, you can see craters on the moon, constellations, and the Milky Way. Some reasonably priced equipment can make other sights visible. _____.
If you have more than a passing interest in the hobby, you may want to invest in an inexpensive telescope, so you can see planets and distant stars more clearly.

   A   In conclusion, comets and nebulae are easy to see with an inexpensive pair of binoculars.

   B   For example, with an inexpensive pair of binoculars, you can see comets and nebulae.

   C   Meanwhile, you can see comets and nebulae with an inexpensive pair of binoculars.

   D   As a result, binoculars will allow you to see sights such as comets and nebulae.

Read each topic sentence. Then choose the answer that best develops the topic sentence.

6. Have your special-occasion dinners at Mario's Restaurant.

   F   Mario's is located at the intersection of Twentieth and Lake Streets. Lake Street was recently blocked due to the sanitation workers' protest.

   G   Mario's has lovely decor and the finest food in town. Our chefs are trained at the best schools in the United States and in Italy.

   H   My cousin works as a dishwasher at Mario's. His hours aren't too bad, and he has met a lot of friends there.

   J   Mario Randazzo opened Mario's Restaurant in 1972. Before that, he was headwaiter at Donatello's, which closed down after a fire.

7. Mary and Phil keep finding more reasons to love their new neighborhood.

   A   The park across from their apartment hosts a wonderful farmer's market every Thursday and Saturday. The restaurant around the corner has been rated the best in the area.

   B   Like many other Americans, Mary and Phil move frequently. They were able to sublet their last apartment to another young couple.

   C   Unfortunately, their current apartment is more expensive than their last one. In addition, it is on the third floor, and the building has no elevator.

   D   The couple was married just over a year ago. They can afford this new apartment because Mary just got a nice promotion, and Phil has finally finished his degree.

8. The Wilson family is trying to decide where to go on vacation.

   F The Wilsons have taken a summer vacation every year for the past five years. Luckily, everyone has been able to take time off during the same week.

   G Most families take their vacations in late July or in early August. Other popular times for family vacations are during the winter and spring school breaks.

   H Taking a cruise would be relaxing for the parents and fun for the children. Going to the beach would be cheaper, and the family could visit relatives on the way there.

   J Family vacations can often lead to unexpected stress. On a trip, when family members spend almost every minute together, the need to get along can wear on everyone.

9. When the tomb of King Tut was opened, explorers found amazing treasures.

   A Since then, objects from the tomb have been on display all around the world. People in every country are interested in what was found there.

   B The pharaoh of Egypt known as King Tut had assumed the throne around the age of nine. He reigned for only nine years and died at the age of eighteen.

   C It is said that anyone who breaks into King Tut's tomb is cursed. Lord Carnavon, one of the first men to enter the tomb in 1922, died only six weeks after the discovery.

   D One of the most important finds was the king's 22-carat gold coffin, which weighed a staggering 2,448 pounds. Also discovered was the gold mask that covered Tut's head.

Read each paragraph. Then choose the sentence that does not belong in the paragraph.

10. **1.** To its regular customers, Baxter's Coffee Shop feels like home. **2.** The owner greets his customers by name every morning as they come through the door. **3.** The waitress brings her favorite customers their preferred morning drink as soon as they sit down. **4.** The coffee shop advertises its specials on a big sign on the front window.

   F Sentence 1

   G Sentence 2

   H Sentence 3

   J Sentence 4

11. **1.** Controlling the height of a hot-air balloon is not complicated. **2.** Balloon enthusiasts find that sunrise and sunset are the best times to take their unusual vehicles for a spin. **3.** When you want the balloon to rise, you heat the air inside it. **4.** To lower it, you simply let the air cool down naturally.

   A Sentence 1

   B Sentence 2

   C Sentence 3

   D Sentence 4

Capitalizing Proper Nouns and *I*

A **proper noun** names a particular person, place, or thing. Every important word in a proper noun is capitalized. A **common noun** is a general name for a person, place, or thing. Common nouns are not capitalized. Short words, such as *the, of,* or *in*, are not considered to be important unless they are the first or the last word in a proper noun. Study the following rules for capitalizing proper nouns.

- **Capitalize the names of persons.** Capitalize every word and initial in a person's name.

  Billie Jean King   S. I. Hayakawa

- **Capitalize titles and abbreviations when used before names.** Do not capitalize titles, such as *doctor* or *mayor*, when used alone. Common title abbreviations include *Dr., Mr., Mrs.,* and *Ms.*

  <u>Dr.</u> Robert Dailey is a new <u>doctor</u> at the clinic.

- **Capitalize words for family relations when they are used with or in place of the names of particular people.** If a family title follows a possessive pronoun such as *my, our,* or *your*, it is not capitalized.

  Grandma Jones   my grandmother

- **Capitalize the names of days, holidays, and months.** Do not capitalize the names of the seasons.

  Monday   Labor Day   September   autumn

- **Capitalize the names of cities, states, countries, and continents.**

  Seattle   Washington   Kenya   Africa

- **Remember that the pronoun *I* should always be capitalized.**

Read each sentence. Circle every word that should be capitalized.

1. The poet emily dickinson was born in amherst, massachusetts, on december 10, 1830.

2. Although my grandfather started the business, aunt nora runs it now.

3. I can't remember a time when coach amos was not a fixture here in the town of hudson.

4. The emperor napoleon was crowned in the city of paris, france.

5. A holiday that is celebrated in both the united states and canada is thanksgiving.

6. The official date for memorial day is the last monday in may.

Practice

Read each item. Capitalize words wherever necessary. Write *Correct* if the item is written correctly.

1. detroit, michigan _____

2. justice antonin scalia _____

3. australia _____

4. fourth of july _____

5. next tuesday _____

6. ralph vaughan williams _____

7. my younger brother _____

8. são paulo, brazil _____

9. the month of may _____

10. the mayor of our city _____

11. sunday, january 5 _____

Read each set of sentences. Then choose the sentence with correct capitalization.

12. **A** One of our Family traditions is christmas dinner with uncle Andy and aunt Marge.

   B One of our family traditions is Christmas dinner with Uncle Andy and Aunt Marge.

   C One of our family traditions is Christmas dinner with uncle Andy and aunt Marge.

13. **F** The queen of England, queen Elizabeth II, was born on april 21, 1926, in London.

   G The Queen of England, Queen Elizabeth II, was born on april 21, 1926, in london.

   H The queen of England, Queen Elizabeth II, was born on April 21, 1926, in London.

14. **A** My sister recently moved from ohio to oregon, and I miss her very much.

   B My sister recently moved from Ohio to Oregon, and I miss her very much.

   C My Sister recently moved from Ohio to Oregon, and i miss her very much.

15. **F** Our most popular tour of Europe includes eight days in Germany and Switzerland.

   G Our most popular Tour of Europe includes eight days in germany and switzerland.

   H Our most popular tour of europe includes eight days in Germany and Switzerland.

Apply

Read each item. Then write a sentence that includes an example of the pair of nouns described. Be sure you use correct capitalization.

1. the name of a person and a city

   _____

2. the name of a person and the name of a person with a title

   _____

3. the name of a day and a holiday

   _____

4. the name of a holiday and the name of a country

   _____

5. the name of a family relation and the name of a country

   _____

6. the name of a city and the name of a state

   _____

7. the name of a person with a title and the name of a month

   _____

8. the name of a family relation and the pronoun *I*

   _____

Read the following paragraph. Then rewrite it using correct capitalization.

A special holiday in alaska is seward's day. It celebrates the day on which the united states bought alaska from russia. It was secretary william h. seward who arranged the purchase in march of 1867. Both he and president andrew johnson were criticized at the time. Most americans thought that alaska was just a frozen wasteland.

_____

_____

_____

_____

Check Up

Read each set of sentences. Choose the sentence that has correct capitalization.

1. A The new security regulations take effect on Monday, November 4.

    B Give these files to the Office Manager, mr. Fielding.

    C My Aunt and I are planning a Family reunion for next Summer.

    D The Annual rainfall in Phoenix, arizona is only eight inches.

2. F The number one Holiday for candy sales is halloween.

    G I think dr. Stanley is scheduled to perform your surgery.

    H The inventor of the electric light, Thomas a. Edison, was born in Milan, ohio.

    J India, one of the larger countries in Asia, is also one of the oldest democracies in the world.

3. A The first observance of Mother's day was in grafton, west virginia.

    B The Superintendent has called a meeting for Friday Morning.

    C Both my grandfather and my father have red hair.

    D About 4,000 scientists live in Antarctica every Summer.

4. F The country of San marino is one of the smallest in europe.

    G The first prime minister of Israel, Golda Meir, was born in Russia.

    H The Day Of The Dead is a holiday celebrated in Mexico.

    J My crew can start painting your house on thursday.

Read the following paragraph and look at the numbered, underlined parts. Choose the answer that is written correctly for each underlined part.

(5)   In 1876 Nellie Tayloe Ross was born in st. Joseph, missouri. Forty-nine years
(6) later, in 1925, she was elected to succeed her husband, William b. Ross, as the
(7) Governor of Wyoming. She served for two years as the first woman governor in
(8) the country. For the rest of her long life, Mrs. Nellie Ross was involved in public service.
    She died on December 19, 1977.

5. A St. Joseph, missouri

    B st. Joseph, Missouri

    C St. Joseph, Missouri

    D Correct as it is

6. F William B. Ross

    G William b. ross

    H william b. Ross

    J Correct as it is

7. A governor of wyoming

    B Governor of wyoming

    C governor of Wyoming

    D Correct as it is

8. F mrs. Nellie Ross

    G Mrs. nellie Ross

    H Mrs. nellie ross

    J Correct as it is

Capitalizing Proper Nouns and Proper Adjectives

Study the following rules of capitalization.

- **Capitalize the names of streets, buildings, institutions, and bridges.**

    Basin Street   White House   Boston College   Concord Bridge

- **Capitalize geographical names such as mountains and rivers.** Do not capitalize words such as *north*, *east*, and *west* when they are used to indicate direction. Capitalize them when they refer to a section of the country.

    The raft drifted south down the Mississippi River.

    The Northeast is a highly urbanized part of the country.

- **Capitalize names of ethnic groups, nationalities, and languages.**

    Italian Americans   French   Arabic

- **Capitalize the names of government agencies.**

    House of Representatives   Federal Aviation Administration

- **Capitalize the names of clubs, organizations, and businesses.**

    Aces Tennis Club   National Honor Society   Barnes and Noble, Booksellers

- **Capitalize the names of historical and special events.**

    Revolutionary War   the Olympics

- **Capitalize proper adjectives.** Proper adjectives are words formed from proper nouns.

    Parisian café   Canadian bacon   Biblical scholars

Read each phrase. If the phrase is capitalized correctly, write *Correct* on the line. If it is not capitalized correctly, rewrite it correctly on the line.

1. by a chinese philosopher   _____

2. on the shores of the lake   _____

3. with the department of agriculture   _____

4. to the continental divide   _____

5. by the coleman candle company   _____

6. at the lincoln memorial   _____

7. of latinos   _____

Practice

Many proper nouns have more than one word, for example, *Department of the Treasury.* If a proper noun has more than one word, capitalize all important words, but do not capitalize the short words such as *the, of,* or *in.* Occasionally, a short word is the first or the last word in the name; then it should be capitalized.

Read each set of sentences. Choose the sentence that is capitalized correctly.

1. **A** The debate was sponsored by the League of women voters.
   B The Debate was sponsored by the League Of Women Voters.
   C The debate was sponsored by the League of Women Voters.

2. **F** The recent outbreak of measles was reported to the board of health.
   G The recent outbreak of measles was reported to the Board of Health.
   H The recent outbreak of measles was reported to The Board Of Health.

3. **A** The industrial revolution was a time of dramatic change in the Lives of many People.
   B The Industrial Revolution was a time of dramatic change in the lives of many people.
   C The industrial Revolution was a time of Dramatic change in the lives of many people.

4. **F** Our house is on the south side of Skyline Drive.
   G Our house is on the South Side of Skyline drive.
   H Our house is on the South side of Skyline Drive.

5. **A** The sumner technical school offers night classes on computer repair.
   B The sumner Technical School offers Night Classes on computer repair.
   C The Sumner Technical School offers night classes on computer repair.

Read each sentence. Circle the words that should be capitalized.

6. The highland mystery book club will meet at stacy's books on railroad avenue.

7. The accident shut down both lanes heading east on the putnam memorial bridge.

8. You can get a sample of soda bread at the irish exhibit at the sterling multicultural fair.

9. The university of colorado hopes to receive an award from the national science foundation.

10. This article lists many of the scientific contributions of african americans.

11. Located in new york harbor, the statue of liberty was a gift from the french people.

Apply

Read each item. Then write a sentence that includes an example of the noun or nouns described. Be sure you use correct capitalization.

1. the name of a street and the name of a structure

   _____

2. the name of a historical event

   _____

3. a geographical name

   _____

4. the name of a business and the name of a street

   _____

5. the name of a government agency

   _____

6. the name of a special event

   _____

7. a proper adjective

   _____

8. the name of a club or an organization

   _____

Read the following paragraph. Then rewrite it using correct capitalization.

Millions of european immigrants entered the united states in the early 1900s. After crossing the atlantic ocean in crowded ships, they arrived at ellis island. There they were processed by the bureau of immigration. During the first world war, immigration decreased, and soon the facilities at ellis island were closed.

_____

_____

_____

_____

Check Up

Read each set of sentences. Choose the sentence that has correct capitalization.

1. **A** Avoid mayfield road because of the heavy traffic at rush hour.
   B The Baltimore Orioles play in Oriole Park at Camden Yards.
   C Passports are issued by the United States state department.
   D The campground is six miles North of Lake Amador.

2. **F** These textbooks are also available in spanish.
   G The Alamo appliance store offers free delivery of all purchases.
   H The Skipton castle dates from the Middle ages.
   J Many Indian foods are quite spicy.

3. **A** The hurricane is threatening the States in the southeast.
   B The Golden Gate bridge is an example of a suspension bridge.
   C This newspaper serves the hispanic community in the area.
   D The Acton Amateur Radio Club sponsors an annual radio equipment sale.

Read the following paragraph and look at the numbered, underlined parts. Choose the answer that is written correctly for each underlined part.

(4)   During World war II, the U.S. military was seeking an effective way to send coded
(5) messages that would not be understood by the enemy. The United States marine corps
(6) turned to the Navajo people for help. The Navajo are a native american tribe with villages
(7) in several states in the southwest. Their language is extremely complex. The code they
      supplied was never broken by the enemy.

4. **F** world war II
   G World War II
   H world War II
   J Correct as it is

5. **A** United States Marine Corps
   B United states Marine corps
   C United States marine Corps
   D Correct as it is

6. **F** native american Tribe
   G Native american Tribe
   H Native American tribe
   J Correct as it is

7. **A** several States in the southwest
   B several States in the Southwest
   C several states in the Southwest
   D Correct as it is

Capitalizing First Words, Titles, and Abbreviations

Capitalize the first word of every sentence.

We cannot hear you.   Please speak louder!

Capitalize the first word of a quotation.

"The forecasters predict rain today," said Shelly.

Tina replied, "Have you seen my umbrella?"

Capitalize the first word, the last word, and any other important words in a title. Do not capitalize articles and short words such as *the, in, for, from, a, an, of, on, to,* or *by* unless they are the first or last words in the title.

The Old Man and the Sea (book and movie)

The Teahouse of the August Moon (play and movie)

"Write Your Own Will" (brochure)

Capitalize many abbreviations. Abbreviations are shortened forms of words or phrases.

Mail your payments to P.O. Box 1021.

Guided tours leave at 11:00 A.M. and 2:00 P.M.

Read each pair of sentences. Circle the letter of the sentence that is capitalized correctly.

1. **A** I rented P.O. Box 43 for my business mail.

   B I rented p.o. box 43 for my business mail.

2. **A** I am sure the class, "Photography for beginners," would help me take better pictures.

   B I am sure the class, "Photography for Beginners," would help me take better pictures.

3. **A** "Take advantage of our wonderful bargains on cruises," said the travel agent.

   B "take advantage of our wonderful bargains on cruises," said the travel agent.

4. **A** My friend asked, "Have you finished the crossword puzzle in today's newspaper?"

   B my friend asked, "have you finished the crossword puzzle in today's newspaper?"

5. **A** The last train leaves the downtown terminal at 1:10 a.m.

   B The last train leaves the downtown terminal at 1:10 A.M.

6. **A** Bob loves old horror movies, such as *house of wax.*

   B Bob loves old horror movies, such as *House of Wax.*

Practice

Read each title. Then rewrite it using correct capitalization. If it is capitalized properly, write *Correct* **on the line.**

1. "yellow rose of Texas" (song) _____

2. *the Phantom of the opera* (musical and movie) _____

3. "gunga din" (poem) _____

4. *Dayton Daily news* (newspaper) _____

5. *family ties* (television program) _____

6. "The Tragedy At Marsdon Manor" (short story) _____

7. *entertainment Weekly* (magazine) _____

8. *the Wall Street journal* (newspaper) _____

9. *the Shipping news* (book and movie) _____

10. "how to care for roses" (brochure) _____

Read the following paragraph and look at the numbered, underlined parts. Choose the answer that is written correctly for each underlined part.

(11)   Ralph Gleason, the star of the popular show, *a Decorator's touch*, will
(12) speak at the University Club this Saturday at 10:00 a.m. and 1:00 P.M. Tickets
         for the sessions are free to the first 150 people who send a self-addressed
(13) envelope to P.O. Box 682, Los Angeles, CA. After listening to Mr. Gleason, you
(14) will surely say, "no decorating job is too tough for me!"

11. **A** *A Decorator's touch*

    B *a Decorator's Touch*

    C *A Decorator's Touch*

    D Correct as it is

12. **F** 10:00 A.M. and 1:00 P.M.

    G 10:00 A.M. and 1:00 p.m.

    H 10:00 a.m. and 1:00 p.m.

    J Correct as it is

13. **A** p.o. box 682

    B P.O. box 682

    C P.o. Box 682

    D Correct as it is

14. **F** say, "No Decorating Job

    G Say, "No decorating job

    H say, "No decorating job

    J Correct as it is

Apply

Read each sentence. Then rewrite it using correct capitalization.

1. the crowd quietly listened to a reading of "casey at the bat."

_____

2. do you know the words to "birds of a feather"?

_____

3. the flight has been postponed from 11:35 a.m. to 12:20 p.m.

_____

4. my sister raved, "this month's issue of *fine cooking* has the best holiday recipes."

_____

5. "please forward my mail to p.o. box 32," he requested.

_____

6. *all quiet on the western front* was both a great book and a riveting movie.

_____

7. my doctor gave me a brochure called "a guide to immunizations."

_____

8. episodes of *I love lucy* will be shown this Sunday from 6:00 a.m. to 11:30 p.m.

_____

9. we are eating more healthfully after taking the class "introduction to vegetarian cooking."

_____

Read the following paragraph. Then rewrite it using correct capitalization.

I start my day reading *the washington post*. My copy usually arrives by 6:30 a.m. In the afternoon, I read *time* or *newsweek*. In the evening, I always watch *world news of the day*. Clearly, I like to know about current events.

_____

_____

_____

_____

Check Up

Read each set of sentences. Then choose the sentence with correct capitalization.

1. **A** The auctioneer announced, "the bidding begins at fifty dollars."

   B "is this a new prescription?" asked the pharmacist.

   C "Turn off all cell phones before the performance," said the manager.

   D "he is the best singer in the whole world!" gushed Marcy.

2. **F** I read a favorable review of a local production of *kismet*.

   G Tom tried out for the role of stage manager in the play *Our town*.

   H *The Bridge On The River Kwai* won an Academy Award in 1957.

   J The film *The African Queen* was shot on location.

3. **A** My sister's baby was born at 4:40 A.M.

   B The best view of the meteor shower will be after 1:00 a.m.

   C There is free parking on the city streets after 5:00 p.m.

   D The repairman assured me he would be here by 4:00 P.m.

4. **F** One famous short story, "The Lottery," is unusual and shocking.

   G hardly anyone watched *My mother the car* on TV.

   H The barbershop quartet sang, "Shine On harvest moon."

   J This brochure, "tips for House Painters," was helpful.

5. **A** The newscaster warned, "the rain will be heavy at times."

   B "what is your account number?" asked the teller.

   C "This camera has all the features I need," said Jay.

   D The promoter said, "due to slow ticket sales, the concert has been canceled."

6. **F** Please send my mail to p.o. Box 58 instead of my home address.

   G Online bidding for this item ends at 8:00 P.M. tomorrow.

   H This is a designated car-pool lane from 5:30 to 9:00 a.m.

   J All letters addressed to Santa Claus are placed in p.o. box 1225.

7. **A** the song "Mrs. Robinson" runs through the movie *the Graduate*.

   B Have you read the book *Playing by the rules*?

   C our manager subscribes to *Business week* for the office.

   D *The Hartford Courant* is an old, respected newspaper.

8. **F** "The tow truck will be there soon," promised the mechanic.

   G Hollywood has produced yet another remake of *a Christmas Carol* by Charles Dickens.

   H Be sure to read the article "Investing For Today."

   J The foreman said, "the night shift begins at 5:00 p.m."

Review

Proper Nouns, Proper Adjectives, and *I*

Capitalize the names of people. Capitalize titles and abbreviations when used before names.

> Dr. Grace M. Duncan is our family doctor.

Capitalize words for family relations when they are used with or in place of the names of specific people.

> Uncle Martin   my uncle

Capitalize the pronoun *I*.

Capitalize the names of days, months, and holidays.

> Tuesday   August   Independence Day

Capitalize the names of cities, states, countries, and continents.

> Las Vegas   Nevada   Chile   South America

Capitalize the names of streets, buildings, institutions, and bridges.

> Grant Avenue   Windsor Castle   University of Florida

Capitalize geographical names. Capitalize direction words (*north, south, east, west*) only when they refer to a section of the country.

> Missouri River   South Pole   in the Northwest

Capitalize the names of ethnic groups, nationalities, and languages.

> Native American   Egyptian   German

Capitalize the names of clubs, organizations, government agencies, and businesses.

> National Geographic Society   Department of Justice

Capitalize the names of historical and special events.

> Reconstruction   Super Bowl

Capitalize proper adjectives, that is, adjectives made from proper nouns.

> Shakespearean themes   Roman columns

First Words, Titles, and Abbreviations

Capitalize the first word of every sentence. Capitalize the first word of every direct quotation.

> "Who likes onion pizza?" asked Anna.   Everyone said, "I do."

Capitalize the first, last, and any other important words in a title.

> *The Right Stuff* (movie)   "The Fun They Had" (short story)

Capitalize many abbreviations, such as P.O., A.M., and P.M.

Assessment

Read each paragraph and look at the numbered, underlined parts. Choose the answer that is written correctly for each underlined part.

(1)   One of the most respected <u>american composers and bandmasters</u> was an
(2) energetic man named <u>john philip sousa</u>. Although Sousa wrote many kinds of music, he is best known for his marches. He composed many of them during the
(3) years he spent as <u>leader of the United States marine band</u>. His most popular
(4) march, perhaps the most popular march ever written, is <u>"the stars and stripes forever."</u>

1. A American Composers and Bandmasters

   B american Composers and Bandmasters

   C American composers and bandmasters

   D Correct as it is

2. F John philip Sousa

   G John Philip Sousa

   H john philip Sousa

   J Correct as it is

3. A leader of the United States Marine Band

   B Leader of The United States Marine Band

   C Leader of the United states Marine band

   D Correct as it is

4. F "The Stars And Stripes Forever."

   G "the Stars and Stripes forever."

   H "The Stars and Stripes Forever."

   J Correct as it is

Did you ever wonder how we came to celebrate each of our national holidays? The story of one holiday began in 1909. After listening to a sermon on Mother's Day, a young woman named Sonora Dodd decided that a day should be set aside
(5) for fathers, too. Her father was a veteran of <u>the civil war</u> and a widower who had raised his six children by himself. Sonora wrote a petition for the creation of
(6) <u>Father's Day</u>. The idea caught on, and the people of Sonora's hometown of
(7) <u>spokane, Washington</u>, celebrated the holiday in 1910. It was not until 1972,
(8) however, that <u>president Richard Nixon</u> made it a legal national holiday.

5. A The Civil War

   B the Civil war

   C the Civil War

   D Correct as it is

6. F father's day

   G Father's day

   H father's Day

   J Correct as it is

7. A Spokane, Washington

   B Spokane, washington

   C spokane, washington

   D Correct as it is

8. F president richard Nixon

   G President Richard Nixon

   H president richard nixon

   J Correct as it is

(9)   The taj mahal, an impressive building, is a huge white marble structure

(10)   located in northern India. This beautiful building is actually a tomb. The ruler Shah

(11)   Jahan ordered it built in memory of his beloved wife, empress Mumatz Mahal.

(12)   According to tradition, the tomb was designed by a turkish architect. Completing
the amazing tomb took twenty-two years and the labor of over twenty
thousand workers.

9. **A**   Taj Mahal

    B   Taj mahal

    C   taj Mahal

    D   Correct as it is

11. **A**   Empress mumtaz mahal

     B   Empress Mumtaz Mahal

     C   empress Mumtaz mahal

     D   Correct as it is

10. **F**   Northern India

     G   Northern india

     H   northern india

     J   Correct as it is

12. **F**   Turkish Architect

     G   turkish Architect

     H   Turkish architect

     J   Correct as it is

(13)   The Department of public works has announced that a major construction

(14)   project will soon begin on taylor road. Signs have been posted warning drivers

(15)   that the street will be closed from the hours of 11:30 p.m. until 5:30 a.m. for two

(16)   weeks starting Monday, august 5.

13. **A**   Department Of Public Works

     B   department of Public works

     C   Department of Public Works

     D   Correct as it is

15. **A**   11:30 P.m. until 5:30 A.m.

     B   11:30 P.M. until 5:30 A.M.

     C   11:30 P.M. until 5:30 a.m.

     D   Correct as it is

14. **F**   Taylor Road

     G   Taylor road

     H   taylor Road

     J   Correct as it is

16. **F**   monday, august 5

     G   monday, August 5

     H   Monday, August 5

     J   Correct as it is

       One of the most awesome natural wonders of North America is

(17)   niagara falls. It is made up of two waterfalls and lies on the border
between the United States and Canada. The falls are about halfway

(18)   between lake Erie and lake Ontario.

17. **A**   Niagara falls

     B   niagara Falls

     C   Niagara Falls

     D   Correct as it is

18. **F**   Lake erie and Lake ontario

     G   lake erie and lake ontario

     H   Lake Erie and Lake Ontario

     J   Correct as it is

Read each set of sentences. Choose the sentence that has correct capitalization.

19. A My Sister and i are quite close.

   B Severe thunderstorms have struck the Southwestern states.

   C We visited Mount Vernon, the home of George Washington.

   D the used book Store has moved to maple Street.

20. F Scientists believe the earliest human beings lived in Africa.

   G Many flights to the northeast have been delayed due to fog.

   H The oldest College in the United States is Harvard University.

   J The Tournament Of Roses parade takes place on January 1.

21. A The chinese are the largest asian American ethnic group.

   B For many people, Finnish is a very difficult Language to learn.

   C The return address on this letter is P.O. Box 12, Ames, Iowa.

   D a member of the Newcomers' club greeted us at our new home.

22. F I was surprised that mayor Gray decided not to run for re-election.

   G Many movies have been filmed in the lovely Monument valley.

   H We're late because we missed the exit for the Stanley Bridge.

   J My Instructor from the Sure way driving School was very patient.

23. A The Hospital has added another Doctor to its staff.

   B The song, "Happy days are here Again," was used as a campaign song for Franklin d. Roosevelt.

   C This Television Station is geared toward the hispanic population.

   D "Don't let yourselves become too confident," said Coach Adams.

24. F My grandparents remember the great depression very well.

   G A scene of *King kong* takes place on the Empire state building.

   H The strong winds made driving on the falcon bridge difficult.

   J A water main break flooded Cedar Road.

25. A This issue of *Fitness And You* gives tips on weightlifting.

   B I cruised to the Virgin Islands.

   C Many irish people lined the street for the St. Patrick's day parade.

   D My mortgage payments are due on the first Day of the Month.

26. F The train headed for cleveland, ohio, will leave at 5:02 a.m.

   G Japan lies off the Northeast Coast of Asia.

   H Over 125,000 houses have been built by Habitat for Humanity.

   J Send your complaint to the Department of consumer affairs.

End Marks

A statement is followed by a **period.**

> The museum is open until five o'clock.

A question is followed by a **question mark.**

> Where are the Impressionist paintings?

An exclamation is followed by an **exclamation point.**

> What a wonderful use of light and shadow!

A command may be followed by either a period or an exclamation point, depending on the amount of feeling expressed.

> Tell me the title of that painting.

> Run to the gift shop before it closes!

Decide which end mark is needed for each sentence.

1. How slowly the freeway traffic is moving today
   A .   B ?   C !   D None

2. I have worked as a daycare provider for the last five years
   F .   G ?   H !   J None

3. Hand your résumé to the secretary
   A .   B ?   C !   D None

4. Take the first exit, and then turn right at the end of the ramp
   F .   G ?   H !   J None

5. Would you like to order an appetizer
   A .   B ?   C !   D None

6. Our bus is coming down the street, so hurry up!
   F .   G ?   H !   J None

7. What a powerful speech that was
   A .   B ?   C !   D None

8. When do you expect to complete the project
   F .   G ?   H !   J None

Practice

Write a period, a question mark, or an exclamation point at the end of each sentence.

1. Are you going out to dinner with Celeste

2. Your order will be shipped in two days

3. Take a five-minute break

4. Look out below

5. How much sugar does this recipe call for

6. It's your turn to take the dog for a walk

7. Tell me about your problem

8. What strength that marathon runner has

9. Does anyone know how old these leftovers are

10. I never want to see him again as long as I live

11. Go away and leave me alone

12. This gift shop has an excellent variety of items

Read the paragraph and look at its blank spots. Choose the correct end mark for each blank spot.

(13)   I went to see Les Raven's new flick, *Horror Movie*__ I
(14) wondered if it would be as bad as his last movie__ Now, after sitting
       through over two hours of bad acting and worse dialogue, I am ready
(15) to give you my review. What a waste of time and talent__ Go to
(16) see this movie only if you have absolutely nothing better to do__

13. **A** .   **B** ?   **C** !

14. **F** .   **G** ?   **H** !

15. **A** .   **B** ?   **C** !

16. **F** .   **G** ?   **H** !

Apply

Read each situation. Then write a pair of sentences in response to the situation. The sentences in each pair should have different end marks.

1. Your favorite television show has just been canceled.

   _____

   _____

2. You overslept.

   _____

   _____

3. You are at the zoo.

   _____

   _____

4. An old friend shows up unexpectedly.

   _____

   _____

5. You are meeting your new neighbors.

   _____

   _____

6. You hear a loud crash.

   _____

   _____

7. You are driving, and another driver pulls ahead of you and slows down.

   _____

   _____

8. Your boss gives you an unexpected pay raise.

   _____

   _____

Check Up

Decide which end mark, if any, is needed for each sentence.

1. The clerk brought out ten pairs of shoes, but the customer still wasn't satisfied

   A .   **B** ?   **C** !   **D** None

2. What is the interest rate on a car loan from this bank

   F .   **G** ?   **H** !   **J** None

3. What a sad ending to the story

   A .   **B** ?   **C** !   **D** None

4. The plot of this mystery is complicated

   F .   **G** ?   **H** !   **J** None

Read each set of sentences. Choose the sentence that has the correct end mark.

5. **A** Measure the length of the counter!

   B I heard that this restaurant serves vegetarian meals?

   C How dark the sky looks!

   D Do you have a driver's license.

6. **F** What a lovely wedding that was?

   G Please arrange the papers in this folder according to date!

   H These tomatoes are not ripe yet.

   J What kind of flower is this!

7. **A** Call the fire department?

   B I want to get an office job after I graduate!

   C How rude that man is?

   D Sid wants to play tennis with me.

8. **F** When is the next available appointment for a manicure?

   G How loud that car's radio is?

   H Fill out this rebate form completely?

   J This position includes evening and weekend work!

9. **A** Call me when you get home.

   B I can't believe how much this video game costs?

   C Fear of the dark is a common phobia!

   D How much does that job pay.

10. **F** Run for your life.

    G Do you understand the VCR instructions for setting the time?

    H Leave your coat in the hallway!

    J What an amazing story that was?

11. **A** Did you receive my message!

    B Drive carefully or you'll slide right off these icy roads!

    C Recycle your cans and bottles?

    D I hired an accountant to help me with my income tax forms?

12. **F** Where should I park my car.

    G The Voters Against Unfair Taxes are protesting the tax increase?

    H I could pay in cash or by check?

    J Stop talking and listen to me!

Commas: Compound Sentences and Introductory Phrases

A compound sentence has two or more independent clauses. An **independent clause** has a subject and a predicate and can stand on its own. The clauses may be connected by one of the following conjunctions: *and, or, nor, but, yet, so,* and *for*. Place a comma after the first independent clause, before the conjunction.

> The trees have changed color, and soon we will be raking leaves.

> Meet me for lunch today, but do not come before noon.

If a sentence has a compound element, such as a compound subject or compound predicate, do not place a comma between the parts.

> Hikers and cyclists shared the same path in the park. (compound subject)

> Either type or print the required information. (compound verb)

Read each pair of sentences. Circle the letter of the sentence in which commas are used correctly.

1. **A** An evergreen or a rose bush would fill in that bare spot in the garden.

   B An evergreen, or a rose bush would fill in that bare spot in the garden.

2. **A** Ms. Steele was offered a promotion, but she did not get the raise she wanted.

   B Ms. Steele was offered a promotion but she did not get the raise she wanted.

3. **A** Either Beverly is late this morning or, she decided to take a vacation day.

   B Either Beverly is late this morning, or she decided to take a vacation day.

4. **A** Azzam began work as a clerk and now, he is manager of the department.

   B Azzam began work as a clerk, and now he is manager of the department.

5. **A** Phil neither cleaned nor repaired the garden equipment.

   B Phil neither cleaned, nor repaired the garden equipment.

6. **A** This bed, and breakfast, is highly recommended, for the owners are gracious hosts.

   B This bed and breakfast is highly recommended, for the owners are gracious hosts.

7. **A** Dale and Kim finished one pie and began another.

   B Dale, and Kim finished one pie, and began another.

8. **A** Buy the computer now, or wait for a sale later.

   B Buy the computer now or wait for a sale later.

Practice

Commas are needed after some words or phrases that come at the beginning of a sentence. Use commas in the following situations:

- When *yes* or *no* is used to answer a question or make a comment

  <u>Yes,</u> you may borrow the car tonight.

- To set off a long introductory phrase from the rest of the sentence

  <u>Somewhere along this winding road with many intersections,</u> we lost our way.

- To set off a short introductory phrase of four words or less if the sentence is hard to understand without the comma

  <u>By the way,</u> Rebecca and Gary will be joining us for dinner.

Underline the introductory word or phrase in each sentence. Add commas as needed.

1. Despite the disappointing test results the company decided to continue its research.

2. With several branches broken off the tree slowly began to die.

3. No Mr. Granger has not called to confirm his appointment.

4. Whistling softly Zeke began the difficult task of clearing the underbrush.

5. Of all the varieties of apples Jonathans are my favorite.

Read the following paragraph and look at the numbered, underlined parts. Choose the answer that is written correctly for each underlined part.

(6)   Every fall <u>bags of little red cranberries</u> appear in the supermarket.
(7) Cranberries grow wild along <u>streams but</u> growers raise them in special bogs.
(8) <u>Rich in vitamin C, cranberries</u> are used in sauces, jellies, and fruit drinks.
(9) <u>Indeed this cheerful little berry</u> is a part of many holiday meals.

6. A fall, bags of little red cranberries

   B fall bags of little red cranberries,

   C fall, bags of little red cranberries,

   D Correct as it is

7. F streams, but

   G streams, but,

   H streams but,

   J Correct as it is

8. A Rich in vitamin C cranberries

   B Rich in vitamin C cranberries,

   C Rich in vitamin C, cranberries,

   D Correct as it is

9. F Indeed this cheerful little berry,

   G Indeed this, cheerful little berry

   H Indeed, this cheerful little berry

   J Correct as it is

Apply

Read each sentence. Place commas wherever they are needed. Put an *X* over any comma that is incorrect. Write *C* on the line if the sentence is correct.

1. From a distance, the horses, and riders looked like tiny specks in my camera. _____

2. No your order is not ready today, nor will I have it done tomorrow. _____

3. To be perfectly frank I think you are making a grave mistake. _____

4. Yes, Aunt Carla is seventy today but she looks much younger. _____

5. Feeling foolish Dominic excused himself, and left the room. _____

6. After raking all the leaves we were totally exhausted. _____

7. Either purchase a new tire, or have the old one repaired. _____

8. After painting the windows we forgot to open them, and now many are stuck. _____

9. Yes current magazines are on the shelves but older ones are in storage. _____

10. George, and Nora were excellent guides for they had been to Greece many times. _____

11. In the morning, we quickly packed our bags, and caught the early flight home. _____

12. After putting on his glasses Grandfather read us his favorite poem. _____

Read each independent clause. Then form a compound sentence by adding a conjunction from the box and another independent clause. Use commas wherever they are needed.

and	or	nor	but	for	yet	so

13. Tyler sent his résumé to several companies _____

_____

14. Remove that weed from the garden now _____

_____

15. This refrigerator is nearly fifteen years old _____

_____

Check Up

Read each sentence and look at the underlined part. Choose the answer that is written correctly for the underlined part.

1. Coming to a fork in the road we stopped and looked at the map.

   A road, we stopped,

   B road we stopped,

   C road, we stopped

   D Correct as it is

2. Trevor wanted to continue the search, but Isolde and I wanted to stop.

   F search but Isolde

   G search, but Isolde,

   H search but, Isolde

   J Correct as it is

3. Yes either dog or cat fur may be making you sneeze.

   A Yes either dog, or cat

   B Yes, either dog or cat

   C Yes, either dog, or, cat

   D Correct as it is

4. At work, Ivan is very serious and few people know about his great sense of humor.

   F At work Ivan is very serious

   G At work Ivan is very serious,

   H At work, Ivan is very serious,

   J Correct as it is

5. Excited by the appearance of land, the captain, and crew cheered loudly.

   A land, the captain

   B land the captain

   C land the captain,

   D Correct as it is

6. The plaza is crowded for many people enjoy eating outdoors.

   F The plaza is crowded,

   G The plaza is, crowded,

   H The plaza, is crowded

   J Correct as it is

7. Enjoying the moment the happy couple smiled, and waved to their relatives and friends.

   A moment, the happy couple smiled

   B moment the happy couple smiled,

   C moment, the happy couple smiled,

   D Correct as it is

8. For one thing, you did not arrive on time, nor did you tell me you would be late.

   F thing you did not arrive on time

   G thing, you did not arrive on time

   H thing you did not arrive on time,

   J Correct as it is

9. The young actor sang and danced well, yet few people appreciated his talents.

   A sang, and danced well

   B sang, and danced well,

   C sang and danced well

   D Correct as it is

10. No, I haven't seen this video but we could watch it later this evening.

   F No I haven't seen this video, but

   G No, I haven't seen this video but,

   H No, I haven't seen this video, but

   D Correct as it is

Commas: Complex Sentences and Relative Clauses

A **complex sentence** is made up of one independent clause and one or more dependent clauses (which can't stand alone). The dependent clause is joined to the main clause by a conjunction like *although, because, if, when, after, since, though, until,* or *that.*

When the dependent clause comes at the start of the sentence, put a comma after it and before the independent clause.

> If that car alarm doesn't stop, I'm going to scream.

When the dependent clause comes at the end of the sentence, don't use a comma.

> I'm going to scream if that car alarm doesn't stop.

For each item, circle the letter of the sentence that is punctuated correctly.

1. **A** If you need to reach me, I'll be at the beach.

   B If you need to reach me I'll be at the beach.

2. **A** The invention of flight was an event, that changed the world.

   B The invention of flight was an event that changed the world.

3. **A** Because Colette's little boy wants to be a superhero he wears a cape.

   B Because Colette's little boy wants to be a superhero, he wears a cape.

4. **A** Jay nibbled the burger to be polite although he doesn't like meat.

   B Jay nibbled the burger to be polite, although he doesn't like meat.

5. **A** After Gabrielle jumped for the ball and hit the floor, she heard a crunch.

   B After Gabrielle jumped for the ball, and hit the floor, she heard a crunch.

6. **A** When Susan B. Anthony was born women were not allowed to vote.

   B When Susan B. Anthony was born, women were not allowed to vote.

7. **A** They say that Emperor Nero fiddled while the city of Rome burned.

   B They say, that Emperor Nero fiddled, while the city of Rome burned.

8. **A** Sara Paretsky's mystery novels are popular because she created an appealing private detective.

   B Sara Paretsky's mystery novels are popular, because she created an appealing private detective.

Practice

A **relative clause** is an adjective clause introduced by a pronoun. They're called *relative* because they relate adjective clauses to the words they modify. The pronouns that can introduce a relative clause are *who, whom, whoever, whomever, what, whatever, which,* and *whichever.* Set off a relative clause with commas when the clause is not essential to the sentence.

> My uncle, who is a doctor, will be visiting us this weekend.

> Whatever Barbara says, John plans to attend the concert.

Do not set off a relative clause with commas if it is essential to the sentence.

> Whatever Barbara says must be true.

Underline the relative clause in each sentence. Add commas as needed.

1. Dennis who is Polly's new boyfriend seems like a nice guy.

2. Whichever answer I choose it seems I'm always wrong.

3. That author's new novel which is on the bestseller list isn't very good.

4. I was wondering what movie you'd like to see.

Read the paragraph below. Look at the parts that are numbered and underlined. Choose the answer that is written correctly for each underlined part.

(5)   Thousands of years ago, ice dams in Idaho gave way which sent a
(6) towering wall of water toward the Pacific Ocean. Whatever else it caused the flood moved massive amounts of rock and left dry land behind. It was J. Harlen
(7) Bretz, a high-school science teacher who first identified the flood geology. It took
(8) nearly eighty years for the experts to believe him. What a sweet moment, it was when he was finally awarded geology's highest honor at age 96.

5. **A** gave way which,

   B gave way, which

   C gave way who

   D Correct as it is

6. **F** it caused, the

   G it, caused the

   H it; caused the

   J Correct as it is

7. **A** teacher, who first

   B teacher which first

   C teacher who first,

   D Correct as it is

8. **F** What, a sweet moment it

   G What a sweet moment it

   H What, a sweet moment, it

   J Correct as it is

Apply

Read each sentence. Place commas wherever they are needed. Place an X over any comma that is not needed. Write C on the line if the sentence is correct.

1. Even winters here are warm which is why I like this place. _____

2. "Although you can run you can't hide," Tyrone's brother shouted. _____

3. Whoever you want to be for the night you can find the perfect costume at the Alter Ego store. _____

4. Because Mandy was having trouble with algebra, Grace tutored her. _____

5. Elizabeth Garcia, who was my grandmother was a jazz singer. _____

6. Lester will go on to college, if he can raise his grades a little.

7. It gets colder in winter because of the angle of the sun.

8. Emeralds which are Jennifer's favorite gems, are less expensive than diamonds.

9. George found out, that Richard had lied to him.

10. When the cat's away the mice will play.

Read each independent clause. Then form a complex sentence by adding a conjunction or pronoun from the box and a dependent clause. Place commas wherever they are needed.

although	because	if	who	which

1. Making sand paintings is a satisfying hobby.

_____

_____

2. The full moon shed almost enough light to read by.

_____

_____

3. Emory Blackburn was my great-grandfather.

_____

_____

4. The kitten cried.

_____

_____

Check Up

Read each sentence and look at the underlined part. Choose the answer that is written correctly for the underlined part.

1. Independence <u>Day which</u> is a holiday, is July 4.

   A Day; which

   B Day, which

   C Day, which,

   D Correct as it is

2. Although Norm eats very nutritious <u>foods he still</u> has high cholesterol.

   F foods, he still

   G foods, he still,

   H foods he still,

   J Correct as it is

3. Leaves turn colors in the <u>fall because the trees</u> stop making chlorophyll.

   A fall, because the trees

   B fall because the trees,

   C fall because, the trees

   D Correct as it is

4. Albert <u>Camus who was</u> one of the founders of existentialism, was from Algeria.

   F Camus; who was

   G Camus who was,

   H Camus, who was

   J Correct as it is

5. When Calvin heard the <u>wolves howl it</u> sent shivers down his spine.

   A wolves howl it,

   B wolves howl, it

   C wolves, howl it

   D Correct as it is

6. If the sky isn't <u>crystal clear Shannon</u> can't get more than three channels on her TV.

   F crystal, clear Shannon

   G crystal clear, Shannon

   H crystal clear Shannon,

   J Correct as it is

7. Leonard will play <u>chess with whomever</u> is available.

   A chess, with whomever

   B chess with, whomever

   C chess with whomever,

   D Correct as it is

8. The oil spill was still causing <u>damage to the ocean, after</u> twenty years.

   F damage, to the ocean after

   G damage, to the ocean, after

   H damage to the ocean after

   J Correct as it is

9. Did you tell <u>the principal, that I wanted to talk to her?</u>

   A the principal that I wanted

   B the principal that, I wanted,

   C the principal that I wanted,

   D Correct as it is

10. Which dish Mary Kay <u>feels like cooking, depends</u> on the weather.

    F feels, like cooking depends

    G feels like, cooking depends

    H feels like cooking depends

    J Correct as it is

Commas: Series and Parenthetical Expressions

Sentences with a series of three or more words or short phrases need commas to separate the items. Place a comma after each word or phrase except the last one.

> Sparrows, blue jays, and cardinals nibble on seeds and berries.

> John got off the Mega Coaster with his head spinning, his knees shaking, and his stomach churning.

When two or more adjectives are in a series, try saying the word *and* between each set of consecutive adjectives to see if it makes sense. If it does, place a comma between the adjectives. If it does not, leave the comma out.

> When will you replace that worn, faded, broken recliner? (*Worn and faded and broken recliner* makes sense.)

> The sad, lonely old man went to visit his wife's grave every day. (*Sad and lonely old man* makes sense; *sad and lonely and old man* does not.)

Do not use commas if the items in a series are joined with connecting words.

> Streak of green and red and blue made the glass vase sparkle with color.

Read each sentence. Place commas wherever they are needed. If a sentence is correct as it is, write *C* on the line.

1. Louisiana Mississippi and Florida had hurricane warnings last night. _____

2. Does the deli serve chicken soup or corned beef or cheesecake? _____

3. Suzanne stuffs envelopes gives out bumper stickers and answers the phone. _____

4. The old desk contained some notebooks a few coins and rusted paper clips. _____

5. An old lone tree clung to the edge of the stream. _____

6. Beware of jellyfish and sharks and jagged coral when swimming in this area. _____

7. Deliveries generally are made in early morning mid-afternoon and late evening. _____

8. Repair repaint or replace those old windows before the weather turns colder. _____

9. A short stone moss-covered fountain leaned against the garden fence. _____

10. Either Carla or Joyce or Clay should have a key to the storeroom. _____

Practice

A **parenthetical expression** is a word, phrase, or clause that adds emphasis, information, or a comment to the main idea of a sentence. This expression, however, can be dropped without changing the meaning of the sentence. In most cases, place a comma before and after a parenthetical expression to separate it from the rest of the sentence.

> <u>Oh</u>, what difference will that make?
>
> The bank, <u>as usual</u>, was crowded with customers.
>
> He discovered the molecule, <u>it is true</u>, after experimenting for years.

Read each pair of sentences. Circle the letter of the sentence in which commas are used correctly.

1. **A** You remembered, of course, to pay the electric bill.
   B You remembered of course, to pay the electric bill.

2. **A** The surprise, as you may have guessed is that I've been promoted.
   B The surprise, as you may have guessed, is that I've been promoted.

3. **A** We'll take say five pounds of that Swiss cheese.
   B We'll take, say, five pounds of that Swiss cheese.

4. **A** Oh well, perhaps we can meet for lunch another time.
   B Oh, well perhaps we can meet for lunch another time.

5. **A** The decision was too important, she declared, to be left until next week.
   B The decision was too important she declared, to be left until next week.

Underline the parenthetical expression in each sentence. Add commas wherever they are needed.

6. Hal will be better prepared next time to be sure.

7. Your camera I suppose fell into the pool when you did.

8. They were surprised indeed at the success of their fundraising efforts.

9. The test scores as might be expected were extremely high.

10. Fortunately we were not injured in the automobile accident.

11. Nova Scotia according to this brochure is a scenic place to visit.

12. Senator Smedlap if you believe this poll is in danger of losing the election.

Apply

Read each sentence. If it needs commas, rewrite it correctly on the line. If the sentence is punctuated properly, write *Correct* on the line.

1. Lamps picture frames and small tables are located on the third floor.

   _____

2. Lillian was surrounded as usual by ribbons craft supplies and gadgets of every kind.

   _____

3. The first aid kit is supplied with bandages and ointment and eye wash.

   _____

4. This painting as you see shows a delicate serious graceful ballerina.

   _____

5. Our baskets are made by hand carefully crafted and guaranteed to last.

   _____

6. Neither ice nor snow nor freezing wind keeps me from the ski slope.

   _____

7. Could we leave for the theater at say 6:30 P.M.?

   _____

8. The last game of the season according to the paper was not well attended.

   _____

9. Rollie's dog begs rolls over and plays dead if you give him a treat.

   _____

10. This model shreds paper and heavy cardboard and even some plastics.

    _____

11. Do you find it annoying for example when telemarketers call at dinnertime?

    _____

12. Well have you decided whether to purchase this piano?

    _____

Check Up

Read the following paragraph and look at the numbered, underlined parts. Choose the answer that is written correctly for each underlined part.

(1)   Healthy eating according to almost every reliable source means
(2) adding more fresh fruits vegetables and grains to your diet. Choose lean
(3) meats and low-fat dairy products. It helps, of course to cut back on fats
(4) and sweets. A good diet may lead to better health a longer life and a
      more positive outlook.

1. A eating, according to almost every,
     reliable source

   B eating, according to almost, every,
     reliable source

   C eating, according to almost every
     reliable source,

   D Correct as it is

2. F fruits, vegetables and

   G fruits, vegetables, and

   H fruits, vegetables, and,

   J Correct as it is

3. A It helps of course,

   B It helps, of course,

   C It helps of course

   D Correct as it is

4. F better health a longer life,

   G better health, a longer life

   H better health, a longer life,

   J Correct as it is

Read each sentence and look at its underlined part. Choose the answer that is written correctly for the underlined part.

5. Frankie will rotate the tires check the battery and change the oil in your car for one low price.

   A tires, check the battery, and

   B tires check the battery, and

   C tires, check the battery, and,

   D Correct as it is

6. Salmon or tuna or shrimp are excellent choices for outdoor grilling.

   F Salmon, or tuna, or shrimp

   G Salmon, or, tuna, or, shrimp,

   H Salmon, or tuna or shrimp

   J Correct as it is

7. Dozens of knives, forks, and spoons were neatly arranged on the tables.

   A knives forks and spoons

   B knives, forks, and, spoons

   C knives, forks and spoons

   D Correct as it is

8. Brussels sprouts, and cabbage as you may know are in the same family of vegetables.

   F sprouts, and cabbage, as you may know,

   G sprouts and cabbage, as you may know

   H sprouts and cabbage, as you may know,

   J Correct as it is

Other Uses of Commas

When a person or thing is directly addressed in a sentence, the name must be set off with commas. The following examples show the correct placement of commas for words of **direct address** at the beginning, end, or middle of a sentence.

> Dr. McGrath, you have an urgent call on line two.
>
> Why are you so slow today, you stupid computer!
>
> If you carry the largest package, Jeannine, I can handle the rest.

When the names of a city and a state occur in a sentence, place a comma between them. If the sentence continues, use a second comma after the name of the state.

> Did you visit the Arch when you were in St. Louis, Missouri?
>
> Kevin lives in Phoenix, Arizona, in a new condominium.

Read each pair of sentences. Circle the letter of the sentence in which commas are used correctly.

1. **A** Ms. Grimes do you know if, Mr. Wilson, has left the office yet?

   B Ms. Grimes, do you know if Mr. Wilson has left the office yet?

2. **A** Be sure to stop in Old Town when you get to Albuquerque, New Mexico, Ted.

   B Be sure to stop in Old Town when you get to Albuquerque, New Mexico Ted.

3. **A** Hold the ruler straight, son, or your measurement will not be exact.

   B Hold the ruler straight son, or your measurement will not be exact.

4. **A** No, you greedy cat you can't have any more fish.

   B No, you greedy cat, you can't have any more fish.

Underline the word or words of direct address in each sentence. Add commas wherever they are needed.

5. Charlene thanks for offering to drive today.

6. Tell me Martin how do you like working as a security guard?

7. Will you accept a verbal request sir or should I put it in writing?

8. The meeting is closer to Towson Maryland than it is to Baltimore William.

9. Uncle Angelo when are you and Aunt Louisa leaving for Italy?

Practice

An **appositive** is a word or phrase added to a sentence to explain another word. It means the same thing as the word it explains. Use commas to set off an appositive from the rest of the sentence.

> Our dog, Grover, is ten years old.

> We went to Handy Helper, a do-it-yourself store, for the tools.

If words such as *or* or *namely* introduce the appositive, include them within the commas.

> Several potsherds, or broken pieces of old pottery, were discovered at the ancient site.

Underline the appositive in each sentence. Place commas wherever they are needed.

1. My mother-in-law Irene works at the county courthouse.

2. Sweetbriar Commons the biggest mall in the area has a large food court.

3. Ben Davis the mayor of Centerville is noted for his well-run administration.

4. A large ruby a red stone hung from a gold chain around her neck.

5. Josie and Al owners of the corner deli work long hours seven days a week.

6. His youngest daughter Veronica just won a college scholarship.

7. An amphora an oval jar with two handles was used long ago to store oil or wine.

8. The salesperson urged us to try the Tornado a vacuum cleaner with extra power.

Use an appositive from the list provided and complete each sentence. Place commas correctly.

owners of the daycare	the receptionist
my sister-in-law	singers popular in the '60s
our good friends	one of your classmates
the plumber	a strong-minded individual

9. Jamal _____

10. Sam and Tillie _____

11. Donita _____

12. Barbara Syms _____

13. Mr. Waveland _____

Apply

Read each item. Following the directions, write a sentence using the underlined word in direct address. Be sure to add all necessary punctuation.

1. Recommend a good restaurant to <u>Brittany</u>.

_____

2. Tell <u>Owen</u> what TV program you like to watch.

_____

3. Make a dental appointment with <u>Dr. Pinkton</u>.

_____

4. Ask <u>Mrs. Arnold</u> about insurance for your car.

_____

5. Explain to <u>Miguel</u> why you were late.

_____

Rewrite each sentence, adding commas wherever they are needed.

6. My personal trainer Samantha Engstrom often travels to Miami Florida.

_____

7. Henry have you seen a copy of *Back Roads* the new travel magazine?

_____

8. Your pancakes Mrs. Bronson were light and fluffy.

_____

9. Ken's nephew Steven is attending graduate school in Boulder Colorado.

_____

10. Bridget's Breads our local bakery makes tasty Irish soda bread.

_____

11. The ship's galley or kitchen could seat four people comfortably.

_____

Check Up

Read each set of sentences. Then choose the sentence that is punctuated correctly.

1. **A** Niagara Falls, an impressive waterfall, lies on the border between the United States and Canada.

   B That's a good picture of you Kim on the beach in Florida.

   C Jannette Ricci, an old friend from Bangor, Maine called me today.

   D Ned, are you working at that new amusement park Shady Creek?

2. **F** Our trip from Seattle, Washington to Springfield, Illinois took several days.

   G Darrin, is studying marine biology at Woods Hole Oceanographic Institution a research center on Cape Cod.

   H Gregory Higgins, a successful businessman donated a large sum of money to the youth center.

   J Drive two miles down this street, ma'am, and you'll see the road sign for Virginia Beach, Virginia.

3. **A** Those boots would be perfect for you Grandmother.

   B Marvin is an avid philatelist, or stamp collector.

   C Dorothy look for grackles, a kind of blackbird, in the cornfield.

   D If you write the invitations Monica, I'll mail them for you.

4. **F** Check the atlas, Stanley, to find the location of Kokomo, Indiana.

   G The narwhal, a type of whale has a long tusk on the upper jaw.

   H Jamie do you think this chair is a good replacement for the old one?

   J Our neighbors Larry and Diana just moved from Dubuque, Iowa.

5. **A** Cut through the outer plastic covering first Ranelle, and the package will open easily.

   B Prince, our Great Dane won a second place ribbon at the show.

   C The hobby shop owner, Jeff Waters has a large collection of baseball cards.

   D Abdul, show Arianna, the new lab technician, where we keep supplies.

6. **F** Durum a type of hard wheat is often used to make pasta.

   G Will you please return these books to the library, Marsha?

   H Foot Company, a shoe warehouse specializes in hard-to-find sizes.

   J Emily, my daughter, works for Miles and Sharp a law firm.

7. **A** Where in this messy drawer did I leave you my trusty flashlight?

   B Ms. Simmons your luggage has been found in Nome Alaska.

   C Our concentration was broken by a sudden noise, a knock on the door.

   D *The Four Seasons* a concerto by Vivaldi, has lively music.

8. **F** Mount Rushmore, the giant memorial to four U.S. presidents is near Rapid City, South Dakota.

   G A supernova an extremely bright exploding star, creates a huge cloud of dust and gas.

   H Is it true, Pat, that you and Ivan are in line for a promotion?

   J Mr. Bingham your appointment is with, Dr. Locke, on Friday.

Semicolons and Colons

You can use a **semicolon** to join the independent clauses of a compound sentence. A semicolon may not be used to join a dependent clause with an independent clause. When you use a semicolon, do not use a conjunction such as *and* or *but*.

Correct: The singer stood at the front of the stage; the dancers performed behind her.

Incorrect: The singer stood at the front of the stage; and the dancers performed behind her.

Incorrect: While the singer stood at the front of the stage; the dancers performed behind her.

A semicolon should be placed between the clauses of a compound sentence when a transitional phrase joins the clauses. A comma must be inserted after the transitional phrase. Common transitional phrases include the following: *accordingly, for example, however, in fact, for instance,* and *nevertheless.*

The actors are enthusiastic; however, the play is in need of fine-tuning.

A semicolon should be placed between items in a series if those items contain commas.

The musical is scheduled to play in St. Louis, Missouri; Chicago, Illinois; and Cleveland, Ohio.

Read each sentence. Insert semicolons wherever they are needed.

1. The spaniel refused to obey its owner consequently, the owner took it to obedience school.

2. In his garden, Jeff grew red, green, and yellow peppers yellow, green, and pole beans and summer, spaghetti, and acorn squash.

3. Lila works for a temporary agency she enjoys the variety of her assignments.

4. Saturday dawned bright and sunny therefore, the Scotts decided to go to the beach.

5. The maids arrived at the home early they washed, dusted, and vacuumed before noon.

6. The cab driver expected to have a quiet night instead, he was busy answering one call after the other.

7. The hotel was fully booked even the honeymoon suite was taken.

8. The movie credits listed the writer, Leslie Watts the producer, James Anderson and the director, Maura Blake.

Practice

A **colon** is used to introduce a list of items. A word or phrase naming the items, such as *the following, these,* or a number, must appear before the list.

      Correct: In this gallery, the following artists are shown: Renoir, Degas, and Monet.

      Correct: In this gallery, three artists are shown: Renoir, Degas, and Monet.

      Incorrect: In this gallery, the artists are: Renoir, Degas, and Monet.

Use a colon between numerals that tell the hour and the minute.

      The meeting was called to order at 10:15 A.M.

Use a colon after the greeting in a business letter.

      Dear Sir: Dear Dr. Walsh:

Read each set of sentences. Choose the sentence in which semicolons and colons are used correctly.

1. **A** Teresa has held the following positions: clerk, receptionist, and secretary.

   B Teresa has held the following positions; clerk, receptionist, and secretary.

   C Teresa has held the following positions; clerk; receptionist; and secretary.

2. **F** Before he left at 445, Vince printed the report.

   G Before he left at 4:45, Vince printed the report.

   H Before he left at 4:45; Vince printed the report.

3. **A** Louisa had never been to Japan, in fact: she had never traveled out of her home state.

   B Louisa had never been to Japan, in fact; she had never traveled out of her home state.

   C Louisa had never been to Japan; in fact, she had never traveled out of her home state.

Read each sentence. Add semicolons or colons wherever they are needed. Place an X over any semicolon or colon that is used incorrectly.

4. The plane's wings needed de-icing for that reason, the flight was delayed until 745.

5. The breakfast buffet featured: pancakes, scrambled eggs, and fresh fruit.

6. Should we go to: Las Vegas, Nevada New Orleans, Louisiana or Orlando, Florida?

7. Voting is both a duty and a privilege nevertheless, many Americans don't bother to vote on Election Day.

8. I scheduled three students for the 930 A.M. make-up test Evan, Karina, and Dennis.

Apply

Read each sentence. If semicolons and colons aren't used correctly, rewrite the sentence on the lines. If semicolons and colons are used correctly, write *Correct*.

1. Art won: a stuffed bear, a doll, and a pair of dice at the first booth, a cap at the second booth, and a balloon, a popcorn ball, and a gift certificate at the last booth.

   _____

   _____

2. We lost power during the windstorm, it leveled houses; throughout the city.

   _____

3. Whenever Bruce leaves his house at 7:45, he arrives at work with time to spare.

   _____

4. The caterers offered possible clients desserts such as these, peach tarts; apple strudel; chocolate eclairs; and cherry cheesecakes.

   _____

   _____

5. Gwen had forgotten her keys again, fortunately; Bonita had remembered hers.

   _____

Rewrite the following paragraph, using semicolons and colons correctly.

On that February morning, weather forecasters said that there would be a blizzard. Smart skiers would have stayed home, however; eight skiers thought they could handle bad weather. They headed out without proper equipment such as: waterproof sleeping bags and tents. Suddenly the snow began. The skiers became confused: consequently they were soon lost. When the skiers didn't return; rescue parties were sent out. The story had a happy ending, all the skiers got home safely. From now on; they will respect the power of snow and wind.

_____

_____

_____

_____

_____

_____

Check Up

Read each set of sentences. Choose the sentence that uses semicolons and colons correctly.

1. **A** An accident has closed the freeway; and traffic is being rerouted.

   B Elena likes strange food combinations; for example, she enjoys jelly and cucumbers.

   C On Wednesday, my night class begins at 7;15.

   D Though Bryan is a professional chef; he eats simply at home.

2. **F** The couple didn't have much money: nevertheless they were happy.

   G I work Friday nights, otherwise; I would come to your party.

   H The movie was hilarious audiences laughed from start to finish.

   J Items on sale include the following: caps, T-shirts, and sunglasses.

3. **A** Tonight is clear; and it is also cold.

   B My dog can do tricks: playing dead, rolling over, and giving his paw.

   C A gas line exploded; the noise shook the quiet neighborhood.

   D Ellen wants to buy a house, however; she is having trouble saving money.

4. **F** Jeri introduced us to Mr. Thompson, her history teacher; Ms. Dean, her English teacher; and Dr. Walters, her principal.

   G Since she joined the fitness club; Marcia has swum every day.

   H Our busiest days are: Friday, Saturday, and Monday.

   J Jesse studied acting; but he wasn't able to make a living at it.

Read the following paragraph and look at the numbered, underlined parts. Choose the answer that is written correctly for each underlined part.

(5)   Whenever Hannah feels down; she knows a trip to the shopping mall will cheer
(6) her up. When visiting a mall, Hannah doesn't have a set plan in mind; she simply
     enjoys being out among the mall's sights, sounds, and smells. Occasionally she browses
(7) among items such as these, CDs, sweaters, or books. Sometimes she meets friends
(8) while shopping: however; that's not important. The mall gives Hannah a welcome
     break from her everyday routine.

5. **A** feels down, she

   B feels down. She

   C feels down: she

   D Correct as it is

6. **F** in mind, she

   G in mind; and she

   H in mind she

   J Correct as it is

7. **A** such as: these

   B such as these;

   C such as these:

   D Correct as it is

8. **F** shopping however;

   G shopping; however,

   H shopping, however;

   J Correct as it is

Review

End Marks

Use a **period** to end all statements and most commands. Place a **question mark** at the end of a question. Put an **exclamation point** after any sentence that expresses great excitement or emotion.

Commas

Use **commas** for the following purposes:

- to separate independent clauses in a compound sentence that are joined by a conjunction such as *and, or, nor, but, yet, so,* and *for*
- to separate a dependent clause at the beginning of a complex sentence from the independent clause. Conjunctions include *although, because, if, when,* and *that.*
- to set off a relative clause in a sentence. Relative pronouns are *who, whom, whoever, whomever, what, whatever, which,* and *whichever.*
- to set off the introductory words *yes* or *no* when they are used to reply to a question
- to set off certain short phrases and all long phrases that begin a sentence
- to separate words or phrases written in a series of three or more
- to separate adjectives written in a series of two or more
- to set off a parenthetical expression from the rest of its sentence
- to separate the name of someone being addressed from the rest of the sentence
- to separate the name of a city, a state, and the rest of a sentence
- to set off an appositive from the rest of the sentence

Semicolons

Use **semicolons** for the following purposes:

- to separate independent clauses in a compound sentence if there is no conjunction
- to separate the first clause in a compound sentence from the transitional phrase that follows it; place a comma after the transitional phrase.
- to separate items in a series if those items have commas

Colons

Use **colons** for the following purposes:

- to introduce a list of items; the list must be preceded by a word or phrase naming its items, such as *these things* or *the following* or a number.
- to separate numerals that name the hour and the minute
- to end the greeting in a business letter

Assessment

Decide which punctuation mark, if any, is needed in each sentence.

1. Carlos and Lorita and Jamie resemble their maternal grandparents.

    A ;   **B** ,   **C** :   **D** None

2. Max where did you store the electric drill?

    F ,   **G** :   **H** ;   **J** None

3. My watch was off I left work ten minutes early.

    A :   **B** ;   **C** ,   **D** None

4. Bruce left his wallet in the bank but a teller found it.

    F ,   **G** ;   **H** .   **J** None

5. Who left the milk out on the counter

    A .   **B** !   **C** ?   **D** None

6. Grab the rope and hold on

    F ?   **G** ;   **H** !   **J** None

Read each sentence and look at its underlined part. Choose the answer that is written correctly for the underlined part.

7. The elevator was <u>filled nevertheless</u> more people tried to squeeze inside.

    A filled, nevertheless,

    B filled, nevertheless;

    C filled; nevertheless,

    D Correct as it is

8. The following items were arranged in the cabinet: <u>drywall screws and nails on the left;</u> nuts, bolts, and washers on the right; and wrenches and hammers in the middle.

    F drywall, screws, and nails on the left,

    G drywall screws and nails, on the left;

    H drywall, screws and nails on the left;

    J Correct as it is

9. Tiger <u>Woods who may be</u> the best golfer in the world, started playing at age two.

    A Woods which may be

    B Woods, which may be

    C Woods, who may be

    D Correct as it is

10. <u>Yes, Denise</u> I'll help you make cookies.

    F Yes Denise

    G Yes, Denise,

    H Yes; Denise,

    J Correct as it is

Assessment continued

Read each paragraph and look at the numbered, underlined parts. Choose the answer that is written correctly for each underlined part.

(11)   Before today's interstate superhighways were <u>constructed, people</u> traveled on
(12)   <u>smaller less speedy</u> national roads. One such highway was Route 66. Running
(13)   between Chicago, Illinois, and <u>Los Angeles California</u> Route 66 was an important
(14)   highway <u>for truckers, farmers and tourists</u> alike. Dozens of small towns and rural
(15)   areas were linked together by <u>Route 66 "The</u> Main Street of America."

11. **A** constructed; people

    B constructed people,

    C constructed people

    D Correct as it is

12. **F** smaller, less speedy, national,

    G smaller less speedy, national

    H smaller, less speedy national

    J Correct as it is

13. **A** Los Angeles, California,

    B Los Angeles, California;

    C Los Angeles, California

    D Correct as it is

14. **F** for truckers, farmers, and tourists

    G for truckers; farmers; and tourists

    H for: truckers, farmers, and tourists

    J Correct as it is

15. **A** Route 66, "The

    B Route 66: "The

    C Route 66; "The

    D Correct as it is

(16)   <u>Gutzon Borglum an American sculptor</u> is not as well known as his most
(17)   famous <u>work, the</u> Mount Rushmore National Memorial. Borglum worked
       under difficult and dangerous conditions for many years. Cutting
(18)   directly into a <u>mountain, he</u> carved huge portraits of four American
(19)   <u>presidents,</u> Washington, Jefferson, Lincoln, and Teddy Roosevelt.

16. **F** Borglum, an American sculptor

    G Borglum an American sculptor,

    H Borglum, an American sculptor,

    J Correct as it is

17. **A** work: the,

    B work; the

    C work the

    D Correct as it is

18. **F** mountain he

    G mountain: he

    H mountain. He

    J Correct as it is

19. **A** presidents

    B presidents:

    C presidents;

    D Correct as it is

Read each set of sentences. Choose the sentence that is punctuated correctly.

20. **F** Jean's water skiing adventure ended, much to her surprise, with a stiff neck, a pulled muscle, and an unexpected dunk in the lake.

    G If you miss the 8;15 bus, Joel, try to catch the one at 9;00.

    H Angie recently acquired a *solidus* an ancient Roman coin!

    J Cut some of that wood for the fire and, stack it along the fence.

21. **A** Victor usually reads: the national news, the stock market report, and the sports pages in the newspaper.

    B She chose naturally, the most expensive ring, bracelet and necklace in the store.

    C Ed's favorite hobby, gardening, keeps him busy all summer.

    D Who left dirty dishes in the sink.

22. **F** Did you really miss the bus or did you oversleep again, Ms. Allensby.

    G Edgar Allan Poe wrote "The Black Cat," a short story; "To Helen," a poem; and "The Poetic Principle," an essay.

    H Yes I'll be sure to watch the program at 10:30 tonight.

    J Golly, what an amazing comeback?

23. **A** The street vendor offered us handmade sweaters, and caps, and scarves at a reasonable price.

    B You are half an hour early Grace; it is only 8:30.

    C That's a great idea, Hiromi!

    D Marsha wants a June wedding, Lawrence isn't so sure?

24. **F** This craft requires: narrow, medium, and wide ribbon; round, oval, and square buttons; and two yards of calico.

    G No, do not call before 7:00 A.M., Jenny.

    H The shoplifter should have realized of course, that Super Electronics has cameras everywhere in the store.

    J Your efforts to improve the environment, by the way, will have a positive effect on the neighborhood Mrs. DeVoe.

25. **A** Frankly, Sylvia I do not care to travel all the way to Beaver, Oklahoma, for the county fair.

    B Ten pounds of potatoes, I guess, should make enough salad for the family picnic.

    C While looking for the defroster, Ellen mistakenly turned on the lights, the wipers, and, the radio instead.

    D Be careful cutting the roast, the knife is razor sharp.

26. **F** The plastic fish that wiggled its tail moved its head and sang a song was only a passing fad, thank goodness.

    G Please return the following items to the library: the atlas, the dictionary, and the video.

    H Every evening several deer come out of the woods, and graze in our garden.

    J The Water Festival in Newport, Rhode Island, is lots of fun, in fact, we plan to attend.

Direct and Indirect Quotations

A **direct quotation** is a speaker's exact words. When a direct quotation is written, the speaker's words are enclosed in quotation marks (" "). The quotation marks are placed before and after the words the speaker says. The end mark for the quotation should be placed within the quotation marks. The first word of a direct quotation should be capitalized.

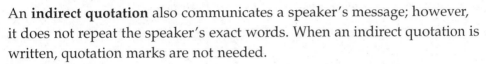

> The nurse said, "Please come into the examining room."
>
> "How do you feel today?" the doctor asked.

An **indirect quotation** also communicates a speaker's message; however, it does not repeat the speaker's exact words. When an indirect quotation is written, quotation marks are not needed.

> **Indirect:**   The doctor told Rachel to take two aspirin.
>
> **Direct:**   The doctor said, "Rachel, take two aspirin."

Usually, an indirect quotation reports on a statement that a speaker has made. Sometimes, however, the indirect quotation reports on a question that a speaker has asked. Remember that the indirect quotation itself is a statement, not a question, so its end mark should be a period, not a question mark.

> **Incorrect:**   The nurse asked Rachel if she was feeling better yet?
>
> **Correct:**   The nurse asked Rachel if she was feeling better yet.

Read each sentence. If it is an indirect quotation, write *I* on the line. If it is a direct quotation, write *D* on the line, and add quotation marks wherever they are needed.

1. _____ This bus is too crowded! complained Courtney.

2. _____ The suspect said that he could not remember where he was on July 14.

3. _____ My high school teacher said that success is a result of hard work and luck.

4. _____ Heidi announced, The messenger has come for the package.

Read each set of sentences. Circle the letter of the sentence that is capitalized and punctuated correctly.

5. **A**   "I enjoy almost all kinds of music, said Michelle."

   B   "I enjoy almost all kinds of music," said Michelle.

6. **A**   Daniel asked Michelle if she liked jazz and rap.

   B   Daniel asked Michelle "if she liked jazz and rap"?

Practice

When writing direct quotations, be sure to place commas correctly.

Whenever the phrase that identifies the speaker comes before the quotation, place a comma after the phrase and outside the opening quotation mark.

Rachel replied, "I am feeling much better, thank you."

When the phrase that identifies the speaker comes after the quotation, and the quotation is a statement, use a comma instead of a period. The comma should be placed within the quotation marks. (Remember that question marks and exclamation points that are part of the quotation should also be placed within the quotation marks.)

"Your cold should improve in a few days," said Doctor Lehman.

"I hope my son doesn't catch this cold!" Rachel exclaimed.

Each of the following sentences contains one or more capitalization or punctuation errors. Rewrite each sentence correctly.

1. Arthur said "we should learn some Spanish before we go to Mexico"

   _____

2. "repeat after me" said the language teacher patiently.

   _____

3. "does my accent sound natural yet" asked Emily.

   _____

4. Kristen exclaimed "I can hardly wait to get on the plane"!

   _____

5. "maybe we should travel to Italy next year" said Terry.

   _____

6. "how many languages do you speak"? asked William.

   _____

7. "some people simply have a gift for learning languages" volunteered Amy.

   _____

8. Rex said "it's easiest to learn foreign languages when you are young"

   _____

Apply

Read each sentence. If it is a direct quotation, rewrite it as an indirect quotation. If it is an indirect quotation, rewrite it as a direct quotation.

1. Debra asked if anyone wanted to go out to lunch with her.

   _____

2. The officer sternly told me, "You were exceeding the speed limit."

   _____

3. "We were awarded first prize!" announced the winning team.

   _____

4. The roofer said that repairs could cost about two thousand dollars.

   _____

5. Ms. Dwyer asked, "When will the report be finished?"

   _____

6. One pollster predicts that the governor will win re-election easily.

   _____

Read the following conversation. Then continue the conversation on the lines below. Write at least two more sentences for each speaker. Be sure to capitalize and punctuate your sentences correctly.

"What do you think we should do this weekend?" Kara asked.

"We could go out to dinner and then take in a movie," suggested Ernie.

Penny chimed in, "We need more excitement in our weekends."

Kara said, "I'm getting tired of the same old routine, too."

   _____

   _____

   _____

   _____

   _____

   _____

   _____

Check Up

Read each sentence and look at its underlined part. Choose the answer that is written correctly for the underlined part.

1. Janine said, <u>These</u> commercials always seem louder than the shows."

   A Janine said these

   B "Janine said, These

   C Janine said, "These

   D Correct as it is

2. Dr. Watkins asked Jay <u>if he smoked cigarettes.</u>

   F Jay, "If he smoked cigarettes."

   G Jay if he smoked cigarettes?

   H Jay "If he smoked cigarettes."

   J Correct as it is

3. The motel clerk <u>said "breakfast is</u> available in the lobby each morning."

   A said, "Breakfast

   B said, "breakfast

   C said "Breakfast

   D Correct as it is

4. The ticket taker at the box office told us that <u>"we were right on time."</u>

   F "We were right on time".

   G "We were right on time."

   H we were right on time.

   J Correct as it is

Read each set of sentences. Choose the sentence that is written correctly.

5. A "The movie is about to begin," said Doug.

   B Tracy complained "I can barely see the screen from this seat".

   C "Did one person both write and direct this film" asked Faith?

   D The people sitting behind us "told us to stop talking."

6. F The speaker asked how many audience members were parents?

   G "Raising children is a difficult job," said Dr. Brown.

   H "I couldn't agree more"! said the mother of two toddlers.

   J "Here are some tips that you might find useful, said the speaker."

7. A "train travel should be relaxing," said Regina.

   B "The conductor said that the train would reach the station on time".

   C The anxious passengers asked why the train had stopped.

   D Lillian asked; "Would you like part of the sandwich I packed"?

8. F "I'm crazy about downhill skiing"! said Yoshi.

   G Kurt said. "My skis are waxed and I'm ready to go".

   H "how much snow has fallen already,"? asked Cynthia.

   J Jane admitted, "What I like best about skiing is sitting by the fire after a day on the slopes."

Quotations and Quotation Marks

A **divided quotation** is a type of direct quotation. In a divided quotation, a phrase that identifies the speaker interrupts the speaker's words.

"It's a lovely night," said Salma, "so let's walk in the garden."

Follow these rules when writing a divided quotation:

- Enclose each part of the quotation in its own set of quotation marks.
- If the second part of the quotation is a separate sentence, place a period after the interrupting phrase, and capitalize the first word of the second sentence.

  "The mosquitoes are terrible tonight," complained Eduard. "We should go inside."

- If the second part of the quotation is not a separate sentence, place a comma after the interrupting phrase, and do not capitalize the first word of the continuation of the quotation.

  "It might help," said Salma, "to put on some of this mosquito repellant."

Sometimes, a question or exclamation may contain a direct quotation. In that case, place the question mark or exclamation point outside the quotation marks. No end mark is needed within the quotation marks.

Did that sign say, "Exit here for Apple Creek Island"?

What colossal egotism it took to say, "My project is sure to win"!

Read each divided quotation. Add quotation marks wherever they are needed.

1. Playing in the street, explained Doris, is not a good idea in this neighborhood.

2. Let's eat, said Eddie. I'm starved!

3. Did the clerk say, Show your receipt to the guard at the door ?

4. If we want good tickets, said Alyssa, we'll need to get in line early.

5. Jeremy has found a job in Denver, said Meryl. We're looking for a house there.

6. Did I hear you say, I'm sorry?

7. Before dinner, said Nathan, we played a little basketball.

8. This computer has been giving me trouble lately, complained Jesse. I need a new one.

9. What a relief it was to hear the pilot say, The weather is clearing up !

Practice

Use quotation marks to set off titles of short works, including poems, short stories, songs, reports, articles, and chapters of books. (Remember that every important word in a title is capitalized.)

> "Paul Revere's Ride" (poem)
>
> "The Pit and the Pendulum" (short story)
>
> "The Star-Spangled Banner" (song)
>
> "Stock Market Rises on Strong Earnings" (article)

In a sentence, if a title of a short work is followed by a comma or a period, put the comma or period inside the quotation marks.

> The words to the national anthem, "The Star-Spangled Banner," were written by Francis Scott Key.
>
> Henry W. Longfellow wrote a poem called "Paul Revere's Ride."

In a sentence, if a title of a short work is followed by a question mark or an exclamation point, put the question mark or exclamation point outside the quotation marks.

> Did Henry W. Longfellow write the poem called "Paul Revere's Ride"?

Read each pair of sentences. Circle the letter of the sentence that is punctuated correctly.

1. **A** When will the choir sing "Climb Ev'ry Mountain"?

   B When will the choir sing "Climb Ev'ry Mountain?"

2. **A** One chilling short story by Edgar Allan Poe is "The Fall of the House of Usher".

   B One chilling short story by Edgar Allan Poe is "The Fall of the House of Usher."

3. **A** What a stirring rendition of "Amazing Grace!"

   B What a stirring rendition of "Amazing Grace"!

4. **A** Did James work on the research article named "Vitamin C and You"?

   B "Did James work on the research article named Vitamin C and You?"

5. **A** My favorite fairy tale, "Rumpelstiltskin," was written by the Brothers Grimm.

   B My favorite fairy tale, "Rumpelstiltskin", was written by the Brothers Grimm.

6. **A** I have read only the first chapter, called "My Story Begins".

   B I have read only the first chapter, called "My Story Begins."

Apply

Read each sentence. If it is capitalized and punctuated correctly, write *Correct* **on the line. If it isn't, rewrite it correctly on the line.**

1. When you reach the corner, said Mallory "Turn right."

_____

2. "This register is open now, said the clerk. please step over here."

_____

3. Do you know the words to Battle Hymn of the Republic?

_____

4. I can't believe the judge just said, "Nate Dixon has won the competition"!

_____

5. "I know it's early said Victoria, "But I'm really tired"!

_____

6. The speech was entitled "Tapping Your potential".

_____

7. Haven't you heard Mr. Farley say, The customer is always right.

_____

8. "If that phone rings," said Ms. Graves, "you should answer it right away."

_____

9. "The plane will land soon, said Travis. let's pull our seats upright."

_____

10. As Mom read Ian his favorite folktale, The Three Sillies, he fell sleep.

_____

11. Eric's rock group wrote this song, "Pay Me Back", for a radio contest.

_____

12. "if you feel like singing" said the announcer; Feel free to join in."

_____

Check Up

Read each set of sentences. Choose the sentence that is written correctly.

1. **A** "That book," said Akram, "cost me ten dollars."

   B Does it include a story called "The Phantom Strikes Again?"

   C That book was expensive, said Abby, because it is so rare.

   D Did you say, "I left my book on the bus?"

2. **F** The show's theme song, "Take It or Leave It", has become a hit.

   G Does that sign say, "These kittens are free".

   H Have you read the poem "Hamburgers in Heaven"?

   J Did you read the final chapter, "Made In The Shade?"

3. **A** "I fell asleep," said the distraught bus rider, "and missed my stop"!

   B "What do you call this color"? asked Suzanne. "It's beautiful"!

   C Freeway traffic is heavy, "said Roberto." Let's take back roads.

   D "The actors aren't great," said Cecily, "but the story is cute."

4. **F** Did Lauren say, "Call me before you leave".

   G Who wrote the story called "The Necklace"?

   H "You can pay me now" said the painter. "Or I can send you a bill.

   J What a joy it was to hear the doctor say, "it's a girl."!

Read each sentence and look at its underlined part. Choose the answer that is written correctly for the underlined part.

5. "If you like the jacket," said Yakima, "why don't you buy it?"

   A Yakima, "Why

   B Yakima. "Why

   C Yakima, why

   D Correct as it is

6. "This book is overdue." said Rita. "Will you return it for me?"

   F overdue," said Rita.

   G overdue," said Rita,

   H overdue" said Rita.

   J Correct as it is

7. Does that ticket say? "admit one guest"?

   A say "admit

   B say? "Admit

   C say, "Admit

   D Correct as it is

8. "When I count to three," said Ariel. "smile and I'll take your picture."

   F three, said Ariel,

   G three. "said Ariel,"

   H three," said Ariel,

   J Correct as it is

Apostrophes in Contractions and Possessives

In a **contraction**, two words are joined and one or more letters are left out. Contractions are used most in informal conversations and letters. When a contraction is written, an apostrophe (') stands for the letters that have been left out.

In some contractions, a helping verb and the word *not* are combined. The apostrophe replaces the letters *no* or *o*. Pay special attention to the contraction *won't*, which combines *will* and *not* in an unusual way.

can + not = can't	have + not = haven't
could + not = couldn't	should + not = shouldn't
did + not = didn't	was + not = wasn't
does + not = doesn't	were + not = weren't
has + not = hasn't	will + not = won't

Contractions can also be formed by combining a pronoun and a verb, as in these examples:

he + is = he's	they + are = they're
she + had = she'd	we + would = we'd
it + is = it's	we + will = we'll
I + am = I'm	what + is = what's
I + have = I've	you + will = you'll

Underline the contraction in each sentence. On the lines, write the two words that were joined to make the contraction.

1. _____ + _____ We hadn't been home long before the doorbell rang.

2. _____ + _____ Claire's friends report that she's happy in her new job.

3. _____ + _____ We will pick the tomatoes when they're ripe and deep red.

4. _____ + _____ Most employees weren't happy with the new regulations.

In each sentence, underline two consecutive words that can be joined in a contraction. Then write that contraction on the line.

5. Imani does not eat red meat more than once per week. _____

6. Jen asked if I would mind caring for her toddler tonight. _____

7. Unless we hurry, we are going to be late for the ceremony. _____

8. What is the most important benefit of long-distance running? _____

Practice

A **possessive noun** is written with an apostrophe to show possession or ownership of the noun that follows it. Remember the following rules when writing possessive nouns.

- Add an apostrophe and an *s* to a singular noun.

  Tiffany's necklace

- Add only an apostrophe to a plural noun that ends in *s*.

  the players' helmets

- Add an apostrophe and an *s* to a plural noun that does not end in *s*.

  children's stories

In conclusion, apostrophes have two major functions: they replace letters that have been omitted from contractions, and they indicate possession when used in possessive nouns. They do not belong in the plural form of other nouns.

> **Incorrect:** The couple ordered hamburger's and soda's for lunch.
>
> **Correct:** The couple ordered hamburgers and sodas for lunch.

Do not use an apostrophe in the possessive form of personal pronouns, such as *hers, its, ours, yours,* and *theirs.*

Read each set of sentences. Choose the sentence in which apostrophes are used correctly.

1. **A** The homeowners asked to see the officers' badge when he came to their door.

   B The homeowner's asked to see the officer's badge when he came to their door.

   C The homeowners asked to see the officer's badge when he came to their door.

2. **F** Those teenager's radios are playing too loudly.

   G Those teenagers' radios are playing too loudly.

   H Those teenagers' radio's are playing too loudly.

3. **A** The waiter picked up the diners' plates and then showed them the dessert menu.

   B The waiter picked up the diner's plates and then showed them the dessert menu.

   C The waiter picked up the diners' plate's and then showed them the dessert menu.

4. **F** After only a few minutes on the trail, the hiker's boots were muddy.

   G After only a few minutes on the trail, the hiker's boot's were muddy.

   H After only a few minutes on the trail, the hikers' boots' were muddy.

5. **A** Valena's twin's are taking turns waking their mother up at night.

   B Valena's twins are taking turns waking their mother up at night.

   C Valena's twins are taking turns' waking their mother up at night.

Apply

Each sentence has one or more apostrophe errors. Rewrite each sentence correctly.

1. The artists' price for his painting is $8,000, but hes willing to negotiate.

_____

2. The next time wer'e near the Miller's house, well stop in for a visit with Mr. Miller.

_____

3. Mrs. Wright will pick up the players uniform's; shel'l bring them back clean on Monday.

_____

4. The showers' in the mens' locker room need a good cleaning.

_____

5. Its Sheila's dream to visit Paris, Rome, and other European citie's some day.

_____

6. This companys' policy has always been to invite stockholder's to it's annual meeting.

_____

Read the following paragraph. Each numbered line has one apostrophe error. Find and underline the word that has been written incorrectly. Then write the word correctly on the corresponding line below.

(7)   Richards car has been giving him quite a bit of trouble lately. For example,
(8) Richard cant' count on it to start on cold mornings. The engine simply refuses
(9) to turn over until Richard pumps the gas several time's. Once the car is started,
(10) it runs well until it has to stop for a while, for example, at a stoplight. If its
(11) stopped too long, the car wont start again for about five minutes. Richard has
(12) taken his car to three neighborhood mechanics. He has followed the mechanic's'
(13) suggestions, but nothing seems to be helping. Hes about ready to give up on
(14) this car and buy a new one, but he is saving for his childrens' education and
     doesn't have any extra cash right now. Is it time for a fourth mechanic?

7. _____   11. _____

8. _____   12. _____

9. _____   13. _____

10. _____   14. _____

Check Up

Read each set of sentences. Choose the sentence in which apostrophes are used correctly.

1. **A** Id love to know how you made you're special brownies.

   B Whenever Im' invited to a party, I always bring an appetizer.

   C I've tried Kim's recipe for strawberry cheesecake.

   D My friends and I have been sharing our mother's recipes.

2. **F** I can hear the birds in the trees, but they're difficult to spot even with my binoculars.

   G That trees' branches are scraping our roof.

   H Is the car in the driveway her's or your's?

   J One writers' idea has been copied by many others.

3. **A** All the neighbors fence's need painting rather badly.

   B We'd rather take a fall vacation than a summer vacation.

   C My grandmothers' voice was warm and reassuring.

   D After the students scores were posted, everyone gathered to see how he or she had done.

4. **F** Small boats that dont' come into port tonight may be damaged.

   G Ed's sailboat is outfitted with an orange and blue spinnaker.

   H These ships' captains' were trained at the naval academy.

   J You can rent canoe's or kayak's at this shop.

Read the following paragraph and look at the numbered, underlined parts. Choose the answer that is written correctly for each underlined part.

(5)   Some doctors' suggestion's are easier to follow than others. The latest dietary advice from doctors is this: eat your dessert first. More exactly, doctors are saying
(6) that yo'ull be better off if you eat a fatty food before you begin your meal. The fat slows down your digestion, so you feel full faster. Which fatty foods are best?
(7) Although this diner's preferences include morsels of chocolate cake or brownies,
(8) doctors suggest healthier food's such as guacamole or a few nuts.

5. **A** doctors' suggestions

   B doctors suggestion's

   C doctors' suggestions'

   D Correct as it is

6. **F** youl'l

   G youll'

   H you'll

   J Correct as it is

7. **A** this diner's preferences'

   B this diners preference's

   C this diners' preference's

   D Correct as it is

8. **F** foods

   G food is

   H foods'

   J Correct as it is

Writing Business Letters

Written communications between companies and their customers or clients are called **business letters.** Such letters usually follow a single, widely accepted format. As you read these descriptions of the parts of a business letter, refer to the sample letter below.

Heading: This is the date on which the letter is written. In the letter below, note the placement of the comma—between the day of the month and the year.

Inside address: This is the recipient's address. The inside address usually has three lines: 1) the name of the individual or business; 2) the street address or post office box; 3) the city, state, and zip code. If both an individual and a company are listed, the inside address requires four lines. All proper nouns and their abbreviations must be capitalized. Any abbreviation in the address must be followed by a period. A comma should be placed between the names of the city and the two-letter abbreviation of the state. Do not place a comma between the state and the zip code.

Salutation: This is the greeting. The salutation may begin with the capitalized word *Dear*, or it may begin with *To Whom It May Concern*. It always ends with a colon. If the name of the recipient is unknown, a general greeting such as *Dear Sir or Madam* or *To Whom It May Concern* is acceptable.

Body: This is the writer's message. The first line of each paragraph is indented.

Closing and Signature: Capitalize only the first word of the closing and insert a comma after it. A handwritten signature follows the closing. Below the signature, clearly print the name of the sender.

(Heading)	October 15, 2006
(Inside Address)	Sunburst Resort 14507 Circle Dr. Miami Beach, FL 33139
(Salutation) **(Body)**	Dear Sir or Madam: I am planning a visit to Florida in February. Please send me a brochure about your resort.
(Closing)	Sincerely yours,
(Signature)	*Darrell Hayes*
(Name)	Darrell Hayes

Read each item. Then rewrite it correctly on the line.

1. dear mr. taylor, _____

2. tiffin OH 44883 _____

3. august, 10, 2006 _____

4. Truly Yours: _____

5. 134 ninth St _____

Practice

Read the following letter parts. Then write each part in its correct place in the letter form below. Correct any errors in capitalization or punctuation.

p.o. box 314	Sydney Redmond
tarrytown NY 10591	Dear Sir Or Madam,
Kerry Landscapers	April 23 2005
Respectfully Yours;	*Sydney Redmond*

    I would like to be considered for the job opening you advertised in the *Daily Herald* last Sunday. For the last two summers, I was part of a landscaping crew at Meadows Landscaping in Syracuse, New York, so I am familiar with the job of a landscaper. I am available for an interview at any time. My phone number is 555-1235.

_____

_____

_____

_____

_____

_____

_____

_____

_____

_____

_____

_____

Apply

On the lines below, write a business letter. Give the letter today's date. The letter should go to Mom's Homestyle Restaurant, located at 3561 Depot Street in Mayfield, Ohio. The zip code is 44124. You should address the letter to the owner of the restaurant, Mrs. Gertrude Zoeller. In the body of the letter, explain that you think you left a book at the restaurant when you visited it, and ask if anyone has found it. Request that the book be returned to you at your home address. Be sure to capitalize and punctuate the letter correctly.

_____

_____

_____

_____

_____

_____

_____

_____

_____

_____

_____

_____

_____

_____

_____

_____

Check Up

Read the following letter and look at the numbered, underlined parts. Choose the answer that is written correctly for each underlined part.

(1) june 3, 2005

Harold's Painting and Plastering
(2) 1457 Collins ave
(3) omaha, ne, 68102

(4) Dear Mr. Harold:

I am writing to recommend Arnold Pruitt for a job with your company. Arnie has worked with me for three years as a painter's assistant. He always comes to work on time and handles his duties quietly and efficiently. He is quick to learn new techniques for painting, plastering, and general home repair and restoration. I am sure that anyone who hires him will find him a valuable employee.

(5) Yours Truly,
Daniel Holloway
Daniel Holloway

1. **A** june 3 2005
   B June 3, 2005
   C June, 3 2005
   D Correct as it is

2. **F** 1457 Collins Ave.
   G 1457 Collins Ave
   H 1457, collins ave.
   J Correct as it is

3. **A** Omaha ne 68102
   B Omaha, NE: 68102
   C Omaha, NE 68102
   D Correct as it is

4. **F** Dear mr. harold:
   G Dear Mr. Harold,
   H dear Mr. Harold:
   J Correct as it is

5. **A** yours truly,
   B Yours truly,
   C Yours truly:
   D Correct as it is

Review

Quotations and Quotation Marks

A **direct quotation** is a speaker's exact words. Direct quotations are enclosed in quotation marks. Note the placement of commas and end marks in the direct quotations below.

> "How much does that television cost?" Selena asked.
>
> Rob said, "I think it costs about four hundred dollars."
>
> "That seems like a lot," said Selena, "for a little TV."

An indirect quotation communicates a speaker's message without using his or her exact words. No quotation marks are used in an indirect quotation.

> Selena asked when the televisions might go on sale.

When a question or an exclamation contains a direct quotation, place the question mark or exclamation point outside the quotation marks.

> Did the salesman say, "This is a state-of-the-art television"?

Use quotation marks to set off the titles of short works such as poems, short stories, songs, reports, articles, and chapters of books.

Apostrophes in Contractions and Possessive Nouns

In a **contraction,** two words are joined and one or more letters are left out. An apostrophe (') stands for the letters that have been left out. A **possessive noun** shows possession, or ownership, of the noun that follows it. To form a possessive noun, add an apostrophe and an *s* to a singular noun. Add just an apostrophe to a plural noun that ends in *s*. Add an apostrophe and an *s* to a plural noun that does not end in *s*.

> Geneva's children   students' exams   women's opinions

Writing Business Letters

Here is a business letter that is capitalized and punctuated correctly.

> **(Heading)**   October 16, 2005

(Inside Address)   Fanelli's Garden Shop
2694 Cedar Rd.
Los Angeles, CA 90071

(Salutation)   Dear Sir or Madam:
(Body)   My final payment is enclosed. Thank you for your help in making my home beautiful.

> **(Closing)**   Yours truly,
> **(Signature)** *Dean Bond*
> **(Name)**   Dean Bond

Assessment

Read each set of sentences. Choose the sentence that is written correctly.

1. **A** Melisa asked, "Can I park on this street overnight"?

   B Elise replied "I've seen the police giving out tickets to overnight parkers."

   C "Where am I supposed to park my car?" asked Tierra.

   D "you can get a permit," explained Alison, "to park on the street".

2. **F** Steve said that "he would give his cat's kittens to a good home."

   G A neighbor asked how old the kittens were?

   H The vet says, "that my cat needs to be given vitamin pills."

   J Eric complained that his dog had run away for the third time this week.

3. **A** I'll ask my cousins if theyre coming to the reunion?

   B It's fascinating to read the diary I kept when I was a teenager.

   C Each season of the year has it's own beauty.

   D I'm sure that these books are their's.

4. **F** "My child's teacher," said Tony, "assigns homework every night."

   G "Do you help him? asked Rose. I help my son with math every night."

   H "Jill and I both help", replied Tony. "and he's doing better now."

   J "In our house, its homework first," said Monique, "And then Josh can watch a little TV."

5. **A** The handymans tool's are all new.

   B Nicoles' brother and his friend are painting her kitchen.

   C Elouise is painting her childrens' room a bright blue.

   D The Kramers' house is more than 100 years old.

6. **F** "Can you direct me to the cafeteria"? asked Gavin.

   G Did Brandon say, "I'll meet you in the parking lot"?

   H Zia wondered whether everyone had gotten her message?

   J Didn't Derek insist, "that the dinner would be his treat?"

7. **A** All the workers' paychecks will be sent to their homes.

   B If an employees' performance is superior, will he or she get a bonus?

   C To learn the director's opinions, Dale sent them detailed questionnaires.

   D Ray has been keeping track of customers suggestion's and will report on them to the board.

8. **F** The attorney asked if he could approach the judges bench?

   G "My client," she said, "Has been under enormous stress."

   H The judge said, "Consider the evidence carefully before arriving at a verdict."

   J it was a wonderful surprise when the jury foreman said "we find the defendant not guilty"!

Assessment continued

Read the following letters and the paragraph and look at the numbered, underlined parts. Choose the answer that is written correctly for each underlined part.

(9)   February 8 2005

Appliance Rebate Center
(10) P.o. box 357
(11) Red wing, MN; 55066

(12) To whom it may concern,
        Three months ago, I sent in a rebate coupon along with a sales receipt for a new coffeemaker. According to the instructions, I was supposed to
(13) receive a check in the amount of $6.00 in six to eight weeks. I have'nt received that check yet. I am requesting that someone look into this problem and send me my check as soon as possible. If you need to get in touch with me, my phone number is 555-555-3672.

(14) Yours truly
      Martin Sowinski
      Martin Sowinski

9. A February 8, 2005
    B february, 8, 2005
    C February, 8, 2005
    D Correct as it is

10. F p.o. box 357
    G P.o. Box 357
    H P.O. Box 357
    J Correct as it is

11. A Red Wing, Mn, 55066
    B Red Wing, MN 55066
    C Red wing, mn 55066
    D Correct as it is

12. F To Whom It May Concern:
    G To whom it may concern:
    H To Whom it may Concern,
    J Correct as it is

13. A hav'ent
    B havent'
    C haven't
    D Correct as it is

14. F Yours Truly:
    G Yours truly,
    H Yours truly;
    J Correct as it is

(15) may 19, 2006

ShopNet, Inc.
3674 Tremont Ave.
(16) New york, Ny 10036

(17) Dear sir or madam:

    I recently purchased a gold necklace from the ShopNet television network. The necklace was supposed to be 18 inches long; however, it's only 12 inches long. Perhaps I was sent the wrong necklace. I don't want this necklace and am returning it. Please subtract the price of the necklace from my credit card account.

(18) Your Customer
    Christina Jackson
    Christina Jackson

15. **A** May 19, 2006

   B May, 19, 2006

   C May 19: 2006

   D Correct as it is

16. **F** New York: NY, 10036

   G New york, Ny, 10036

   H New York, NY 10036

   J Correct as it is

17. **A** Dear sir or madam,

   B Dear Sir or Madam:

   C Dear Sir Or Madam;

   D Correct as it is

18. **F** Your customer,

   G Your Customer,

   H Your Customer:

   J Correct as it is

    Borrowing money is often unavoidable; however, it should be approached with care, or so say some of our wisest writers. For example, Thomas Tusser says, "Who goeth a-borrowing goeth a-sorrowing." Did Benjamin Franklin say,
(19) "If you'd know the value of money, go and borrow some." Anyone familiar with William Shakespeare's *Hamlet* has memorized the words of Polonius who
(20) says, "Neither a borrower nor a lender be." Even the Bible warns, us that the borrower is the lender's servant." So if you must borrow money, you might want to keep all of these words of wisdom in mind.

19. **A** borrow some?"

   B borrow some"?

   C borrow some".

   D Correct as it is

20. **F** "warns us that the borrower is the lender's servant".

   G warns us, "that the borrower is the lender's servant."

   H warns us that the borrower is the lender's servant.

   J Correct as it is

Posttest

Decide which punctuation mark, if any, is needed in each sentence.

1. There's nothing better to quench your thirst on a hot day than cool water

   A ?   **B** .   **C** !   **D** None

2. Although she had lost the election by a wide margin, Marilyn promised shed run again.

   F "   **G** '   **H** :   **J** None

3. Jahja can your name be translated into English?

   A .   **B** ;   **C** ,   **D** None

4. "I object," said the lawyer. This witness is only repeating hearsay."

   F ,   **G** '   **H** "   **J** None

5. We'll meet at the restaurant at 730.

   A :   **B** ;   **C** "   **D** None

6. If Susan takes your shift tonight can you work Thursday?

   F ,   **G** :   **H** ;   **J** None

7. Anton Chekhov who is best known for his plays, was a writer and a physician.

   A '   **B** ;   **C** ,   **D** None

Choose the word or phrase that best completes each sentence.

8. Professor Deems delivered his address _____ than the other speakers.

   F most expressively

   G more expressively

   H most expressive

   J more expressive

9. Long before the Civil War began, Robert E. Lee _____ his own slaves.

   A had freed

   B had been freeing

   C has freed

   D was freeing

10. Jonelle's collection of jigsaw puzzles _____ an entire closet.

    F fill

    G have filled

    H are filling

    J fills

11. The governor _____ toured the areas affected by the flood.

    A he

    B himself

    C hisself

    D themselves

Read each set of sentences. Choose the sentence that is written correctly and has correct capitalization and punctuation.

12. **F** Van tripped on a step he fell the rest of the way down the stairs.

    G Sounding like a bowling ball rolling down the steps.

    H Everyone came running to see what had happened.

    J Van's embarrassing moment.

13. **A** What is the most noisiest hand-held machine in use today?

    B Leaf blowers must be the loudest.

    C When I walk near one, I walk more quicker to get past it fast.

    D I can't imagine feeling any more unhappily about any machine.

14. **F** Richard doesn't never want to take a night bus again.

    G He didn't think it would be hard to sleep during the trip.

    H But there wasn't hardly a minute when no one was talking to him.

    J He couldn't barely wait to get off the bus and take a nap!

15. **A** Some children at the department store were playing silly games.

    B Running up the down escalator, adult customers were bumped.

    C This is my last and final warning!

    D Their mother had to scold them and taking them home.

16. **F** Melvin works in a pizza shop when he was in high school.

    G After he flattened the dough, he had spread tomato sauce over it.

    H He checked each order to see what toppings had been requested.

    J After he graduated, he is training to be a pizza shop manager.

17. **A** Every guest at the baby shower wrapped their presents in pink.

    B How did all them guests know that Rona was expecting a girl?

    C The party was so enjoyable that it went on longer than planned.

    D Rona and her husband thanked his guests sleepily.

18. **F** Last Summer, morris took a tour of the american southwest.

    G On Independence day, his group was in tucumcari, New mexico.

    H They were on their way West from texas to arizona.

    J He liked the Grand Canyon best.

19. **A** When Tina lay down on a couch for a moment, she fell asleep.

    B She had barely lain her head down when she started to nap.

    C Lie the blame on her hard work!

    D She should lay down in a comfortable bed.

Read each set of underlined sentences. Then choose the sentence that best combines the underlined sentences.

20. Cherise ran into one of her old teachers recently.
She had not seen the teacher for years.

    F Whenever Cherise ran into one of her old teachers, she had not seen the teacher for years.

    G Cherise ran into one of her old teachers recently, and, for years, she had not seen the teacher.

    H Recently Cherise ran into one of her old teachers, whom she had not seen for years.

    J Cherise ran into one, whom she had not seen for years, of her old teachers recently.

21. Mike searched for his lost contact lens.
Other students in his class searched for Mike's lost contact lens.
Mike's teacher searched for Mike's lost contact lens.

    A Mike searched for his lost contact lens, and other students in his class, and Mike's teacher searched for Mike's lost contact lens.

    B After Mike searched for his lost contact lens, other students in his class and his teacher searched for it, too.

    C Mike searched for his lost contact lens that other students in his class and his teacher searched for.

    D Mike, other students in his class, and his teacher searched for Mike's lost contact lens.

22. We heard geese.
The geese were flying overhead.
They were honking noisily.

    F Flying overhead, we heard geese honking noisily.

    G We heard the geese that were flying overhead honk noisily.

    H Honking noisily, we heard geese flying overhead.

    J Geese that were flying overhead and honking noisily, we heard them.

23. Ted cleaned his garden tools.
The tools were rusty.
Ted used steel wool.

    A Ted cleaned his rusty garden tools with steel wool.

    B Ted cleaned his garden tools that were rusty with steel wool.

    C Ted cleaned his rusty garden tools, and Ted used steel wool.

    D Steel wool was what Ted used to clean his garden tools, which were rusty.

Read each paragraph. Then choose the sentence that best fills the blank.

24.   _____. It has long been suspected that many of the glues and solvents used there are hazardous to the health of those who touch or breathe them. The factory itself is hot and is not well ventilated. Workers use dangerous machinery and are not properly trained in safety procedures. They complain about the repetitive work they are expected to perform and say that it has become a strain on their bodies.

  F   The employees of the local factory work under terrible conditions.

  G   Research has shown that heat is an important factor in worker productivity.

  H   Last year, the local factory had its most profitable year ever.

  J   The employees of the local factory are on strike for higher wages.

25.   Helen had several framed photographs she wanted to display on a wall. First, she measured the wall space she wanted to fill. Then she outlined a square of that same size on the floor. _____. After she had the photos grouped in a pleasing arrangement on the floor, she carefully hung the pictures on the wall.

  A   She selected pictures of her family and photos she took on her travels.

  B   Next she arranged the photos on the floor.

  C   Next she tapped several nails into the wall at the appropriate places.

  D   Pictures can be arranged formally or informally, depending upon one's preferences.

26.   Alex can't decide whether to rent an apartment or buy a home. He is earning enough to buy the home, and he has squirreled away money for a small down payment. _____. If he moves away soon, it would be easier to leave an apartment than it would be to sell a home. But he feels that paying rent isn't a good choice because it doesn't allow him to build any equity. This is a puzzle that Alex is having trouble solving.

  F   Therefore, he may move away from Georgia before the end of the year.

  G   For that reason, he doesn't know how long he will be living in Georgia.

  H   On the other hand, he doesn't know how long he will be living in Georgia.

  J   For example, a move to a new city in a different state is certainly possible.

27.   _____. Residents can be seen flying kites or throwing Frisbees in Tiananmen Square. Vendors in street stalls sell fruits and vegetables, along with fabrics, kitchenware, and hundreds of other items. Street performers along the sidewalks add excitement. After sundown, groups of friends squat beneath streetlights to play cards and chat. Young people dance to rock music beneath the Imperial Palace walls.

  A   The street life in Beijing, China, is among the liveliest in the world.

  B   Most of the world's kite-flying and Frisbee champions hail from Beijing, China.

  C   Beijing, China, is full of shopping bargains.

  D   Many card games have their origins in the streets of Beijing, China.

28.   What do elephants and sea turtles have in common? Elephants have been hunted mercilessly for their tusks, which can be used in decorative knickknacks and jewelry. _____. Unfortunately, unless humans stop killing these creatures, they may disappear from the face of the earth forever.

    F   However, sea turtles are hunted for their beautiful shells, used in making jewelry such as earrings, combs, and tie clips.

    G   Similarly, sea turtles have been trapped and killed for their beautiful shells, which can be made into earrings, combs, and tie clips.

    H   Consequently, the beautiful shells of sea turtles can be made into items such as earrings, combs, and tie clips.

    J   Instead, sea turtles have beautiful shells that can be made into jewelry such as earrings, combs, and tie clips.

29.   In April 1917, upon hearing that the United States had entered World War I, entertainer George Cohan sat down and wrote a stirring patriotic song he called "Over There." _____. Following its introduction, the song became a national hit; millions of Americans were humming its catchy tune and buying sheet music to play it on their pianos. Years later, in recognition of the way the song inspired so many Americans at such a difficult time, President Franklin Roosevelt awarded Cohan a Congressional Medal.

    A   Cohan wrote another song, "When You Come Back and You Will Come Back" after the war, but it was never as popular as "Over There."

    B   The song was introduced to the world at a Red Cross benefit in the fall of 1917.

    C   George Cohan was a former vaudeville actor who wrote more than 500 songs.

    D   Cohan had written and sold his first song in 1894, so in 1917 he was already an accomplished songwriter.

Read each topic sentence. Then choose the answer that best develops the topic sentence.

30. It is important for all of us employees to socialize outside of work on a regular basis.

    F   The Cavern, just a block west of the office building, is a pleasant restaurant that always offers a number of delicious appetizers in the evening. Our employees should stop by after work.

    G   Many of the employees in our company have been working here for years. Quite a few of them are preparing to retire soon.

    H   In a nonwork setting, we could get to know each other as people, not just as fellow employees. Knowing each other better, we might begin taking each other's feelings into account when we make work-oriented decisions and might be able to work together more smoothly.

    J   The annual company picnic is one example of a low-stress way of socializing, but it happens only once a year. Getting together more often would be good for us all.

31. A few simple rules can help turn dinnertime into a time of family sharing.

    A Another time when parents can catch up on their children's lives is when they drive their children to school, sports events, or music lessons. And on the weekends, parents can set aside time for a family meeting, where common concerns are discussed.

    B Modern families are pulled in many directions, even at dinnertime. Parents have work and volunteer commitments, and children are often involved in sports and lessons.

    C Most families today eat at the kitchen table, not in the formal dining room. In fact, the dining room is used so rarely that today's architects are not even including them.

    D Decide to meet as a family for an evening meal at least once a week; don't let meetings and classes constantly pull you away. Also, make the rule that no one can take a phone call during the meal; let the answering machine record messages while you have a chance to catch up on one another's lives and enjoy good food.

Read each paragraph. Then choose the sentence that does <u>not</u> belong in the paragraph.

32.   **1.** Your favorite color may reveal more about you than you would have thought possible. **2.** Many people associate these character traits with people whose favorite color is red: energy, courage, and enthusiasm. **3.** My favorite color happens to be purple. **4.** Those who like yellow best are often seen as intellectual and creative.

    F Sentence 1

    G Sentence 2

    H Sentence 3

    J Sentence 4

33.   **1.** The Museum of Art offers free admission on Tuesdays. **2.** Tierra visits the Museum of Art regularly and especially enjoys seeing the museum's world-renowned collection of Chinese statues. **3.** Wandering into the Impressionist Room, she often allows herself to fall under the spell of the light-filled scenes by painter Pierre-Auguste Renoir. **4.** On the way out, she usually swings by more of her favorites, the paintings of giant flowers by Georgia O'Keeffe.

    A Sentence 1

    B Sentence 2

    C Sentence 3

    D Sentence 4

Read the following paragraphs and the letter and look at their numbered, underlined parts. Choose the answer that is written correctly for each underlined part.

(34)   Despite the fact that it's almost seventy years old, a film made in 1939 that people enjoyed so many years ago is still enjoyed today and draws a huge audience every time it's shown on TV. As you
(35) have probably guessed, I'm talking about *the Wizard Of Oz*. Every child
(36) roots for Dorothy as she and Toto battles the Wicked Witch with the
(37) help of the Scarecrow Tinman, and Cowardly Lion.

34.
F Although it's almost seventy years old but still good, a film made in 1939 is still enjoyed a lot today and draws

G A film that people enjoyed almost seventy years ago still draws

H An old film can still draw

J Correct as it is

35. A *The Wizard Of Oz*

B *The Wizard of Oz*

C *the Wizard of Oz*

D Correct as it is

36. F she and Toto battle

G her and Toto battles

H she and Toto is battling

J Correct as it is

37. A the: Scarecrow, Tinman, and

B the Scarecrow, Tinman, and,

C the Scarecrow, Tinman, and

D Correct as it is

(38)   "Doesn't your vacation start tomorrow, Santos, Ginny asked? Are you going anywhere?"
     "If the airport isn't shut down by this snowstorm," Santos answered, "we're
(39) flying to San Juan to visit relatives. I looked forward to the sunshine."
(40)   Ginny predicted, "All of your coworkers will envy you, shoveling snow."
(41) "Well, the time will go much too fast for my wife and I," Santos said.

38. F Santos," Ginny asked. "Are

G Santos?" Ginny asked. "Are

H Santos?" Ginny asked, "are

J Correct as it is

39. A I have been looking

B I had looked

C I will have looked

D Correct as it is

40. F coworkers will envy shoveling you snow

G coworkers will envy you and shovel snow

H coworkers, shoveling snow, will envy you

J Correct as it is

41. A I and my wife

B my wife and me

C my wife and myself

D Correct as it is

(42) August 5 2005

Learn by Doing, Corp.
(43) P.O. Box 225
(44) San Jose, ca 95113

Dear Sir or Madam:
(45)   For my child's second birthday last March, my Mother gave my daughter
your Build-a-House kit. The kit came with a two-year guarantee. Less than six
(46) months later, the paint on the wooden blocks are chipping off. I complained
(47) to the manager of the store where the kit was bought; however, he only said
(48) "that I should go directly to you." I would prefer a refund but will accept a
replacement because my daughter enjoys using the kit. I have enclosed copies of
both the sales slip and the guarantee. I hope to hear from you soon.

Yours truly,
Ronald Meeks
Ronald Meeks

42. **F** August, 5, 2005

    G August 5, 2005

    H august 5, 2005

    J Correct as it is

43. **A** p.o. box 225

    B P.O. box 225

    C PO. Box 225

    D Correct as it is

44. **F** San jose, ca 95113

    G San Jose, Ca 95113

    H San Jose, CA 95113

    J Correct as it is

45. **A** birthday last March, my mother

    B Birthday last March, my Mother

    C birthday last march, my mother

    D Correct as it is

46. **F** later the paint on the wooden blocks are

    G later, the paint on the wooden blocks have been

    H later, the paint on the wooden blocks is

    J Correct as it is

47. **A** bought; however he

    B bought, however, he

    C bought: however, he

    D Correct as it is

48. **F** said that "I should go directly to you."

    G said that I should go directly to you.

    H said, "that I should go directly to you."

    J Correct as it is

Posttest Answer Key and Evaluation Chart

This Posttest has been designed to check your mastery of the language skills studied. Circle the question numbers that you answered incorrectly and review the practice pages covering those skills.

Key

1.	B	25.	B
2.	G	26.	H
3.	C	27.	A
4.	H	28.	G
5.	A	29.	B
6.	F	30.	H
7.	C	31.	D
8.	G	32.	H
9.	A	33.	A
10.	J	34.	G
11.	B	35.	B
12.	H	36.	F
13.	B	37.	C
14.	G	38.	G
15.	A	39.	A
16.	H	40.	H
17.	C	41.	B
18.	J	42.	G
19.	A	43.	D
20.	H	44.	H
21.	D	45.	A
22.	G	46.	H
23.	A	47.	D
24.	F	48.	G

Tested Skills	Question Numbers	Practice Pages
pronouns	11, 41	23–26, 27–30
antecedent agreement	17	31–34
verbs	9, 10, 16, 39	35–38, 39–42, 43–46
subject/verb agreement	36, 46	47–50
easily confused verbs	19	51–54
adjectives and adverbs	8, 13	55–58, 59–62, 63–66
use of negatives	14	67–70
sentence recognition	12	75–78, 79–82
sentence combining	20, 21, 22, 23	83–86, 87–90, 91–94
sentence clarity	15, 34, 40	95–98, 99–102, 103–106
topic sentences	24, 27	111–114, 115–118
supporting sentences	30, 31	119–122
sequence	25, 29	123–126
unrelated sentences	32, 33	127–130
connectives and transitions	26, 28	131–134
proper nouns and proper adjectives	18, 45	139–142, 143–146
first words and titles	35	147–150
end marks	1	155–158
commas	3, 6, 7, 37	159–162, 163–166, 167–170, 171–174
semicolons and colons	5, 47	175–178
quotations	4, 38, 48	183–186, 187–190
apostrophes	2	191–194
letter parts	42, 43, 44	195–198

Answer Key

Unit 1 Usage

Nouns

Page 19: 1. Artists (PL, C), paintings (PL, C), cathedral (S, C), **2.** Robert Frost (S, PR), poem (S, C), inauguration (S, C), John F. Kennedy (S, PR), **3.** cars (PL, C), engines (PL, C), line (S, C), **4.** Ben (S, PR), clients (PL, C), attention (S, C), details (PL, C), **5.** Smiths (PL, PR), Appalachian Mountains (PL, PR), **6.** mechanic (S, C), repair (S, C), **7.** accident (S, C), traffic (S, C), freeway (S, C), standstill (S, C)

Page 20: *Nouns are underlined:* **1.** <u>Abraham Lincoln</u> was known for his <u>honesty</u> and <u>compassion</u>. **2.** <u>Dolores</u> will soon become a <u>citizen</u> of the <u>United States</u>. **3.** Correct, <u>audience</u>, <u>actors</u>, <u>bows</u>, **4.** <u>Ms. Baxter</u> called the <u>members</u> of the <u>committee</u> into her <u>office</u>. **5.** <u>Ken</u> and <u>Betsy</u> ordered <u>appetizers</u> and <u>sandwiches</u> at the <u>Copper Pot Restaurant</u>. **6.** <u>Women</u> and <u>children</u> hastily boarded the <u>lifeboats</u>. **7–15.** Answers will vary.

Page 21: Answers will vary.

Page 22: 1. C, **2.** G, **3.** B, **4.** H, **5.** A, **6.** G, **7.** D, **8.** H, **9.** B, **10.** J

Personal Pronouns

Page 23: 1. *Circle:* she; *Draw arrow to:* Grandma, **2.** *Circle:* their; *Draw arrow to:* trees, **3.** *Circle:* I, my; *Draw arrow to:* Greg, **4.** *Circle:* you; *Draw arrow to:* Deeane, **5.** *Circle:* their; *Draw arrow to:* travelers, **6.** *Circle:* its; *Draw arrow to:* play

Page 24: 1. subject, *Underline:* she, **2.** object, *Underline:* him; *Circle:* ask, **3.** object, *Underline:* him, her; *Circle:* led, **4.** subject, *Underline:* they, **5.** subject, *Underline:* we, **6.** object, *Underline:* us; *Circle:* with, **7.** object, *Underline:* me; *Circle:* correct, **8.** subject, *Underline:* I, **9.** object, *Underline:* them; *Circle:* Telephone, **10.** subject, *Underline:* she

Page 25: 1. His, S, M, 3, **2.** its, S, N, 3, **3.** our, P, No gender, 1, **4.** their, P, No gender, 3, **5.** my, **6.** hers, **7.** their, **8.** ours, **9.** theirs

Page 26: 1. B, **2.** H, **3.** B, **4.** F, **5.** C, **6.** J, **7.** A, **8.** G

More Pronouns

Page 27: 1. *Circle:* Whom, I, **2.** *Circle:* This, D, **3.** *Circle:* those, D, **4.** *Circle:* What, I, **5.** *Underline:* that is currently at the top of the charts; *Circle:* that, **6.** *Underline:* who is standing by the door; *Circle:* who, **7.** *Underline:* for whom we voted; *Circle:* whom

Page 28: 1. *Underline:* herself, REF; *Draw arrow to:* Paula, **2.** *Underline:* himself, REF; *Draw arrow to:* artist, **3.** *Underline:* themselves, REF; *Draw arrow to:* players, **4.** *Underline:* Anyone, IND, **5.** *Underline:* Many, IND, **6.** *Underline:* herself, REF; *Draw arrow to:* Dana, **7.** *Underline:* itself, REF; *Draw arrow to:* film, **8.** *Underline:* yourself, REF; *Draw arrow to:* you

Page 29: 1. Many, P, **2.** Everyone, S, **3.** someone, S, **4.** either, S, **5.** Several, P, **6.** All, P, **7.** nothing, S, **8.** none, S, **9.** neither, S, **10.** Most, P, **11.** herself, **12.** who, **13.** those, **14.** himself, **15.** whose, **16.** this *or* these, **17.** whom, **18.** What, **19.** All, Some, Most, *or* None

Page 30: 1. C, **2.** F, **3.** A, **4.** G, **5.** C, **6.** G, **7.** C, **8.** F

Making Pronouns Agree with Their Antecedents

Page 31: 1. *Underline:* her; *Circle:* Mallory, **2.** *Underline:* their; *Circle:* workers, **3.** *Underline:* they; *Circle:* hikers, **4.** *Underline:* he; *Circle:* Mr. Turner, **5.** *Underline:* his, her; *Circle:* Everyone

Page 32: 1. A, **2.** B, **3.** B, **4.** B, **5.** A, **6.** A

Page 33: 1. *Underline:* them; *Circle:* plays, **2.** *Underline:* them; *Circle:* dolls, **3.** *Underline:* his; *Circle:* neither, **4.** *Underline:* her; *Circle:* sister, **5.** *Underline:* he; *Circle:* sailor, **6.** After everybody made his or her guess, the answer was revealed. **7.** The doctor tells her patients to restrict their salt intake. **8.** Both Ned and Van have their own pool tables. **9.** Mrs. Parker put on her glasses because she couldn't read the fine print. **10.** Correct, **11.** A few of the actors forgot their lines. **12.** Did either of those Miss America finalists describe her home state? **13.** Both Jason and Val brought their surfboards to the beach.

Page 34: 1. A, **2.** H, **3.** C, **4.** G, **5.** D, **6.** G, **7.** B, **8.** J

Verbs

Page 35: 1. *Underline:* were, objected; *Write:* cookies, stale, **2.** *Underline:* introduce; *Write:* models, **3.** *Underline:* arrive, get, wait, **4.** *Underline:* finished, is; *Write:* she, blind, **5.** *Underline:* have replaced; *Write:* typewriters, **6.** *Underline:* would like, is; *Write:* dessert, Mona, full, **7.** *Underline:* must finish, leave; *Write:* project

Page 36: 1. *Underline:* have bought, PP, I, **2.** *Underline:* was, P, I, **3.** *Underline:* played, P, R, **4.** *Underline:* had considered, PP, R, **5.** *Underline:* drove, P, I, **6.** *Underline:* has sent, PP, I, **7.** *Underline:* reported, P, R, **8.** *Underline:* has completed, PP, R, **9.** *Underline:* have stood, PP, I

Page 37: 1. *Underline:* were seen, P, **2.** *Underline:* was promoted, P, **3.** *Underline:* prefers, A, *Underline:* are baked, P, **4.** *Underline:* was shattered, P, *Underline:* was dropped, P, **5.** *Underline:* was felled, P, *Underline:* invaded, A, **6.** *Underline:* are grown, P, *Underline:* are used, P, **7–9:** Sentences will vary, but the listed verbs must be used. **7.** breaks, **8.** have taught, **9.** will choose

Page 38: 1. B, **2.** F, **3.** D, **4.** G, **5.** C, **6.** J, **7.** B, **8.** H

Verbs and Their Tenses

Page 39: 1. Present, **2.** Past, **3.** Present, **4.** Past, **5.** Future, **6.** Present, **7.** Future

Page 40: 1. were scanning, **2.** will be casting, **3.** is trying, **4.** are carrying, **5.** will be enjoying, **6.** were walking, **7.** are planning, **8.** will be accepting *or* is accepting, **9.** were visiting, **10.** was running *or* is running, **11.** are eating, **12.** are swimming, **13.** will be raking

Page 41: 1. B, **2.** F, **3.** D, **4.** H, **5.** B, **6.** J

Page 42: 1. B, **2.** H, **3.** C, **4.** F, **5.** C, **6.** J, **7.** D, **8.** F

Perfect Tenses of Verbs

Page 43: 1. has seen, **2.** had borrowed, **3.** has advised, **4.** will have survived, **5.** had carved, **6.** will have used, **7.** has improved, have changed, **8.** had used, **9.** had disappeared, **10.** had developed

Page 44: 1. A, **2.** A, **3.** A, **4.** A, **5.** B, **6.** B, **7.** has *or* have filled, **8.** will have filled, **9.** blow, **10.** had blown, **11.** speak, **12.** will have spoken, **13.** has *or* have tapped, **14.** had tapped, **15.** write, **16.** has *or* have written, **17.** had sung, **18.** will have sung, **19.** squeeze, **20.** had squeezed, **21.** had seen, **22.** will have seen, **23.** has *or* have skipped, **24.** had skipped, **25.** has *or* have opened, **26.** will have opened

Page 45: 1. C, **2.** G, **3.** A, **4.** H, **5.** D, **6.** J, **7.** has cooked, **8.** had bought, **9.** had barked, **10.** has startled

Page 46: 1. A **2.** J, **3.** B, **4.** G, **5.** C, **6.** F, **7.** B, **8.** F

Agreement of Subjects and Verbs

Page 47: 1. S, explains, **2.** S, leaves, **3.** S, arrives, **4.** P, go, **5.** P, pick, **6.** P, include

Page 48: 1. *Underline:* are; *Circle:* boys, **2.** *Underline:* were; *Circle:* girls, **3.** *Underline:* shakes; *Circle:* package, **4.** *Underline:* are; *Circle:* workers, **5.** *Underline:* ring; *Circle:* bells, **6.** *Underline:* jam; *Circle:* letters, **7.** *Underline:* works; *Circle:* girl, **8.** *Underline:* wait; *Circle:* players, **9.** *Underline:* were; *Circle:* cars,

10. *Underline:* sells; *Circle:* house **11.** *Underline:* is; *Circle:* puppy **12.** *Underline:* go; *Circle:* Smiths

Page 49: 1. *Underline:* portraits, mirror; *Circle:* and; *Underline:* hang, **2.** *Underline:* brakes, (steering) mechanism; *Circle:* or; *Underline:* is, **3.** *Underline:* foreman, assistants; *Circle:* or; *Underline:* Has, **4.** *Underline:* Kendra, parents; *Circle:* nor; *Underline:* eat, **5.** *Underline:* mums, (rose) bush; *Circle:* or; *Underline:* Were, **6.** resembles, **7.** is, **8.** Has, **9.** need, **10.** Do, **11.** seems

Page 50: 1. A, **2.** F, **3.** C, **4.** F, **5.** B, **6.** H, **7.** A, **8.** G

Easily Confused Verbs

Page 51: 1. B, **2.** B, **3.** A

Page 52: 1. lay, **2.** rose, **3.** sat, **4.** taught, **5.** laid, **6.** accepted, **7.** raising, **8.** set, **9.** taught, **10.** except, **11.** learn, **12.** risen

Page 53: 1. Correct. **2.** I hope that you accept credit cards because I don't have enough cash on me. **3.** Even though the temperature had risen, the weather was still chilly. **4.** That clock has sat on the mantle for more than twenty years. **5.** I was taught the multiplication tables in third grade. *or* I learned the multiplication tables in third grade. **6.** When Katie raises her voice, you know she is really angry. **7–11.** Sentences will vary.

Page 54: 1. D, **2.** H, **3.** D, **4.** F, **5.** C, **6.** G, **7.** A, **8.** J

Adjectives

Page 55: 1. six, fancy, wooden, **2.** different, finer, small, **3.** Young, imaginary, **4.** delicious, unusual, **5.** more level, **6.** inappropriate, invasive, **7.** gaudiest, costume, **8.** most likely, perfect, birthday, **9.** least expensive, nearest, convention, **10.** keener

Page 56: 1. cleaner, **2.** largest, **3.** softest, **4.** Correct, **5.** Correct, **6.** higher, highest,

7. lonelier, loneliest, (or more lonely, most lonely), **8.** more graceful, most graceful, **9.** more, most, **10.** wetter, wettest, **11.** more honest, most honest, **12.** gentler, gentlest

Page 57: Answers will vary. Possible answers are given for items 1–8. **1.** more exciting, **2.** sharpest, **3.** practical, **4.** juiciest, **5.** most entertaining, **6.** worst, **7.** sudden, **8.** more nutritious, **9–14.** Answers will vary. Each sentence must use the kind of adjective listed to describe one of the subjects in the box.

Page 58: 1. A, **2.** H, **3.** B, **4.** F, **5.** D, **6.** H, **7.** C, **8.** J

Adverbs

Page 59: 1. *Write:* never; *Circle:* thought, **2.** *Write:* painfully; *Circle:* limped, **3.** *Write:* twice; *Circle:* passed, **4.** *Write:* more expertly; *Circle:* carves, **5.** *Write:* superbly; *Circle:* teaches, **6.** *Write:* later; *Circle:* will arrive, **7.** *Write:* more efficiently; *Circle:* would work, **8.** *Write:* thoroughly; *Circle:* enjoyed, **9.** *Write:* Surely; *Circle:* remembered, **10.** *Write:* yesterday; *Circle:* ended, **11.** *Write:* energetically; *Circle:* worked, **12.** *Write:* more gradually; *Circle:* ascends

Page 60: 1. B, **2.** B, **3.** A, **4.** A, **5.** A, **6.** more recently, most recently, **7.** worse, worst, **8.** faster, fastest, **9.** later, latest

Page 61: Answers will vary. Possible answers are given. **1.** accurately, **2.** now, **3.** hardly, **4.** better, **5.** almost, **6.** carefully, **7.** highly, **8.** most perfectly, **9.** tomorrow, **10.** fastest, **11.** soon, **12.** earlier, **13.** *Underline:* entirely; *Write:* Correct, **14.** *Underline:* immediately; *Write:* Correct, **15.** *Underline:* most quickly; *Write:* more quickly, **16.** *Underline:* more convincingly; *Write:* Correct, **17.** *Underline:* most rapidly; *Write:* more rapidly, **18.** *Underline:* well; *Write:* Correct, **19.** *Underline:* hardly; *Write:* Correct, **20.** *Underline:* worsest; *Write:* worst

Page 62: 1. D, **2.** F, **3.** B, **4.** H, **5.** C, **6.** H, **7.** A, **8.** J, **9.** B, **10.** G

Answer Key continued

Adjective or Adverb?

Page 63: 1. *Circle:* advice, ADJ, **2.** *Circle:* stopped, ADV, **3.** *Circle:* substances, ADJ, **4.** *Circle:* is, ADV, **5.** *Circle:* remembered, ADV, **6.** *Circle:* pace, ADJ, **7.** *Circle:* were, ADV, **8.** *Circle:* will be, ADV, **9.** *Circle:* recent, ADV, **10.** *Circle:* screen, ADJ

Page 64: 1. most heavily, **2.** heavier, **3.** heavy, **4.** cleverly, **5.** clever, **6.** most clever, **7.** efficient, **8.** more efficiently, **9.** most efficient

Page 65: 1. Honest, **2.** softest, **3.** gracefully, **4.** courageously, **5.** lowest, **6.** well, **7.** more imaginatively, **8.** firmest, **9.** sympathetic, **10.** badly, **11.** politely, **12.** more robust, **13–20.** Answers will vary. Possible answers are provided. **13.** later, **14.** louder, **15.** wettest, **16.** more expensive, **17.** expectantly, **18.** finest, **19.** barely, **20.** tomorrow

Page 66: 1. A, **2.** J, **3.** B, **4.** G, **5.** C, **6.** F, **7.** D, **8.** G

Using Negative Words

Page 67: 1. *Circle:* didn't, never; DN, **2.** *Circle:* didn't, none; DN, **3.** *Circle:* nowhere, **4.** *Circle:* doesn't, no; DN, **5.** *Circle:* didn't, no; DN, **6.** *Circle:* No, isn't, no; DN, **7.** *Circle:* don't, **8.** *Circle:* didn't, never; DN, **9.** *Circle:* barely, **10.** *Circle:* wasn't, nothing; DN

Page 68: 1. B, **2.** B, **3.** A, **4.** A, **5.** B, **6-9.** Answers will vary. Possible answers are given. **6.** You can hardly find workmanship like this anymore. *or* You can't find workmanship like this anymore. *or* You can find workmanship like this no more. **7.** There was barely enough room for two cars in the garage. *or* There wasn't enough room for two cars in the garage. **8.** Correct, **9.** I'm sure that I didn't order any anchovies on my pizza. *or* I'm sure that I ordered no anchovies on my pizza.

Page 69: 1. anything, **2.** any, **3.** ever, **4.** anywhere, **5.** any, **6.** anybody, **7.** could,

8. anything, **9.** was, **10.** The ad didn't attract anyone who was willing to buy our car. The ad attracted no one who was willing to buy our car. **11.** Pam can't ever find enough time to read the newspaper. Pam can never find enough time to read the newspaper. **12.** Surprisingly, the runner wasn't breathing hard after the race. Surprisingly, the runner was scarcely breathing hard after the race. **13.** My teenage son's jacket doesn't fit him this year. My teenage son's jacket hardly fits him this year.

Page 70: 1. D, **2.** H, **3.** C, **4.** F, **5.** B, **6.** J

Assessment

Pages 72–74: 1. C, **2.** J, **3.** B, **4.** G, **5.** A, **6.** H, **7.** C, **8.** F, **9.** D, **10.** G, **11.** D, **12.** F, **13.** B, **14.** H, **15.** C, **16.** J, **17.** A, **18.** G, **19.** B, **20.** F, **21.** A, **22.** H, **23.** D, **24.** G, **25.** A, **26.** H

Unit 2 Sentence Formation

Complete Sentences and Fragments

Page 75: 1. Correct; *Underline:* Alyssa, *Circle:* just got a promotion at work, **2.** F, **3.** F, **4.** F, **5.** Correct; *Underline:* The art museum, *Circle:* is free on Thursdays, **6.** Correct; *Underline:* Dan, *Circle:* swims five miles every day, **7–10.** Answers will vary.

Page 76: Answers will vary for items 1, 2, 3, 6, and 7. Possible answers are given. **1.** Joan lives on League Street, above the Italian market. **2.** The new grocery store has an enormous selection of fruits and vegetables. **3.** Carolyn hummed her favorite song while she was making coffee. **4.** Correct, **5.** Correct, **6.** The street musician plays guitar every Friday by the fountain in the park. **7.** Because Eliza was doing so well in school, her mother told her she could have a sleepover.

Page 77: 1. After these customers leave, I'll close up for the night. *or* I'll close up for the

night after these customers leave. **2.** Sentences will vary. **3.** Sentences will vary. **4.** As Kevin picked up the grocery bag, he noticed that his eggs had been crushed. *or* Kevin noticed that his eggs had been crushed as he picked up the grocery bag. **5.** Sentences will vary.
6. Sentences will vary. **7.** Sentences will vary.
8. I asked Sherry for help because she's good with numbers. *or* Because she's good with numbers, I asked Sherry for help.
9. Sentences will vary. **10.** Sentences will vary.
11. Sentences will vary. **12.** Sentences will vary.

Page 78: 1. B, **2.** F, **3.** C, **4.** H, **5.** D, **6.** F

Run-On Sentences

Page 79: 1. Marty and Kris had a quiet night at home/they cooked dinner and watched a movie. **2.** It's chilly out tonight/take your jacket. **3.** I'm not familiar with computers/can anyone help me? **4.** Genevieve is going to Greece for the summer/her family lives near Athens. **5.** Ryan was my best friend in grade school/I haven't seen him in thirty years.
6. C, **7.** C, **8.** RO, **9.** RO, **10.** C, **11.** RO, **12.** C, **13.** RO

Page 80: 1. A, **2.** H, **3.** B, **4.** G

Page 81: Answers for numbers 1, 3, 6, 7, 9, and 11 will vary. Possible answers are given.
1. Auditions were held yesterday. Al tried out for the part of the shopkeeper. **2.** Correct,
3. Oliver isn't feeling well; his stomach hurts.
4. Correct, **5.** Correct, **6.** This street used to be quiet; these days, car alarms go off all night long. **7.** Twenty blocks is too far to walk in this weather; therefore, I'll take the bus.
8. Correct, **9.** It rained all morning, but the sun came out around lunchtime. **10.** Correct,
11. Mike's dog has a passion for shoes; he chewed up two pairs last weekend.
12. Correct

Page 82: 1. C, **2.** J, **3.** B, **4.** G, **5.** C, **6.** J

Sentence Combining: Compound Sentence Parts

Page 83: 1. The team is on a winning streak and will probably win the championship.
2. My husband and my friends planned a surprise party for me. **3.** We listened carefully to the speech but didn't understand it. **4.** My brother and two sisters work for the family business. **5.** Brian or Mandy may keep score today. **6.** The kangaroo and the koala are animals native to Australia.

Page 84: 1. A, **2.** B, **3.** B, **4.** B, **5.** A

Page 85: 1. D, **2.** F, **3.** C, **4.** G, **5.** The Valley Photography Shop sells and repairs cameras.
6. Correct, **7.** My grandmother's apple pie and homemade ice cream taste delicious.
8. Sherlock Holmes and Hercule Poirot are famous fictional detectives.

Page 86: 1. C, **2.** G, **3.** B, **4.** J, **5.** D

Sentence Combining: Subordinate Clauses

Page 87: 1. D, **2.** D, **3.** I, **4.** D, **5.** D, **6.** I, **7.** D, **8.** D, **9.** D, **10.** D, **11.** D, **12.** D, **13.** I, **14.** I

Page 88: 1. A, **2.** A, **3.** B, **4.** B

Page 89: Revised sentences may vary. Possible answers are provided. **1.** When Tammy was tired of listening to the concert, she quietly left her seat. **2.** Correct, **3.** When Stanley went hiking in the dark, he fell and broke his leg. **4.** Sarah open a small bookstore, which specialized in English literature. **5.** Correct, **6.** Since the weather was perfect this year, we had an abundance of corn and soybeans.

Page 90: 1. C, **2.** G, **3.** A, **4.** J, **5.** B

Answer Key continued

Sentence Combining: Adding Modifiers

Page 91: 1. That umbrella in the closet has a broken handle. **2.** Melissa ordered a mahogany table for the dining room. **3.** Hiking in the Rockies, we spotted mountain goats on rocky ledges. **4.** The woolen scarf irritated my neck and chin. **5.** Students from Harding School participated in the science fair. **6.** Our old chair near the fireplace needs a new slipcover.

Page 92: 1. E, **2.** C, **3.** B, **4.** A, **5.** D. Placement of adverbs and adverb phrases may vary for items 6–8. **6.** An artisan deftly shaped the clay on the potter's wheel. **7.** Jake and Russ paddled the canoe across the lake. **8.** An officer arrived within a few minutes to assist us.

Page 93: Placement of adverbs and adverb phrases may vary. **1.** We received free tickets to the game. **2.** Correct, **3.** The actor stepped slowly and majestically into the spotlight. **4.** During halftime, the high school band marched around the football field. **5.** Schools of colorful fish darted through the crystal clear water. **6.** Chef Pierre precisely and rapidly sliced the vegetables with a sharp knife.

Page 94: 1. A, **2.** H, **3.** B, **4.** J, **5.** D

Sentence Clarity: Misplaced Modifiers

Page 95: 1. Jumping on the trampoline, the children showed off for Grandma. *or* The children jumping on the trampoline showed off for Grandma. **2.** Milton unplugged the lamp that was wobbly from the outlet on the wall. **3.** The elevator was packed with eight of us leaving the office early. **4.** Someone with his glasses off could get hurt tripping over that cat. *or* With his glasses off, someone could get hurt tripping over that cat. **5.** I finally found my class picture from first grade, lost in the attic for years. **6.** Everyone who was at the restaurant heard a loud boom. **7.** Lea tiptoed past Harold, asleep on the couch. **8.** Looking through the refrigerator for a snack, Maxine found a moldy orange.

Page 96: 1. Before getting to bed, D, **2.** After leaving those scissors outside in the rain, D, **3.** Rusty after being left out in the rain, M, **4.** Losing your temper as easily as you do, D, **5.** with mushrooms in the oven, M, **6.** Sliding downhill on a toboggan, D, **7.** working far into the night, D, **8.** who worked far into the night, M, **9.** Losing many plants to a late frost, D, **10.** After clearing the table, D, **11 & 12.** Corrections to sentences will vary.

Page 97: 1. C, **2.** F, **3.** C. Answers will vary for items 4 & 5. Possible answers are given. **4.** Eloise greeted her unexpected visitors and wished she had cleaned her apartment. **5.** Walking across an intersection, Mr. and Mrs. Vance were almost run over by a car.

Page 98: 1. D, **2.** H, **3.** A, **4.** H, **5.** B, **6.** J

Sentence Clarity: Parallel Structure

Page 99: 1. B, **2.** A, **3.** B, **4.** B, **5.** B, **6.** A

Page 100: 1. B, **2.** H, **3.** A, **4.** H, **5.** C, **6.** G

Page 101: 1. A, **2.** H, **3.** D, **4.** H, **5.** Martin would prefer to fish or to hike or to canoe down the river. **6.** Abby's whistling of old songs, her humming of a single note, and her tapping of her fingers are signs that she is nervous.

Page 102: 1. B, **2.** H, **3.** B, **4.** F, **5.** C, **6.** J

Answer Key continued

Sentence Clarity: Verbosity and Repetition

Page 103: 1. B, **2.** H

Page 104: 1. B, **2.** A, **3.** B, **4.** B, **5.** C, **6.** F, **7.** B, **8.** J

Page 105: 1. C, **2.** G, **3.** A, **4.** F, **5–8.** Answers will vary. Possible answers are given. **5.** The family enjoyed a pleasant day at the beach. **6.** Over-enthusiastic fans pushed towards the stage, shoving others aside. **7.** Carrie usually watered the plants with a plastic milk bottle. **8.** Please call me when you have some free time.

Page 106: 1. C, **2.** G, **3.** D, **4.** F

Assessment

Pages 108–110: 1. D, **2.** F, **3.** C, **4.** H, **5.** B, **6.** J, **7.** C, **8.** F, **9.** B, **10.** H, **11.** A, **12.** G, **13.** B, **14.** F, **15.** C, **16.** G

Unit 3 Paragraph Development

The Main Idea of a Paragraph

Page 111: 1. C, **2.** J

Page 112: 1. C, **2.** D, **3.** B, **4.** E **5.** A

Page 113: Answers will vary. Possible answers are given. **1.** Butterflies and moths are different in a number of ways. **2.** Judging by the way she furnishes her apartment, I'd say my friend is stuck in the seventies. **3.** It is surprising that ginger can be used in so many ways. **4.** Maureen's beautiful wedding dress was like something out of a fairy tale. **5.** We can get the protein we need from a variety of sources.

Page 114: 1. B, **2.** F, **3.** C, **4.** G

Finding the Topic Sentence

Page 115: 1. C

Page 116: 1. It is important to get enough calcium in your diet. **2.** The legendary Ella Fitzgerald became a singer almost by accident. **3.** More than anyone else I know, Uncle Angelo lives by the motto "Always leave things a little better than you found them." **4.** Although he doesn't play an instrument, Lester's life has always revolved around music. **5.** The winter of 1977 was an unusual one all across the United States. **6.** Natalia has been weighing all of the pros and cons but can't decide what to do.

Page 117: Answers will vary. Possible answers are given. **1.** Since my wife took up jogging, she's been buying out the athletic supply store. **2.** Christopher has a real fascination with frogs. **3.** We tried everything to get the couch in through the doorway. **4.** Owning a car in the city might be more trouble than it's worth.

Page 118: 1. D, **2.** F, **3.** C, **4.** G

Supporting Sentences

Page 119: 1. reasons, **2.** examples

Page 120: 1. compare and contrast, B, **2.** facts and figures, F

Page 121: Answers will vary.

Page 122: 1. D, **2.** G, **3.** C, **4.** J

Recognizing Sequence

Page 123: The wording of the answers may vary. **1.** She was diagnosed with a mild case of tuberculosis. **2.** The man spread the word that there was a great woman doctor in town.

Page 124: The wording of the answers may vary for items 1–2. **1.** He simmers the covered mixture for fifteen minutes. **2.** He puts a sprig

Answer Key continued

of parsley on it. **3.** B, C, A, D

Page 125: 1. 2, 3, 4, 1, **2.** 3, 2, 4, 1, **3.** 1, 4, 2, 3, **4.** 3, 4, 2, 1

Page 126: 1. C, **2.** F, **3.** D

Identifying an Unrelated Sentence

Page 127: 1. (wording may vary) Different colors affect rooms in different ways. **2.** Darlene's living room is painted an elegant light green. **3.** (wording may vary) All the Turners gathered for the holiday. **4.** It's annoying when planes are delayed during the holiday season.

Page 128: 1. A, **2.** B, **3.** B, **4.** A

Page 129: 1. *Cross out:* The sun didn't rise this morning until eight o'clock. **2.** *Cross out:* Many unhappy employees long to start their own businesses. **3.** Correct, **4.** *Cross out:* For example, I am never quite sure of what my manager expects of me.

Page 130: 1. D, **2.** H, **3.** A, **4.** G

Transition and Connective Words and Phrases

Page 131: 1. On the other hand, B, **2.** When they reached the top of the first hill, F, **3.** For instance, A

Page 132: 1. B, **2.** F, **3.** C, **4.** G, **5.** D

Page 133: Answers will vary. Make sure the transitional words and phrases used are appropriate for the type of relationship described in the directions. Possible answers are given. **1.** Nevertheless, it felt natural to hold her new nephew. **2.** Before he reached his back door, the rain began to fall. **3.** Therefore, he went to his neighbor and asked to use the phone. **4.** Similarly, Tony is teaching himself German using a computer program. **5.** A noisy group of teenagers were standing behind them. **6.** In conclusion, our city should create a recycling program immediately. **7.** Even more important, sports build character and a willingness to cooperate with others. **8.** For example, I have always wanted to be an airplane pilot.

Page 134: 1. B, **2.** F, **3.** D, **4.** H

Assessment

Pages 136–138: 1. C, **2.** J, **3.** A, **4.** H, **5.** B, **6.** G, **7.** A, **8.** H, **9.** D, **10.** J, **11.** B

Unit 4   Capitalization

Capitalizing Proper Nouns and *I*

Page 139: 1. Emily Dickinson, Amherst, Massachusetts, December, **2.** Aunt Nora, **3.** Coach Amos, Hudson, **4.** Emperor Napoleon, Paris, France, **5.** United States, Canada, Thanksgiving, **6.** Memorial Day, Monday, May

Page 140: 1. Detroit, Michigan, **2.** Justice Antonin Scalia, **3.** Australia, **4.** Fourth of July, **5.** next Tuesday, **6.** Ralph Vaughan Williams, **7.** Correct, **8.** São Paulo, Brazil, **9.** the month of May, **10.** Correct, **11.** Sunday, January 5, **12.** B, **13.** H, **14.** B, **15.** F

Page 141: 1–8. Sentences will vary. They should include the required proper nouns and be capitalized correctly.

A special holiday in Alaska is Seward's Day. It celebrates the day on which the United States bought Alaska from Russia. It was Secretary William H. Seward who arranged the purchase in March of 1867. Both he and President Andrew Johnson were criticized at the time. Most Americans thought that Alaska was just a frozen wasteland.

Page 142: 1. A, **2.** J, **3.** C, **4.** G, **5.** C, **6.** F, **7.** C, **8.** J

Capitalizing Proper Nouns and Proper Adjectives

Page 143: 1. by a Chinese philosopher, **2.** Correct, **3.** with the Department of Agriculture, **4.** to the Continental Divide, **5.** by the Coleman Candle Company, **6.** at the Lincoln Memorial, **7.** of Latinos

Page 144: 1. C, **2.** G, **3.** B, **4.** F, **5.** C, **6.** Highland Mystery Book Club, Stacy's Books, Railroad Avenue, **7.** Putnam Memorial Bridge, **8.** Irish, Sterling Multicultural Fair, **9.** University of Colorado, National Science Foundation, **10.** African Americans, **11.** New York Harbor, Statue of Liberty, French

Page 145: 1–8. Sentences will vary. They should include the required proper nouns and be capitalized correctly.

Millions of European immigrants entered the United States in the early 1900s. After crossing the Atlantic Ocean in crowded ships, they arrived at Ellis Island. There they were processed by the Bureau of Immigration. During the First World War, immigration decreased, and soon the facilities at Ellis Island were closed.

Page 146: 1. B, **2.** J, **3.** D, **4.** G, **5.** A, **6.** H, **7.** C

Capitalizing First Words, Titles, and Abbreviations

Page 147: 1. A, **2.** B, **3.** A, **4.** A, **5.** B, **6.** B

Page 148: 1. "Yellow Rose of Texas", **2.** *The Phantom of the Opera,* **3.** "Gunga Din", **4.** *Dayton Daily News,* **5.** *Family Ties,* **6.** "The Tragedy at Marsdon Manor", **7.** *Entertainment Weekly,* **8.** *The Wall Street Journal,* **9.** *The Shipping News,* **10.** "How to Care for Roses", **11.** C, **12.** F, **13.** D, **14.** H

Page 149: 1. The crowd listened quietly to a reading of "Casey at the Bat." **2.** Do you know the words to "Birds of a Feather"? **3.** The flight has been postponed from 11:35 A.M. to 12:20 P.M. **4.** My sister raved, "This month's issue of *Fine Cooking* has the best holiday recipes." **5.** "Please forward my mail to P.O. Box 32," he requested. **6.** *All Quiet on the Western Front* was both a great book and a riveting movie. **7.** My doctor gave me a brochure called "A Guide to Immunizations." **8.** Episodes of *I Love Lucy* will be shown this Sunday from 6:00 A.M. to 11:30 P.M. **9.** We are eating more healthfully after taking the class "Introduction to Vegetarian Cooking."

I start the day reading *The Washington Post.* My copy usually arrives by 6:30 A.M. In the afternoon, I read *Time* or *Newsweek.* In the evening, I always watch *World News of the Day.* Clearly, I like to know about current events.

Page 150: 1. C, **2.** J, **3.** A, **4.** F, **5.** C, **6.** G, **7.** D, **8.** F

Assessment

Pages 152–154: 1. C, **2.** G, **3.** A, **4.** H, **5.** C, **6.** J, **7.** A, **8.** G, **9.** A, **10.** J, **11.** B, **12.** H, **13.** C, **14.** F, **15.** B, **16.** H, **17.** C, **18.** H, **19.** C, **20.** F, **21.** C, **22.** H, **23.** D, **24.** J, **25.** B, **26.** H

Unit 5   Punctuation

End Marks

Page 155: 1. C, **2.** F, **3.** A, **4.** F, **5.** B, **6.** J, **7.** C, **8.** G

Page 156: 1. ? **2.** . **3.** . **4.** ! **5.** ? **6.** . **7.** . **8.** ! **9.** ? **10.** ! **11.** ! **12.** . **13.** A, **14.** F, **15.** C, **16.** F

Page 157: Sentences will vary. They should relate to the given situations and have the proper end marks. Each pair of sentences should have two different types of sentences.

Page 158: 1. A, **2.** G, **3.** C, **4.** F, **5.** C, **6.** H, **7.** D, **8.** F, **9.** A, **10.** G, **11.** B, **12.** J

Answer Key continued

Commas: Compound Sentences and Introductory Phrases

Page 159: 1. A, **2.** A, **3.** B, **4.** B, **5.** A, **6.** B, **7.** A, **8.** A

Page 160: 1. <u>Despite the disappointing test results</u>, the company decided to continue its research. **2.** <u>With several branches broken off</u>, the tree slowly began to die. **3.** <u>No</u>, Mr. Granger has not called to confirm his appointment. **4.** <u>Whistling softly</u>, Zeke began the difficult task of clearing the underbrush. **5.** <u>Of all the varieties of apples</u>, Jonathans are my favorite. **6.** A, **7.** F, **8.** D, **9.** H

Page 161: 1. *X* on comma after *horses*. **2.** Insert comma after *No*. **3.** Insert comma after *frank*. **4.** Insert comma after *today*. **5.** Insert comma after *foolish*. *X* on the given comma. **6.** Insert comma after *leaves*. **7.** C, **8.** Insert comma after *windows*. **9.** Insert commas after *Yes* and *shelves*. **10.** *X* on the given comma. Insert comma after *guides*. **11.** *Xs* on given commas. **12.** Insert comma after *glasses*. **13-15.** Answers will vary, but each compound sentence must include a comma at the end of the given independent clause, before the connecting word.

Page 162: 1. C, **2.** J, **3.** B, **4.** G, **5.** A, **6.** F, **7.** A, **8.** J, **9.** D, **10.** H

Commas: Complex Sentences and Relative Clauses

Page 163: 1. A, **2.** B, **3.** B, **4.** A, **5.** A, **6.** B, **7.** A, **8.** A

Page 164: 1. Dennis, <u>who is Polly's new boyfriend</u>, seems like a nice guy. **2.** <u>Whichever answer I choose</u>, it seems I'm always wrong. **3.** That author's new novel, <u>which is on the bestseller list</u>, isn't very good. **4.** I was wondering <u>what movie you'd like to see</u>. **5.** B, **6.** F, **7.** A, **8.** G

Page 165: 1. Insert comma after *warm*. **2.** Insert comma after *run*. **3.** Insert comma

after *night*. **4.** C. **5.** Insert comma after *grandmother*. **6.** *X* on comma after *college*. **7.** C. **8.** Insert comma after *emeralds*. **9.** *X* on comma after *out*. **10.** Insert comma after *away*.

Sentences will vary. They should include the required independent clause and be punctuated correctly. Possible answers are provided.

11. Making sand paintings, which is easy to learn, is a satisfying hobby. **12.** Although it was midnight, the full moon shed almost enough light to read by. **13.** Emory Blackburn, who was the mayor of Latrobe, was my great-grandfather. **14.** The kitten cried because she was hungry.

Page 166: 1. B, **2.** F, **3.** D, **4.** H, **5.** B, **6.** G, **7.** D, **8.** H, **9.** A, **10.** H

Commas: Series and Parenthetical Expressions

Page 167: 1. Insert commas after *Louisiana, Mississippi*, **2.** C, **3.** Insert commas after *envelopes, stickers*, **4.** Insert commas after *notebooks, coins*, **5.** C, **6.** C, **7.** Insert commas after *morning, mid-afternoon*, **8.** Insert commas after *Repair, repaint*, **9.** Insert commas after *short, stone*, **10.** C

Page 168: 1. A, **2.** B, **3.** B, **4.** A, **5.** A, **6.** Hal will be better prepared next time, <u>to be sure</u>. **7.** Your camera, <u>I suppose</u>, fell into the pool when you did. **8.** They were surprised, <u>indeed</u>, at the success of their fundraising efforts. **9.** The test scores, <u>as might be expected</u>, were extremely high. **10.** <u>Fortunately</u>, we were not injured in the automobile accident. **11.** Nova Scotia, <u>according to this brochure</u>, is a scenic place to visit. **12.** Senator Smedlap, <u>if you believe this poll</u>, is in danger of losing this election.

Page 169: 1. Insert commas after *Lamps, frames*, **2.** Insert commas after *surrounded, usual, ribbons, supplies*, **3.** Correct, **4.** Insert

commas after *painting, see, delicate, serious,*
5. Insert commas after *hand, crafted,*
6. Correct, **7.** Insert commas after *at, say,*
8. Insert commas after *season, paper,* **9.** Insert
commas after *begs, over,* **10.** Correct, **11.** Insert
commas after *annoying, example,* **12.** Insert
comma after *Well*

Page 170: 1. C, **2.** G, **3.** B, **4.** H, **5.** A, **6.** J, **7.** D,
8. H

Other Uses of Commas

Page 171: 1. B, **2.** A, **3.** A, **4.** B, **5.** <u>Charlene</u>,
thanks for offering to drive today. **6.** Tell me,
<u>Martin</u>, how do you like working as a security
guard? **7.** Will you accept a verbal request, <u>sir</u>,
or should I put it in writing? **8.** The meeting is
closer to Towson, Maryland, than it is to
Baltimore, <u>William</u>. **9.** <u>Uncle Angelo</u>, when are
you and Aunt Louisa leaving for Italy?

Page 172: 1. My mother-in-law, <u>Irene</u>, works at
the county courthouse. **2.** Sweetbriar Commons,
<u>the biggest mall in the area</u>, has a large food
court. **3.** Ben Davis, <u>the mayor of Centerville</u>, is
noted for his well-run administration. **4.** A large
ruby, <u>a red stone</u>, hung from a gold chain
around her neck. **5.** Josie and Al, <u>owners of the
corner deli</u>, work long hours seven days a week.
6. His youngest daughter, <u>Veronica</u>, just won a
college scholarship. **7.** An amphora, <u>an oval jar
with two handles</u>, was used long ago to store oil
or wine. **8.** The salesperson urged us to try the
Tornado, <u>a vacuum cleaner with extra power</u>.
9–13. Answers will vary. Commas must be
placed after each name and after each
appositive.

Page 173: 1–5. Answers will vary. Commas
must set off all underlined words. **6.** My
personal trainer, Samantha Engstrom, often
travels to Miami, Florida. **7.** Henry, have you
seen a copy of *Back Roads*, the new travel
magazine? **8.** Your pancakes, Mrs. Bronson,
were light and fluffy. **9.** Ken's nephew,
Steven, is attending graduate school in

Boulder, Colorado. **10.** Bridget's Breads, our
local bakery, makes tasty Irish soda bread.
11. The ship's galley, or kitchen, could seat
four people comfortably.

Page 174: 1. A, **2.** J, **3.** B, **4.** F, **5.** D, **6.** G, **7.** C,
8. H

Semicolons and Colons

Page 175: 1. Insert semicolon after *owner,*
2. Insert semicolons after *peppers, beans,*
3. Insert semicolon after *agency,* **4.** Insert
semicolon after *sunny,* **5.** Insert semicolon
after *early,* **6.** Insert semicolon after *night,*
7. Insert semicolon after *booked,* **8.** Insert
semicolons after *Watts, Anderson*

Page 176: 1. A, **2.** G, **3.** C, **4.** Insert semicolon
after *de-icing* and colon after *7.* **5.** *X* over
colon. **6.** *X* over colon and insert semicolons
after *Nevada* and *Louisiana.* **7.** Insert
semicolon after *privilege.* **8.** Insert colon after *9*
and *test.*

Page 177: 1. Art won a stuffed bear, a doll, and
a pair of dice at the first booth; a cap at the
second booth; and a balloon, a popcorn ball,
and a gift certificate at the last booth.
2. We lost power during the windstorm; it
leveled houses throughout the city. **3.** Correct,
4. The caterers offered possible clients desserts
such as these: peach tarts, apple strudel,
chocolate eclairs, and cherry cheesecakes.
5. Gwen had forgotten her keys again;
fortunately, Bonita had remembered hers.

On that February morning, weather
forecasters said that there would be a blizzard.
Smart skiers would have stayed home;
however, eight skiers thought they could
handle bad weather. They headed out without
proper equipment such as waterproof sleeping
bags and tents. Suddenly the snow began.
The skiers became confused; consequently,
they were soon lost. When the skiers didn't
return, rescue parties were sent out. The story
had a happy ending; all the skiers got home

Answer Key continued

safely. From now on, they will respect the power of snow and wind.

Page 178: 1. B, **2.** J, **3.** C, **4.** F, **5.** A, **6.** J, **7.** C, **8.** G

Assessment

Pages 180–182: 1. D, **2.** F, **3.** B, **4.** F, **5.** C, **6.** H, **7.** C, **8.** J, **9.** C, **10.** G, **11.** D, **12.** H, **13.** A, **14.** F, **15.** A, **16.** H, **17.** D, **18.** J, **19.** B, **20.** F, **21.** C, **22.** G, **23.** C, **24.** G, **25.** B, **26.** G

Unit 6   Writing Conventions

Direct and Indirect Quotations

Page 183: 1. D. "This bus is too crowded!" complained Courtney. **2.** I, **3.** I, **4.** D. Heidi announced, "The messenger has come for the package." **5.** B, **6.** A

Page 184: 1. Arthur said, "We should learn some Spanish before we go to Mexico." **2.** "Repeat after me," said the language teacher patiently. **3.** "Does my accent sound natural yet?" asked Emily. **4.** Kristen exclaimed, "I can hardly wait to get on the plane!" **5.** "Maybe we should travel to Italy next year," said Terry. **6.** "How many languages do you speak?" asked William. **7.** "Some people simply have a gift for learning languages," volunteered Amy. **8.** Rex said, "It's easiest to learn foreign languages when you are young."

Page 185: 1-6. The wording of the sentences may vary. Possible answers are provided. **1.** Debra asked, "Does anyone want to go out to lunch with me?" **2.** The officer sternly told me that I had been exceeding the speed limit. **3.** The winning team announced that they had been awarded first prize. **4.** "Repairs could cost about two thousand dollars," said the roofer. **5.** Ms. Dwyer asked when the report would be finished. **6.** One pollster predicts, "The governor will win re-election easily."

Quotations in the conversation will vary. Two quotations for each of the three speakers are required. All punctuation and capitalization rules must be followed.

Page 186: 1. C, **2.** J, **3.** A, **4.** H, **5.** A, **6.** G, **7.** C, **8.** J

Quotations and Quotation Marks

Page 187: 1. "Playing in the street," explained Doris, "is not a good idea in this neighborhood." **2.** "Let's eat," said Eddie. "I'm starved!" **3.** Did the clerk say, "Show your receipt to the guard at the door"? **4.** "If we want good tickets," said Alyssa, "we'll need to get in line early." **5.** "Jeremy has found a job in Denver," said Meryl. "We're looking for a house there." **6.** Did I hear you say, "I'm sorry"? **7.** "Before dinner," said Nathan, "we played a little basketball." **8.** "This computer has been giving me trouble lately," complained Jesse. "I need a new one." **9.** What a relief it was to hear the pilot say, "The weather is clearing up"!

Page 188: 1. A, **2.** B, **3.** B, **4.** A, **5.** A, **6.** B

Page 189: 1. "When you reach the corner," said Mallory, "turn right." **2.** "This register is open now," said the clerk. "Please step over here." **3.** Do you know the words to "Battle Hymn of the Republic"? **4.** Correct, **5.** "I know it's early," said Victoria, "but I'm really tired!" **6.** The speech was entitled "Tapping Your Potential." **7.** Haven't you heard Mr. Farley say, "The customer is always right"? **8.** Correct, **9.** "The plane will land soon," said Travis. "Let's pull our seats upright." **10.** As Mom read Ian his favorite folktale, "The Three Sillies," he fell asleep. **11.** Eric's rock group wrote this song, "Pay Me Back," for a radio contest. **12.** "If you feel like singing," said the announcer, "feel free to join in."

Page 190: 1. A, **2.** H, **3.** D, **4.** G, **5.** D, **6.** F, **7.** C, **8.** H

Apostrophes in Contractions and Possessives

Page 191: 1. <u>hadn't</u>, had + not, **2.** <u>she's</u>, she + is, **3.** <u>they're</u>, they + are, **4.** <u>weren't</u>, were + not, **5.** <u>does not</u>, doesn't, **6.** <u>I would</u>, I'd, **7.** <u>we are</u>, we're, **8.** <u>What is</u>, What's

Page 192: 1. C, **2.** G, **3.** A, **4.** F, **5.** B

Page 193: 1. The artist's price for his painting is $8,000, but he's willing to negotiate. **2.** The next time we're near the Millers' house, we'll stop in for a visit with Mr. Miller. **3.** Mrs. Wright will pick up the players' uniforms; she'll bring them back clean on Monday. **4.** The showers in the men's locker room need a good cleaning. **5.** It's Sheila's dream to visit Paris, Rome, and other European cities someday. **6.** This company's policy has always been to invite stockholders to its annual meeting. **7.** <u>Richards</u>, Richard's, **8.** <u>cant'</u>, can't, **9.** <u>time's</u>, times, **10.** <u>its</u>, it's, **11.** <u>wont</u>, won't, **12.** <u>mechanic's'</u>, mechanics' **13.** <u>Hes</u>, He's **14.** <u>childrens'</u>, children's

Page 194: 1. C, **2.** F, **3.** B, **4.** G, **5.** A, **6.** H, **7.** D, **8.** F

Writing Business Letters

Page 195: 1. Dear Mr. Taylor: **2.** Tiffin, OH 44883, **3.** August 10, 2006, **4.** Truly yours, **5.** 134 Ninth St.

Page 196: *Heading:* April 23, 2005 *Inside Address:* (*line 1*) Kerry Landscapers (*line 2*) P.O. Box 314 (*line 3*) Tarrytown, NY 10591 *Salutation:* Dear Sir or Madam: *Body:* (*first line indented*) I would like to be considered for the job opening you advertised in the *Daily Herald* last Sunday. For the last two summers, I was part of a landscaping crew at Meadows Landscaping in Syracuse, New York, so I am familiar with the job of a landscaper. I am available for an interview at any time. My phone number is 555-1235. *Closing:* Respectfully yours, *Signature and Name:* *Sydney Redmond*, Sydney Redmond

Page 197: Wording of the bodies of the letters will vary. Heading, inside address, greeting, and closing must be capitalized and punctuated correctly.

Page 198: 1. B, **2.** F, **3.** C, **4.** J, **5.** B

Assessment

Pages 200–202: 1. C, **2.** J, **3.** B, **4.** F, **5.** D, **6.** G, **7.** A, **8.** H, **9.** A, **10.** H, **11.** B, **12.** F, **13.** C, **14.** G, **15.** A, **16.** H, **17.** B, **18.** F, **19.** B, **20.** H